MATLAB Numerical Calculations

César Pérez López

Apress®

MATLAB Numerical Calculations

Copyright © 2014 by César Pérez López

This work is subject to copyright. All rights are reserved by the Publisher, whether the whole or part of the material is concerned, specifically the rights of translation, reprinting, reuse of illustrations, recitation, broadcasting, reproduction on microfilms or in any other physical way, and transmission or information storage and retrieval, electronic adaptation, computer software, or by similar or dissimilar methodology now known or hereafter developed. Exempted from this legal reservation are brief excerpts in connection with reviews or scholarly analysis or material supplied specifically for the purpose of being entered and executed on a computer system, for exclusive use by the purchaser of the work. Duplication of this publication or parts thereof is permitted only under the provisions of the Copyright Law of the Publisher's location, in its current version, and permission for use must always be obtained from Springer. Permissions for use may be obtained through RightsLink at the Copyright Clearance Center. Violations are liable to prosecution under the respective Copyright Law.

ISBN-13 (pbk): 978-1-4842-0347-7

ISBN-13 (electronic): 978-1-4842-0346-0

Trademarked names, logos, and images may appear in this book. Rather than use a trademark symbol with every occurrence of a trademarked name, logo, or image we use the names, logos, and images only in an editorial fashion and to the benefit of the trademark owner, with no intention of infringement of the trademark.

The use in this publication of trade names, trademarks, service marks, and similar terms, even if they are not identified as such, is not to be taken as an expression of opinion as to whether or not they are subject to proprietary rights.

While the advice and information in this book are believed to be true and accurate at the date of publication, neither the authors nor the editors nor the publisher can accept any legal responsibility for any errors or omissions that may be made. The publisher makes no warranty, express or implied, with respect to the material contained herein.

Managing Director: Welmoed Spahr
Lead Editor: Jeffrey Pepper
Editorial Board: Steve Anglin, Mark Beckner, Gary Cornell, Louise Corrigan, Jim DeWolf, Jonathan Gennick, Robert Hutchinson, Michelle Lowman, James Markham, Matthew Moodie, Jeff Olson, Jeffrey Pepper, Douglas Pundick, Ben Renow-Clarke, Gwenan Spearing, Steve Weiss
Coordinating Editor: Melissa Maldonado
Copy Editor: Barnaby Sheppard
Compositor: SPi Global
Indexer: SPi Global
Artist: SPi Global
Cover Designer: Anna Ishchenko

Distributed to the book trade worldwide by Springer Science+Business Media New York, 233 Spring Street, 6th Floor, New York, NY 10013. Phone 1-800-SPRINGER, fax (201) 348-4505, e-mail orders-ny@springer-sbm.com, or visit www.springeronline.com. Apress Media, LLC is a California LLC and the sole member (owner) is Springer Science + Business Media Finance Inc (SSBM Finance Inc). SSBM Finance Inc is a Delaware corporation.

For information on translations, please e-mail rights@apress.com, or visit www.apress.com.

Apress and friends of ED books may be purchased in bulk for academic, corporate, or promotional use. eBook versions and licenses are also available for most titles. For more information, reference our Special Bulk Sales–eBook Licensing web page at www.apress.com/bulk-sales.

Any source code or other supplementary material referenced by the author in this text is available to readers at www.apress.com. For detailed information about how to locate your book's source code, go to www.apress.com/source-code/.

Contents at a Glance

Contents

About the Author

César Pérez López is a Professor at the Department of Statistics and Operations Research at the University of Madrid. César is also a Mathematician and Economist at the National Statistics Institute (INE) in Madrid, a body which belongs to the Superior Systems and Information Technology Department of the Spanish Government. César also currently works at the Institute for Fiscal Studies in Madrid.

Also Available

- *MATLAB Programming for Numerical Analysis*, 978-1-4842-0296-8
- *MATLAB Control Systems Engineering*, 978-1-4842-0290-6
- *MATLAB Differential Equations*, 978-1-4842-0311-8
- *MATLAB Linear Algebra*, 978-1-4842-0323-1
- *MATLAB Differential and Integral Calculus*, 978-1-4842-0305-7
- *MATLAB Optimization Techniques*, 978-1-4842-0293-7
- *MATLAB Symbolic Algebra and Calculus Tools*, 978-1-4842-0344-6

Introduction

MATLAB is the tool of the modern day mathematician or engineer. The incredible deep functionality of MATLAB makes what would have taken hours 40 years ago, often less than a minute with MATLAB built in functions. MATLAB enables you to explore multiple approaches and reach a solution faster often more accurately than with other tools or traditional programming languages, such as C/C++ or Java. More importantly, it has changed the way we learn and made getting solutions immensely simpler. So, you can now focus on the application, instead of the math. And with that easily available power, you can explore and find more and more functions, test hypotheses and become a significantly more powerful worker.

This book is designed for use, in part, as a tool to enable you to use MATLAB as a scientific/business calculator so that you can get numerical solutions to problems involving a wide array of mathematics using MATLAB. But it is broader in scope than that. The book can be used as an independent resource for MATLAB. A background in the necessary mathematics is assumed, so this book shows you how to interpret your problems to get MATLAB to do what you want it to do. Just look up the function you want in the book and you are ready to use it in MATLAB or use the book to learn about the enormous range of options that MATLAB offers. The book is topical, picking examples to show not only general methods in using MATLAB, but specifics to use MATLAB for advanced mathematical computations while giving a glimpse at their application.

MATLAB Numerical Calculations focuses on MATLAB capabilities to give you numerical solutions to problems you are likely to encounter in your professional or scholastic life. It introduces you to the MATLAB language with practical hands-on instructions and results, allowing you to quickly achieve your goals. Starting with a look at basic MATLAB functionality with integers, rational numbers and real and complex numbers, and MATLAB's relationship with Maple, you will learn how to solve equations in MATLAB, and how to simplify the results. You will see how MATLAB incorporates vector, matrix and character variables, and functions thereof. MATLAB is a powerful tool used to defined, manipulate and simplify complex algebraic expressions. With MATLAB you can also work with ease in matrix algebra, making use of commands which allow you to find eigenvalues, eigenvectors, determinants, norms and various matrix decompositions, among many other features. Lastly, you will see how you can write scripts and use MATLAB to explore numerical analysis, finding approximations of integrals, derivatives and numerical solutions of differential equations.

CHAPTER 1

■ ■ ■

Introduction to MATLAB

1.1 Numerical Calculations with MATLAB

You can use MATLAB as a powerful numerical calculator. While most calculators handle numbers only to a preset degree of accuracy, MATLAB works to whichever precision is necessary for any given calculation. In addition, unlike calculators, we can perform operations not only with individual numbers, but also with objects such as matrices.

Most classical numerical analysis topics are treated by MATLAB. It supports matrix algebra, statistics, interpolation, fit by least squares, numerical integration, minimization of functions, linear programming, numerical solutions of algebraic equations and differential equations and a long list of further techniques.

Here are some examples of numerical calculations with MATLAB (once the commands have been entered to the right of the input prompt "**>>**" simply hit *Enter* to obtain the result):

1. We can calculate 4 + 3 and get 7 as a result. To do this, just type 4 + 3 and then *Enter*:

   ```
   >> 4 + 3
   ```

   ans =

      7

2. We can also find the value of 3 raised to the power 100, without previously fixing the precision. For this it is enough to simply type 3 ^ 100:

   ```
   >> 3 ^ 100
   ```

   ans =

     5. 1538e + 047

3. We can also use the command *format long e* to obtain results in scientific notation with 16 more exponential digits of precision:

   ```
   >> format long e;
   >> 3 ^ 100
   ```

   ans =

     5.153775207320115e+047

4. We can also work with complex numbers. We find the result of the operation raising $(2 + 3i)$ to the power 10 by typing the expression $(2 + 3i) ^ 10$:

```
>> (2 + 3i) ^ 10
```

ans =

   -3 415250000000001e + 005 - 1. 456680000000001e + 005i

The command *format long g* will optimize the output of future calculations.

```
>> format long g
>> (2 + 3i) ^ 10
```

ans =

   -341525 - 145668i

5. The previous result can also be obtained in short format using the command *format short*:

```
>> format short;
>> (2 + 3i) ^ 10
```

ans =

   -3.4152e+005- 1.4567e+005i

6. We can calculate the value of the Bessel function at the point 13.5. To do this, we type Besselj(0,13.5):

```
>> Besselj(0,13.5)
```

ans =

   0.2150

7. We can also perform numerical integration. To calculate the integral between 0 and π of sin(x), we type the expression int(sin(x), 0, pi) after having declared the variable x as symbolic with the command *syms*:

```
>> syms x
>> int(sin(x), 0, pi)
```

ans =

2

These themes will be treated more thoroughly later.

1.2 Symbolic Calculations with MATLAB

MATLAB handles symbolic mathematical computation perfectly, manipulating formulae and algebraic expressions easily and efficiently. You can expand, factor and simplify polynomials, rational functions and trigonometric expressions; you can find algebraic solutions of polynomial equations and systems of equations; you can evaluate derivatives and integrals symbolically and find solutions of differential equations; you can manipulate power series, find limits and explore many other facets of algebraic series.

To perform this task, MATLAB requires that all variables (or algebraic expressions) are previously declared as symbolic using the command *syms*.

Here are some examples of symbolic computations with MATLAB:

1. We find the cube of the algebraic expression: $(x + 1)(x + 2) - (x + 2)^2$. This is done by typing the expression: $expand((x + 1)*(x + 2) - (x + 2)^2)^3)$. The result will be another algebraic expression:

```
>> syms x
>> expand (((x + 1)*(x + 2)-(x + 2)^2)^3).
```

ans =

*-x ^ 3-6 * x ^ 2-12 * x-8*

2. We can factor the result of the above calculation by typing $factor((x + 1) *(x + 2) - (x + 2)^2)^3)$:

```
>> syms x
>> factor(((x + 1)*(x + 2)-(x + 2)^2)^3)
```

ans =

-(x+2) ^ 3

3. We can find the indefinite integral of the function $(x ^ 2)sin(x)^2$ by typing $int(x^2 * sin(x)^2, x)$:

```
>> syms x
>> int(x^2*sin(x)^2, x)
```

ans =

*x ^ 2 * (-1/2 * cos(x) * sin(x) + 1/2 * x)-1/2 * x * cos(x) ^ 2 + 1/4 **
*cos(x) * sin(x) + 1/4 * 1/x-3 * x ^ 3*

4. We can simplify the previous result:

```
>> syms x
>> simplify(int(x^2*sin(x)^2, x))
```

ans =

*-1/2 * x ^ 2 * cos(x) * sin(x) + 1/6 * x ^ 3-1/2 * x * cos(x) ^ 2 + 1/4 **
*cos(x) * sin(x) + 1/4 * x*

5. We can display the previous result in standard mathematical notation:

```
>> syms x
>> pretty(simplify(int('x^2*sin(x)^2', 'x')))
```

$$-1/2 \ x \ cos(x) \ sin(x) + 1/6 \ x - 1/2 \ x \ cos(x) + 1/4 \ cos(x) \ sin(x) + 1/4 \ x$$

6. We can expand the function $x^2 * \sin(x)^2$ as a power series up to order 12, presenting the result in standard form:

```
>> syms x
>> pretty(taylor(x^2*sin(x)^2,12))
```

$$x^4 \ 1/3 \ x^6 + 2/45 \ x^8 - 1/315 \ x^{10} + 0 \ (x^{12})$$

7. We can solve the equation $3ax \ 7x^2 + x^3 = 0$ (where a is a parameter):

```
>> syms x a
>> solve('3*a*x-7*x^2 + x^3 = 0', x)
```

ans =

```
[          0            ]
[7/2 + 1/2 *(49-12*a) ^(1/2) ]
[7/2-1/2 *(49-12*a) ^(1/2)   ]
```

8. We can find the five solutions of the equation $x^5 + 2x + 1 = 0$:

```
>> syms x
>> solve('x^5+2*x+1','x')
```

ans =

```
[-.7018735688558619 -.8796971979298240 * i]
[-.7018735688558619 +.8796971979298240 * i]
[-.4863890359345430                        ]
[ .9450680868231334 -.8545175144390459 * i]
[ .9450680868231334 +.8545175144390459 * i]
```

On the other hand, MATLAB can be used together with the Maple program libraries to work with symbolic mathematics, thus extending its field of action. In this way, MATLAB can be used to work on topics such as differential forms, Euclidean geometry, projective geometry, statistics, etc.

At the same time, we can extend MATLAB's numerical calculation cababilities by using the Maple libraries (combinatorics, optimization, number theory, statistics, etc.)

1.3 MATLAB and Maple

Whenever it is necessary to use a Maple command or function from MATLAB, use the command *maple* followed by the corresponding Maple syntax. ***This functionality is only available if you have installed the symbolic computation Toolbox "Extended Symbolic Math Toolbox"***. This is the tool one uses to work with linear algebra and mathematical analysis.

To use a Maple command from MATLAB, the syntax is as follows:

maple('Maple_command_syntax')

or alternatively:

maple 'Maple_command_syntax'

To use a Maple command with *N* arguments from MATLAB, the syntax is as follows:

maple('Maple_command_syntax', argument1, argument2, …, argumentN)

Let's see some examples:

1. We can calculate the limit of the function *(x^3 -1) / (x-1)* as *x - > 1*:

    ```
    >> maple('limit((x^3-1)/(x-1),x=1)')
    ```

    ans =

    3

    We could also have used the following syntax:

    ```
    >> maple 'limit((x^3-1)/(x-1),x=1)'
    ```

    ans =

    3

2. We can calculate the greatest common divisor of *10,000* and *5,000*:

    ```
    >> maple('gcd', 10000, 5000)
    ```

    ans =

    5000

1.4 General Notation. The Command Window

Whenever a program is used, it is necessary to become familiar with the general characteristics of its notation. Like any program, the best way to learn MATLAB is to use it. Each example consists of the user *input prompt* ">>" followed by the command and the MATLAB response on the next line. See Figure 1-1.

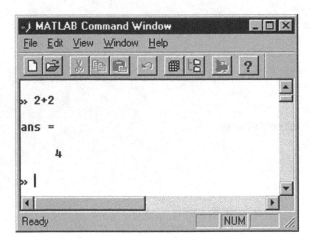

Figure 1-1.

Sometimes, depending on the type of command (user input) given to MATLAB in the Command Window, the response will begin with the expression *ans* =. See Figure 1-2.

Figure 1-2.

It is important to pay attention to uppercase and lowercase characters, parentheses and square brackets, and the use of spaces and punctuation (in particular commas and semicolons).

Like the C programming language, MATLAB is case sensitive; for example, *Sin(x)* is different to *sin(x)*. The names of all built-in functions begin with lowercase letters. Each bracket has its own meaning, as we will see later.

To indicate that two variables must be multiplied you put the symbol * between them, and there cannot be spaces in the names of commands, variables or functions. In other cases, spaces are ignored, but they can be included to make the input more readable.

Once a MATLAB command has been entered, simply press *Enter*. If at the end of the input we put a semicolon, the program runs the calculation and keeps it in memory (*Workspace*), but does not display the result on screen. The *input* prompt ">>" reappears to indicate that you can input a new entry.

```
>> 2 + 3;
>>
```

If the entry is too long and doesn't fit on a single line of the MATLAB Command Window, just put three dots at the end of the line and press *Enter* to continue with the rest of the entry on the next line. Once the entry is complete, press *Enter* to run the command:

```
>> 1254 + 3456789 + 14267890 + 345217 +...
78965 + 125347 + 86500
```

ans =

   18361962
```
>>
```

You can make multiple entries in the same command line by separating them with commas and pressing *Enter* at the end of the last entry. If you use a semicolon at the end of one of the entries of the line, its corresponding output is ignored. If the number of consecutive entries doesn't fit on one line, three dots are used to continue on the next line, as described above:

```
>> 2+2, 5+3, 8+5
```

ans =

   4

ans =

   8

ans =

   13

```
>> 2+2; 5+3, 8+5; 3*4
```

ans =

   8

ans =

   12

To enter a descriptive comment in a command line, just start it with the "%" symbol. When you run the input, MATLAB will ignore the comment and process the rest.

```
>> F = 125 + 2 %F represents units of force
```

$F =$

127

To simplify the process of entering a script to be evaluated by the MATLAB interpreter (via the command window prompt), you can use arrow keys. For example, if you press the up arrow once, you recover the last entry submitted in MATLAB. If you press the up arrow twice, you recover the penultimate entry submitted, and so on.

If you type a sequence of characters in the *input* area and then click the up arrow, you recover the last entry that begins with the specified string.

The commands entered during a MATLAB session are stored temporarily in the buffer (*Workspace*) until the end of the session, at which time you can permanently save the session to file or lose it.

Below is a summary of the keys that can be used in the MATLAB command line, and their functions:

Up Arrow (Ctrl-P)	Retrieves the entry preceding the current one.
Down Arrow (Ctrl-N)	Retrieves the entry following the current one.
Left Arrow (Ctrl-B)	Moves the cursor one character to the left.
Right Arrow (Ctrl-F)	Moves the cursor one character to the right.
CTRL-Left Arrow	Moves the cursor one word to the left.
CTRL-Right Arrow	Moves the cursor one word to the right.
Home (Ctrl-A)	Moves the cursor to the beginning of the current line.
End (Ctrl-E)	Moves the cursor to the end of the current line.
Escape	Clears the command line.
Delete (Ctrl-D)	Erases the character indicated by the cursor.
Backspace	Deletes the character to the left of the cursor.
CTRL-K	Clears (kills) the entire current line.

The command *clc* clears the command window, but does not delete the contents of the work area (the content currently in memory).

1.5 MATLAB and Programming

By properly combining all the features of MATLAB, one can build useful mathematical research programming code. Programs usually consist of a sequence of instructions in which various values are calculated. These sequences of commands are assigned names and can be reused in further calculations.

As in programming languages like C or Fortran, MATLAB supports loops, control flow and conditional statements. MATLAB can write procedural programs, i.e., it can define a sequence of standard steps to run. As in C or Pascal, one can repeat calculations using *Do*, *For*, or *While* loops. The language of MATLAB also includes conditional constructs such as *If Then Else*. MATLAB also supports different logical operators, such as *And*, *Or*, *Not* and *Xor*.

MATLAB supports procedural programming (with iterative processes, recursive functions, loops...), functional programming and object-oriented programming. Here are two simple examples of programs. The first generates the order n Hilbert matrix, and the second calculates the Fibonacci numbers less than 1000.

```
% Generates the order n Hilbert matrix
t = '1/(i+j-1)';
for i = 1:n
     for j = 1:n
          a(i,j) = eval(t);
     end
 end

% Calculates Fibonacci numbers
f = [1 1]; i = 1;
while f(i) + f(i-1) < 1000
        f(i+2) = f(i) + f(i+1);
        i = i+1
end
```

1.6 Translating C, FORTRAN and TEX expressions

MATLAB offers the possibility to translate math expressions to code in other programming languages such as Fortran or C. Additionally, it can also translate expressions to *eqn* and TeX form. To do this, one can use the following commands:

maple('fortran(expression)') Translates the given Maple expression to Fortran.

maple('fortran(expr,optimized)') Translates the given Maple expression to Fortran in an optimized way.

maple('fortran(expr,precision=double)') Translates the Maple expression to Fortran using double-precision.

maple('fortran(expr,digits=n)') Translates the Maple expression to Fortran using n floating point digits.

maple('fortran(procedure)') Translates the given Maple procedure to a Fortran procedure. Also translates Maple arrays and lists to Fortran.

maple('fortran(exp,filename=name)') Translates the given Maple expression to Fortran and saves it in a file named *name*.

maple('C(expression)') Translates the given Maple expression to C. It is necessary to first load the C library with the command *readlib(C)*.

maple('C(expression,optimized)') Translates the given Maple expression into C in an optimized way.

maple('C(expr,precision=single)') Translates the given Maple expression into C using single-precision (double precision is the default).

maple('C(expr,digits=n)') Translates the given Maple expression into C using n floating point digits.

maple('C(procedure)') Translates the given Maple procedure to a C procedure. It also translates Maple arrays and lists to C.

maple('C(procedure, ansi)') Translates the given Maple procedure to C following standard ANSI C syntax for the declaration of the parameters.

maple('C(expr, filename=name)') Translates the given Maple expression to C and saves it in a file with the name *nom*.

maple('latex(expression)') Converts the given Maple expression to TeX.

maple('latex(expr, filename=name)') Converts the given Maple expression to TeX and saves it in a file named *nom*.

maple('eqn(expression)') Translates the given Maple expression to *eqn*. It is necessary to first load the eqn library with the command *readlib(eqn)*.

maple('eqn(expr, filename=name)') Translates the given Maple expression to *eqn* and saves it in a file with the name *name*.

As examples, we translate the integral of $1/(x^4+1)$ to TeX, Fortan and C:

```
>> maple('latex(Int(1/(x^4+1),x))')
```

ans =

```
\int \!\left ({x}^{4}+1\right )^{-1}{dx}
```

```
>> maple('fortran(Int(1/(x^4+1),x))')
```

ans =

```
t0 = Int(1/(x**4+1),x)
```

```
>> maple('readlib(C)'); maple('C(Int(1/(x^4+1),x))')
```

ans =

```
t0 = Int(1/(pow(x,4.0)+1.0),x);
```

CHAPTER 2

■ ■ ■

Integers, Divisibility and Number Systems

2.1 Arithmetic Operations in MATLAB

Arithmetic operations in MATLAB are defined according to the standard mathematical conventions. MATLAB is an interactive program that allows you to perform a wide variety of mathematical operations. Furthermore, it has other properties that make it extremely versatile and complex, applicable to a broad range of subjects from more theoretical mathematics to the more applied.

One of the first applications of MATLAB is its use in realizing arithmetic operations as if it were a conventional calculator, but with one important difference: the precision of calculation. Operations are performed to the greatest accuracy required, or the user may specify the degree of precision in advance. This unlimited precision in calculation sets MATLAB apart from other numerical software, where the accuracy is determined by the word length of the computer, so it is essentially determined by the hardware and cannot be modified. This feature is one of the most important in symbolic calculation.

MATLAB assumes the usual arithmetic operations of sum, difference, product, division and power, with the usual hierarchy between them:

```
x + y sum
x - y difference
x * y or x y product
x/y division
x ^ y power
```

To add two numbers, simply enter the first number, type a plus sign (+) and then enter the second number. Spaces may be included before or after the plus sign to ease readability.

```
>> 53 + 78
```

ans =

    131

We can perform the calculation of powers directly.

```
>> 34 ^ 56
```

ans =

5. *7919e + 085*

Unlike a calculator, when working with integers, MATLAB displays the exact result even when you have more digits than would normally fit across the screen. Here MATLAB returns the exact value of *34 ^ 56*.

```
>> vpa ' 34 ^ 56' 90
```

ans =

57918773205287127842044254126179599852840968492056164062843692360166371779746690236416.

These operations are used to perform calculations of varying degrees of complexity. When combining several operations in the same instruction, one must take into account the usual criteria of priority among them, which determine the order of evaluation of the expression. Consider the following example:

```
>> 2 * 3 ^ 2 + (5-2) * 3
```

ans =

27

Taking into account the usual order of priority of operators, the first to be evaluated is the power operation. The usual order of evaluation can be altered by grouping expressions in parentheses.

In addition to these arithmetic operators, MATLAB is equipped with a set of basic functions, and the user can also define their own functions. Both the embedded MATLAB functions and operators can be applied to symbolic or numeric constants.

EXERCISE 2-1

Perform the following operations:

(a) (-2 + 3 - 5) (4 - 3 + 2)/(15 + 4 - 21)

(b) [(2 - 3)(4 - 3 + 5)]³ [(3 - 2) + (6 - 8 - 5)]

(c) 5 - [4 - 3 + 2 * 7 + 5] + [(3 - 6)² (7 - 9)²]

(d) 6 - 4 * 3/2 - 7 * 2 + 8 - 6/3 - 5² + 3

(e) [5 + 3 * 2/6 - 4].[4/2 - 3 + 6]/[7/2 - 8 - 2]²

We input the above operations in the following way:

```
>> ((-2 + 3 - 5)*(4 - 3 + 2))/(15 + 4 - 21)
```

ans =

6

```
>> ((2 - 3)*(4 - 3 + 5))^3 * (3 - 2 + 6 - 8 - 5)
```

ans =

1296

```
>> 5 - (4 - 3 + 2 * 7 + 5) + (3 - 6)^2 * (7 - 9)^2
```

ans =

21

```
>> 6 - (4 * 3)/2 - 7 * 2 + 8 - 6/3 - 5^2 + 3
```

ans =

-30

```
>> ((5 + (3*2)/6 - 4)*(4/2 - 3 + 6))/(7 - 8/2 - 2)^2
```

ans =

10

EXERCISE 2-2

Perform the following operations:

(a) $6\,a\,b + 3a^2 + 2\,a\,b$

(b) $6\,a^2 + 2\,a - b^2 + 3\,a - 5\,a^2 + b^2$

(c) $6\,a\,b - 2\,a^2 - 4\,a\,b + 3\,a^2$

We input the above operations in the following way:

```
>> syms a b
>> pretty(simplify(6*a*b + 3*a^2 + 2*a*b))
```

$$8\,a\,b + 3\,a^2$$

```
>> pretty(simplify( 6*a^2 + 2*a - b^2 + 3*a - 5*a^2 + b^2))
```

$$a^2 + 5\,a$$

```
>> pretty(simplify(6*a*b - 2*a^2 - 4*a*b + 3*a^2))
```

$$2\,a\,b + a^2$$

The purpose of this exercise is to demonstrate the need to declare symbolic variables as such when they are part of non-numeric expressions.

EXERCISE 2-3

Where $H = 3\,a^2 - 2a + 7$, $F = 6\,a^3 - 5\,a + 2$ and $G = 5\,a^2 + 4a - 3$, calculate:

a) $H + F + G$

b) $H - F + G$

c) $H - F - G$

We input the previous operations in the following way:

```
>> syms a
>> H = 3*a^2 - 2*a + 7, F = 6*a^3 - 5*a + 2, G = 5*a^2 + 4*a - 3
```

$H =$

$3*a^2 - 2*a + 7$

F =

6*a^3 - 5*a + 2

G =

5*a^2 + 4*a - 3

>> pretty(H+F+G)

$$8\,a^2 \;-\; 3\,a \;+\; 6 \;+\; 6\,a^3$$

>> pretty(H-F+G)

$$8\,a^2 \;+\; 7\,a \;+\; 2 \;-\; 6\,a^3$$

>> pretty(H-F-G)

$$-\,2\,a^2 \;-\; a \;+\; 8 \;-\; 6\,a^3$$

We can also perform these operations by using MATLAB's specific symbolic computation command ***symop***. In general, the command *symop* applies the specified operations (*op*) in quotation marks to the symbolic (*sym*) variables in the order presented.

>> pretty(symop(H,'+',F,'+',G))

$$8\,a^2 \;-\; 3\,a \;+\; 6 \;+\; 6\,a^3$$

>> pretty(symop(H,'-',F,'+',G))

$$8\,a^2 \;+\; 7\,a \;+\; 2 \;-\; 6\,a^3$$

>> pretty(symop(H,'-',F,'-',G))

$$-\,2\,a^2 \;-\; a \;+\; 8 \;-\; 6\,a^3$$

When it comes to symbolic operations, it is always possible to make use of the interrelationship between MATLAB and Maple.

>> pretty(sym(maple('3*a^2 - 2*a + 7 + 6*a^3 - 5*a + 2 + 5*a^2 + 4*a - 3')))

$$8\,a^2 \;-\; 3\,a \;+\; 6 \;+\; 6\,a^3$$

```
>> pretty(sym(maple('3*a^2 - 2*a + 7 - (6*a^3 - 5*a + 2) + 5*a^2 + 4*a - 3')))
```

$$8\,a^2 + 7\,a + 2 - 6\,a^3$$

```
>> pretty(sym(maple('3*a^2 - 2*a + 7 - (6*a^3 - 5*a + 2) - (5*a^2 + 4*a - 3')))
```

$$-\,2\,a^2 - a + 8 - 6\,a^3$$

However, in this simple case it is not necessary to use Maple, because MATLAB already executes the operations correctly by introducing symbolic expressions between quotation marks.

```
>> syms a
>> pretty('3*a^2 - 2*a + 7 - (6*a^3 - 5*a + 2) - (5*a^2 + 4*a - 3)')
```

$$-\,2\,a^2 - a + 8 - 6\,a^3$$

2.2 Integers

The MATLAB program can work on different platforms. Depending on the power of the hardware and software, the program will work with greater or lesser precision. The precision with which MATLAB works means that there is virtually no limit to the maximum size of integers that it is capable of handling; the most typical limitation is the amount of computer memory available. Thus, all the usual operations with integers are exact, regardless of the size of the result.

If we want the result of an operation to appear on screen with a certain number of significant figures, we use the symbolic computation command *vpa* (*variable precision arithmetic*), whose syntax is:

vpa 'operation' no_of _ figures

For example, to calculate 7 to the power 400 to 500 significant figures we enter the following:

```
>> vpa '7 ^ 400' 500
```

ans =

*1094500604336113085424254456486662175299754873359706186335419407515439063163492090021478568469687152
8073999537352825386155249571017070263772889172085286838471044006674397286276116996066357907929105887
8933088274875698178024977088223396398265555596916473536792437134632739719389969690630523317113111727
6831958198390034920060979947293122400001.*

The result of the operation is accurate, always placing a point at the end of the result. In this case the result can be expressed in fewer than 500 figures, so the solution is exact. If you request a smaller number of significant figures than the exact result has, MATLAB will round the number to the appropriate multiple of a power of 10. For example, if we perform the above calculation only to 50 significant figures we get:

```
>> vpa ' 7 ^ 400' 50
```

ans =

1. 0945006043361130854242544564866621752997548733597e338

2.3 Divisibility

MATLAB provides multiple commands relating to divisibility. The program implements a variety of *functions with integer arguments* which will be presented below, most of which concern divisibility. Several of these functions are only available if you have installed the extended symbolic mathematics *Toolbox*. A group of the commands are accessible directly, another group first requires the command *maple*, and to gain access to the final group, it is necessary to load the Maple *numtheory* library with the command *maple('with(numtheory)')*.

Among the most typical functions with integer arguments are the following:

>**rem(n,m): the remainder of the division of** *n* **by** *m* **(valid for real** *n* **and** *m*)

>**sign(n): the sign of** *n* **(1 if n > 0, - 1 if n < 0,** *n* **real)**

>**binomial(n,m): the binomial coefficient** *n* **choose** *m* **: n! / (m! (m-n)!)**

>**bernoulli(n): the nth Bernoulli number** B_n**:** $te^{xt}/(e^t - 1) = \Sigma B_n(x) t^n/n!$ **n=0...∞**

>**euler(n) the nth Euler number** E_n**:** $2/(e^t + e^{-t}) = \Sigma En(x) t^n/n!$ **n=0...∞.**

>**max(n1,n2): the maximum of n1 and n2**

>**min(n1,n2): the minimum of n1 and n2**

>**gcd(n1,n2): the greatest common divisor of n1 and n2**

>**lcm(n1,n2): the least common multiple of n1 and n2**

>**maple('irem(n,m)'): the remainder of the division of** *n by m*

>**maple('igcd(n1,n2,...,nk)'): the greatest common divisor of** *k* **numbers**

>**maple('igcdex(n1,n2,...,nk)'): the greatest common divisor of** *k* **numbers using Euclid's algorithm**

>**maple('ilcm(n1,n2,...,nk)'): the least common multiple of** *k* **numbers**

>**maple('max(n1,n2,...,nk)'): the maximum of** *k* **numbers**

>**maple('min(n1,n2,...,nk)'): the minimum of** *k* **numbers**

>**maple('n!'): factorial** *n* **(n! = n(n-1) (n-2)...2.1)**

>**maple('ifactor(n)') or factor(n): factorizes** *n*

>**maple('ithprime(k)'): returns the k-th prime**

>**maple('seq(ithprime(k),k = 1... n') or primes(n): returns the first** *n* **primes**

maple('isprime(n)') or isprime(n): determines whether *n* is prime or not

maple('type(expr,prime)'): determines if the expression is a prime

maple('type(expr,facint)'): determines if the given expression is completely factored or not

maple('isqrt(n)'): determines if *n* is perfect square

maple('nextprime(n)'): finds the smallest prime larger than *n*

maple('prevprime(n)'): finds the largest prime less than *n*

Among the most typical functions with integer arguments for which it is necessary to previously load Maple's *numtheory* library, we have the following:

maple('with(numtheory)') loads the *numtheory* library to be used before the following commands

maple('issqr(n)'): determines if *n* is the square of an integer

maple('issqrfree(n)'): determines if *n* is square-free

maple('ifactors(n)'): returns the prime factors of *n* and their orders

maple('factorset(n)'): returns the set of prime factors of *n*

maple('splitters(n)'): returns a list of the divisors of *n*

maple('sigma(n)'): returns the sum of the divisors of *n*

maple('tau(n)'): returns the number of positive divisors of *n*

maple('bigomega(n)'): returns the number of prime divisors of *n*

maple('iroot(n,m)'): returns the integer part of $n^{1/m}$

maple('iquo(n1,n2)'): returns the integer part of the ratio n1/n2

maple('b(n)'): returns the nth Bernoulli number B_n

maple('fermat(n)'): returns the nth Fermat number: 2^(2^n)+1

Here are some examples:
Factorize the number 24:

```
>> maple ('ifactor(24)')
```

ans =

 (2) ^ 3 * (3)

Factorize the number 999999999999:

```
>> maple ('ifactor(999999999999)')
```

ans =

 (3) ^ 3 *(7) * (11) * (13) * (37) * (101) * (9901)

Find the remainder of the division of 17 by 3:

```
>> rem (17,3)
```

ans =

2

Find the remainder of division of 4.1 by 1.2:

```
>> rem (4.1,1.2)
```

ans =

0.5000

Find the remainder of the division of -4.1 by 1.2:

```
>> rem(-4.1,1.2)
```

ans =

-0.5000

Find the greatest common divisor of 1000, 500 and 625:

```
>> maple ('igcd (1000,500,625)')
```

ans =

125

Find the least common multiple of 1000, 500 and 625:

```
>> maple ('ilcm (1000,500,625)')
```

ans =

5000

Is 99991 a prime number?:

```
>> maple ('isprime (99991)')
```

ans =

true

Indeed, the number is prime.

Find the 100th prime number:

```
>> maple ('ithprime (100)')
```

ans =

541

Find the set of all numbers that divide 24:

```
>> maple('with(numtheory)');maple('divisors(24)')
```

ans =

{1, 2, 3, 4, 6, 8, 12, 24}

Find the prime factors of 12267845 together with their orders of multiplicity:

```
>> maple('with(numtheory)'); maple('ifactors(12267845)')
```

ans =

[1, [[5, 1], [113, 1], [21713, 1]]]

Find the set of prime factors of 135678743:

```
>> maple('with(numtheory)');maple('factorset(135678743)')
```

ans =

{135678743}

Logically, the above number has to be prime:

```
>> maple ('isprime (135678743)')
```

ans =

true

Find the set of prime factors of the number 135678742:

```
>> maple('with(numtheory)');maple('factorset(135678742)')
```

ans =

{2, 1699, 39929}

Find the list of divisors, the number of divisors and the sum of the divisors of 1000000:

```
>> maple('with(numtheory)');maple('divisors(1000000)')
```

ans =

{1, 2, 4, 5, 8, 10, 16, 20, 25, 32, 40, 50, 64, 80, 100, 125, 250000, 3125, 31250, 62500, 125000, 500000, 1000000, 12500, 625, 15625, 25000, 250, 6250, 1250, 500, 2500, 200, 1000, 5000, 400, 2000, 160, 800, 4000, 50000, 10000, 100000, 20000, 200000, 40000, 320, 1600, 8000}

```
>> maple('with(numtheory)');maple('tau(1000000)')
```

ans =

49

```
>> maple('with(numtheory)');maple('sigma(1000000)')
```

ans =

2480437

EXERCISE 2-4

Find the number of different ways of selecting 9 elements from 45 without repetition. Consider the same problem for three elements selected from n.

```
>> maple('binomial(45, 9)')
```

ans =

886163135

```
>> maple('expand(binomial(n, 3))')
```

ans =

*1/6 * n ^ 3-1/2 * n ^ 2 + 1/3 * n*

EXERCISE 2-5

Find the remainder of the division of 2^{134} by 3. Also find the smallest positive integer k such that $k \equiv 12 \bmod 8$.

```
>> rem(2^134,3)
```

ans =

1

```
>> maple('chrem([12],[8])')
```

ans =

4

The syntax of the function *chrem* will be presented in the next section.

EXERCISE 2-6

Find the prime factors and all the divisors of 18900. Also find the 189th prime number.

```
>> maple ('ifactor(18900)')
```

ans =

(2)^2(3)^3*(5)^2*(7)*

```
>> maple('with(numtheory)');maple('divisors(18900)')
```

ans =

{1, 2, 3, 4, 5, 6, 7, 9, 10, 12, 14, 15, 18, 20, 21, 25, 27, 28, 30, 35, 36, 42, 45, 50, 54, 60, 63, 70, 75, 84, 90, 100, 105, 108, 126, 135, 1050, 2700, 18900, 525, 1260, 180, 150, 225, 300, 450, 675, 900, 270, 1350, 540, 140, 175, 189, 210, 252, 315, 350, 378, 420, 630, 700, 756, 945, 1575, 2100, 3150, 4725, 6300, 1890, 9450, 3780}

```
>> maple('ithprime(189)')
```

ans =

1129

EXERCISE 2-7

Two books have 840 and 384 pages, respectively. If they are formed by sections of an equal number of pages (more than 18), calculate the number of pages per section.

```
>> gcd (840, 384)
```

ans =

24

EXERCISE 2-8

Find the smallest number N that when divided by 16, 24, 30 and 32 leaves the remainder 5.

N-5 will be a multiple of 16, 24, 30 and 32, and we are asked to calculate the least number, so N-5 will be the least common multiple of 16, 24, 30 and 32:

```
>> maple ('(16, 24, 30, 32) ilcm')
```

ans =

480

           Therefore N = 480 + 5 = 485.

EXERCISE 2-9

Calculate the factorial of 2000.

We have here an example of the high-precision of MATLAB:

```
>> maple('2000!')
```

ans =

33162750924506332411753933805763240382811172081057803945719354370603807790560082240027323085973259225540235294122583410925808481741529379613138663352634368890563405855616394060511725257187064785639354404540524395746703767410872297043468415834375243158087753364512748799543685924740803240894656150723325065279765575717967153671868935905611281587160171723265715611000421401242043384257371270017588354779689992128352899666585340557985490365736635013338655040117201215263548803826815215224692099520603156441856548067594649705155228820523489999572645081406553667896995321014676226713320268315522051944944616182392752040265297226315025747520482960647509273941658562835317795744828763145964503739913273341772636088524900935066216101444597094127078213137325638315723020199499149583164709427744738703279855496742986088393763268241524788343874695958292577405745398375015858154681362942179499723998135994810165565638760342273129122503847098729096266224619710766059315502018951355831653578714922909167790497022470946119376077851651106844322559056487362665303773846503907880495246007125494026145660722541363027549136715834060978

074945282217490781347709693241556111339828051358600690594619965257310741177081519922564516778
571458056602185654760952377463016679422488444485798349801548032620829890965857381751888619376
692828279888453584639896594213952984465291092009103710046149449915828588050761867924946385180
879874512891408019340074625920057098729578599643650655895612410231018690556060308783629110505
601245908998383410799367902052076858669183477906558544700148692656924631933337612428097420067
172846361939249698628468719993450393889367270487127172734561700354867477509102955523953547941
107421913301356819541091941462766417542161587625262858089801222443890248677182054959415751991
701271767571787495861619665931878855141835782092601482071777331735396034304969082070589958701
381980813035590160762908388574561288217698136182483576739218303118414719133986892842344000779
246691209766731651433494437473235636572048844478331854941693030124531676232745367879322847473
824485092283139952509732505979127031047683601481191102229253372697693236700575656124002905760
438528529029376064795334581796661238396052625491071866638693547661084550461981020840506358270
676526589492393249519685954171672419329530683673495544004586359838161043059449826627530605423
580755894108278880427825951089880635410567917950974017780688782869810219010900148352061688883
720250310665922068601483649830532782088263535655804360568678128416921713304714117631217589577
122637584753123517230990549829210134687304205898014418063875382664169897704237759406280877253
702265426530580862379301422675821187143502918637636340300173251818262076039747369595202642632
364145446851113427202150458383851010136941313034856221916631623892632765815355011276307825059
969158824533457435437863683173730673296589355199694458236873508830278657700879749889992343555
566240682834763784685183844973648873952475103224222110561201295829657191368108693825475764118
886879346725191246192151144738836269591643672490071653428228152661247800463922544945170363723
627940577845420910483054616561906221742869816029733240465202019928138548826819510072828269701
070737500927666487502174775372742351508748246720274170031581122805896178122160747437947510950
620938556674581252518376682157712807861499255876132352950422346387878954508857644661362903940
127665978044202092281337987115900896264878942413210454925003566670632909441579372986743421470
507213588932019580723064781498429522595589012754823971773325722910325760929790733299545056388
362640474650245080809469116072632087494143973000704111418595530278827357654819182002449697761
111346318195282761590964189790958117338627206088910432945244978535147014112442143055486089639
578378347325323595763291438925288393986256273242862775563140463830389168421633113445636309571
965978466338551492316196335675355138403425804162919837822266909521770153175338730284610841886
554138329171951332117895728541662084823682817932512931237521541926970269703299477643823386483
008871530373405666383868294088487730721762268849023084934661194260180272613802108005078215741
006054848201347859578102770707780655512772540501674332396066253216415004808772403047611929032
210154385353138685538486425570790795341176519571188683739880683895792743749683498142923292196
309777090143936843655333359307820181312993455024206044563340578606962471961505603394899523321
800434359967256623927196435402872055475012079854331970674797313126813523653744085662263206768
837585132782896252333284341812977624697079543436003492343159239674763638912115285406657783646
213911247447051255226342701239527018127045491648045932248108858674600952306793175967755581011
679940005249806303763141344412269037034987355799916009259248075052485541568266281760815446308
305406677412630124441864204108373119093130001154470560277773724378067188899770851056727276781
247198832857695844217588895160467868204810010047816462358220838532488134270834079868486632162
720208823308727819085378845469131556021728873121907393965209260229101477527080930865364979858
554010577450279289814603688431821508637246216967872282169347370599286277112447690920902988320
166830170273420259765671709863311216349502171264426827119650264054228231759630874475301847194
095524263411498469508073390080000000000000000000000000000000000000000000000000000000000000000
000000000000000000000000000000000000000000000000000000000000000000000000000000000000000000000
000000000000000000000000000000000000000000000000000000000000000000000000000000000000000000000
000000000000000000000000000000000000000000000000000000000000000000000000000000000000000000000
000000000000000000000000000000000000000000000000000000000000000000000000000000000000000000000
000000000000000000000000000000000000000000000000000000000000000000000000000

EXERCISE 2-10

Calculate the number 2^115-1 and determine whether or not it is prime. If it is compound, break it down into its prime factors. Calculate the closest prime numbers greater than and less than 2^115-1. Verify that the largest of these two numbers is indeed prime.

```
>> 2 ^ 115-1
```

ans =

  4. 1538e + 034

We can now calculate the exact value:

```
>> vpa ' 2 ^ 115-1' 100
```

ans =

41538374868278621028243970633760767

Now let's check if it is prime:

```
>> maple ('isprime(2^115-1)')
```

ans =

false

Thus the number is not prime.

We find the decomposition into prime factors:

```
>> maple ('ifactor(2^115-1)')
```

ans =

*(31) *(47) * (2646507710984041) *(4036961) * (178481) * (14951)*

We now calculate the two prime numbers closest to the above number, one less than the number and the other greater than the number, and we see that the latter is indeed prime.

```
>> maple('prevprime(2^115-1)')
```

ans =

41538374868278621028243970633760701

```
>> maple('nextprime(2^115-1)')
```

ans =

41538374868278621028243970633760839

```
>> maple('isprime(nextprime(2^115-1))')
```

ans =

true

EXERCISE 2-11

Calculate the first 100 prime numbers.

```
>> maple('seq(ithprime(k),k=1..100)')
```

ans =

2, 3, 5, 7, 11, 13, 17, 19, 23, 29, 31, 37, 41, 43, 47, 53, 59, 61, 67, 71, 73, 79, 83, 89, 97, 101, 103, 107, 109, 113, 127, 131, 137, 139, 149, 151, 157, 163, 167, 173, 179, 181, 191, 193, 197, 199, 211, 223, 227, 229, 233, 239, 241, 251, 257, 263, 269, 271, 277, 281, 283293, 307, 311, 313, 317, 331, 337, 347, 349, 353, 359, 367, 373, 379, 383, 389, 397, 401, 409, 419, 421, 431, 433, 439, 443, 449, 457, 461, 463, 467, 479, 487, 491, 499, 503, 509, 521, 523, 541

EXERCISE 2-12

Given the number 51648597:

(a) Determine whether or not it is prime.

(b) If it is composite, break it down into prime factors.

(c) Calculate the set of its prime factors.

(d) Find its prime factors with their multiplicities.

(e) Find the set of its divisors.

(f) Find the sum of its divisors.

(g) Find the number of its divisors.

a)

```
>> maple ('isprime (51648597)')
```

ans =

false

Thus, it is not prime.

b)

```
>> maple('ifactor(51648597)')
```

ans =

(3)^4(7)^3*(11)*(13)^2*

c)

```
>> maple('with(numtheory)');maple('factorset(51648597)')
```

ans =

{3, 7, 11, 13}

d)

```
>> maple('with(numtheory)');maple('ifactors(51648597)')
```

ans =

[1, [[3, 4], [7, 3], [11, 1], [13, 2]]]

e)

```
>> maple('with(numtheory)');maple('divisors(51648597)')
```

ans =

{1, 3, 7, 9, 11, 13, 21, 27, 33, 39, 49, 63, 77, 81, 91, 99, 117, 819, 429, 297, 343, 351, 3972969, 11583, 4459, 14553, 3861, 1053, 231, 147, 1287, 441, 3003, 9009, 693, 51648597, 33957, 5733, 91091, 507, 305613, 120393, 273, 150579, 49049, 637637, 21021, 273273, 63063, 819819, 31941, 7371, 7007, 1565109, 95823, 51597, 24843, 74529, 117117, 81081, 1054053, 27027, 351351, 13377, 173901, 40131, 521703, 1911, 147147, 1912911, 361179, 4695327, 1324323, 17216199, 567567, 7378371, 17199, 223587, 39039, 10647, 13013, 13689, 16731, 50193, 57967, 3549, 4563, 5577, 637, 8281, 1001, 189189, 2459457, 441441, 5738733, 6237, 2079, 1183, 1521, 1859, 11319, 1029, 3087, 1323, 9261, 567, 3969, 27783, 539, 891, 3773, 1617, 4851, 101871, 43659, 169, 670761, 2457, 189, 143}

f)

```
>> maple('with(numtheory)');maple('sigma(51648597)')
```

ans =

106286400

g)

```
>> maple('with(numtheory)');maple('tau(51648597)')
```

ans =

120

2.4 Modular Arithmetic

MATLAB's elementary number theoretic cababilities can be expanded via the *numtheory* library of the *Extended Symbolic Math* toolbox, which incorporates commands related to modular arithmetic. We have the following:

maple('mroot(n1, n2, n3)') is $n1^{1/n2}$ modulo n3

maple('msrqt(n1,n2)') is $n1^{1/2}$ modulo n2

maple('nthpow(n1,n2)') is the largest *n* such that n divides $n1^{n2}$

maple('chrem([n1...nx],[m1...mx])') is the unique integer *n* such that n(mod mi) = ni i=1.....x

maple('imagunit(n)') gives $\sqrt{-1}$ modulo *n*

maple('mlog(p,q,r)') gives the logarithm of *p* to base *q* modulo *r*

maple('phi(n)') gives the number of positive integers less than or equal to *n* that are relatively prime with *n*

maple('invphi(n)') the inverse phi function (i.e. returns the set of positive integers k such that phi(k)=n)

maple('jacobi(n1,n2)') or maple('J(n1,n2)') gives the Jacobi symbol of the integers n1 and n2, i.e. it returns 1 if n1 is relatively prime with n2 and n2 is positive and odd, n2 if n1 is not a positive odd integer, and -1 otherwise

maple('legendre(n1,n2)') or maple('L(n1,n2)') gives the Legendre symbol of the integers n1 and n2, i.e. it returns 1 if n1 is a quadratic residue modulo n2, and -1 if it is not (n1 is a quadratic residue modulo n2 if there exists an integer *m* such that $m^2 \equiv n1$ (mod n2))

maple('lambda(n)') gives the size of the largest cyclic group generated by g^i(mod n)

maple('mersenne(n)') or maple('M(n)') returns 2^n - 1 if it is prime, and if not, returns *false*

maple('mcombine(n1,m1,n2,m2)'): gives an integer *n* such that n ≡ m1(mod n1) and n ≡ m2(mod n2). Returns FAIL if there is no such *n*

maple(' mipolys(n,p)') gives the number of monic univariate irreducible polynomials of degree *n* over Z (mod p)

maple('mipolys(n,p,m)') gives the number of monic univariate irreducible polynomials of degree *n* over the Galois field of order p^m

maple('mobius(n)') gives the positive integer equal to the Möbius function of n

maple('order(n1,n2)') gives the order of the integer n1 in the multiplicative group modulo n2, i.e. gives the smallest positive integer *m* such that n1^m ≡ 1(mod n2)

maple('pprimroot(n)') gives the smallest pseudo primitive root of the positive integer *n*, that is, the generator of the cyclic group under multiplication modulo *n* containing the integers relatively prime with *n*, and if it doesn't exist, gives the least positive integer not exceeding *n* and relatively prime to *n*

maple('pprimroot(n1,n2)') gives the smallest pseudo primitive root of the positive integer n2 that is greater than n1

maple('primroot(n)') gives the smallest primitive root of the positive integer *n*, that is, the generator of the cyclic group under multiplication modulo *n* containing relatively prime integers with *n*

maple('primroot(n1,n2)') gives the smallest primitive root of the positive integer n2 that is greater than n1

maple('quadres(n1,n2)') determines if n1 is a quadratic residue modulo n2

maple('rootsunity(p,n)') give all p-th roots of unity modulo n

maple('safeprime(n)') calculates the smallest prime *p* greater than *n* such that (p-1) / 2 is also prime

Below are some examples:
To find the logarithm of 1000000 in base 8 and modulo 52 we do the following:

```
>> maple('with(numtheory)');maple('mlog(1000000,8,52)')
```

ans =

4

To find the fifth root of 1000000 modulo 52:

```
>> maple('with(numtheory)');maple('mroot(1000000,5,52)')
```

ans =

40

To find the square root of -1 modulo 5:

```
>> maple('with(numtheory)');maple('imagunit(5)')
```

ans =

2

To check if $2^4- 1$ and $2^5- 1$ are primes:

```
>> maple('with(numtheory)');maple('mersenne(4)')
```

ans =

false

```
>> maple('with(numtheory)');maple('mersenne(5)')
```

ans =

31

To find how many positive integers less than or equal to 15 are relatively prime with 15:

```
>> maple('with(numtheory)');maple('phi(15)')
```

ans =

8

EXERCISE 2-13

Find the largest integer n such that n^3 divides 6561. Also find the square root of n modulo 7.

```
>> maple('with(numtheory)'); maple('nthpow (6561,3)')
```

ans =

(9)^3

```
>> maple('with(numtheory)');maple('msqrt(9,7)')
```

ans =

3

EXERCISE 2-14

Find the integer n that simultaneously satisfies the equations n ≡ 1000 (mod 37) and n ≡ 1500 (mod 53). Also find the integer n that simultaneously satisfies the equations n ≡ 500 (mod 3), n ≡ 600 (mod4) and n ≡ 700 (mod 5). Is there an integer m such that m^2 ≡ 1000 (mod 37)? Finally, find the smallest integer k such that 1500^k ≡ 1 (mod 53).

```
>> maple('with(numtheory)');
>> maple mcombine(37,1000,53,1500)
```

ans =

334

```
>> maple chrem([500,600,700],[3,4,5])
```

ans =

20

```
>> maple legendre(1000,37)
```

ans =

1

```
>> maple order (1500,53)
```

ans =

13

We therefore conclude that there is such an integer *m*.

EXERCISE 2-15

Find the number of monic irreducible univariate polynomials of degree 3 over the ring Z (mod 17). Find the number of monic univariate irreducible polynomials of degree 5 over the Galois field of order 7^{11}.

```
>> maple('with(numtheory)');
>> maple mipolys(3,17)
```

ans =

1632

```
>> maple mipolys(5,7,11)
```

ans =

6045360394355011189649410336790819322177683040

EXERCISE 2-16

Find the smallest generator of the cyclic group under multiplication modulo 1500 containing integers relatively prime with 1500. Find such a generator with the condition that it be greater than 11.

```
>> maple('with(numtheory)');
>> maple pprimroot(1500)
```

ans =

7

```
>> maple pprimroot(10,1500)
```

ans =

11

EXERCISE 2-17

Find the fifth roots of unity modulo 11. Also find the smallest prime p greater than 1000 such that (p-1)/2 is also prime.

```
>> maple('with(numtheory)');
>> maple rootsunity(5,11)
```

ans =

1, 3, 4, 5, 9

```
>> maple safeprime(1000)
```

ans =

1019

2.5 Divisibility in Z[√n]

Via the *numtheory* library of the *Extended Symbolic Math* toolbox, MATLAB allows you to perform divisibility tasks in the ring Z[√n], where *n* is any integer. In this regard, the program implements the following functions:

> maple('factorEQ(n,m)') calculates the entire factorization of *m* in the Euclidean ring $Z[n^{1/2}]$

> maple('sq2factor(n)') gives the entire factorization of *n* in Z[√2]

> maple('sum2sqr(n)') gives a list of pairs of numbers whose squares sum to *n*

EXERCISE 2-18

Factorize the following:

(a) 38477343 in the ring Z[√11]

(b) 38434 *√33 in the ring Z[√33]

(c) 408294234124-4242 *√29 in the ring Z[√29]

```
>> maple('with(numtheory)');
>> maple factorEQ(38477343,11)
```

ans =

 *(3) * (125 + 34 * 11 ^(1/2)) * (125-34 * 11 ^(1/2)) *(85 + 16 * 11 ^(1/2)) * (85-16 *
11 ^(1/2))*

Written in radical form, this is:

$$(3)\left(125+34\sqrt{11}\right)\left(125-34\sqrt{11}\right)\left(85+16\sqrt{11}\right)\left(85-16\sqrt{11}\right)$$

```
>> maple factorEQ (38434 * sqrt (33), 33)
```

ans =

(33 ^(1/2)) * (- 23 + 4 * 33 ^(1/2)) * (5/2 + 1/2 * 33 ^(1/2)) * (5/2-1/2 * 33 ^(1/2)) *
(11 + 2 * 33 ^(1/2)) ^ 2 * (58 + 7 * 33 ^(1/2)) * (58-7 * 33 ^(1/2))

Written in radical form, this is:

$$(\sqrt{33})\left(-23+4\sqrt{33}\right)\left(\frac{5}{2}+\frac{1}{2}\sqrt{33}\right)\left(\frac{5}{2}-\frac{1}{2}\sqrt{33}\right)\left(11+2\sqrt{33}\right)^2\left(58+7\sqrt{33}\right)\left(58-7\sqrt{33}\right)$$

```
>> maple factorEQ (408294234124-4242 * sqrt (29), 29)
```

ans =

-(2) *(1/2 + 1/2 * 29 ^(1/2)) * (1/2-1/2 * 29 ^(1/2)) *(5/2-1/2 * 29 ^(1/2)) ^ 4 * (11 + 2 *
29 ^(1/2)) *(4 + 29 ^(1/2)) * (38 + 7 * 29 ^(1/2)) *(955872689/2 + 331629325/2 * 29 ^(1/2))

Written in radical form, this is:

$$-(2)\left(\frac{1}{2}+\frac{1}{2}\sqrt{29}\right)\left(\frac{1}{2}-\frac{1}{2}\sqrt{29}\right)\left(\frac{5}{2}-\frac{1}{2}\sqrt{29}\right)^4\left(11+2\sqrt{29}\right)\left(4+\sqrt{29}\right)\left(11+2\sqrt{29}\right)\left(38+7\sqrt{29}\right)$$

$$\left(\frac{955872689}{2}+\frac{331629325}{2}\sqrt{29}\right)$$

EXERCISE 2-19

Factorize the following in Z[√2]:

a) $(1-\sqrt{2})^{-4}$

b) 83424959

c) 9232-932*√2

```
>> maple('with(numtheory)');
>> maple sq2factor ((1-sqrt (2)) ^(-4))
```

˙ *ans =*

```
(2 ^(1/2) + 1) ^ 4
```

Written in radical form, this is:

$$\left(1+\sqrt{2}\right)^{4}$$

```
>> maple sq2factor (83424959)
```

ans =

```
 (9503 + 1855 * 2 ^(1/2)) *(9503-1855 * 2 ^(1/2))
```

Written in radical form, this is:

$$\left(9503+1855\sqrt{2}\right)\left(9503-1855\sqrt{2}\right)$$

```
>> maple sq2factor (9232-932 * sqrt (2))
```

ans =

```
(2 ^(1/2)) ^ 5 * (2-^(1/2)-1) * (1 + 3 * 2 ^(1/2)) * (5 + 2 ^(1/2)) * (17 + 59 * 2 ^(1/2))
```

Written in radical form, this is:

$$\left(\sqrt{2}\right)^{5}\left(-1+\sqrt{2}\right)\left(1+3\sqrt{2}\right)\left(5+\sqrt{2}\right)\left(17+59\sqrt{2}\right)$$

2.6 Diophantine Equations

Via the *numtheory* library of the *Extended Symbolic Math* toolbox, MATLAB can attempt to solve Diophantine equations, i.e., it can find integer solutions of certain equations, inequalities, systems of equations and systems of inequalities. In this regard, the program implements the following functions:

maple('kronecker({ineq$_1$,...,ineq$_x$},{var$_{1,1}$,...,var$_{1,m}$},{var$_{2,1}$,...,var$_{2,n}$})') gives the Diophantine approximation, in the inhomogeneous case, of the specified inequalities with respect to the given two sets of variables

maple('minkowski({ineq$_1$,...,ineq$_x$},{var$_{1,1}$,...,var$_{1,m}$},{var$_{2,1}$,...,var$_{2,n}$})') gives the Diophantine approximation, in the homogeneous case, of the specified inequalities with respect to the given two sets of variables

maple('thue(f(x,y) = m,[x,y])') solves the equation for f(x,y)$\in$Z[x, y] irreducible over Q[x,y] and integer m

maple('thue(f(x,y)£m, [x, y])') solve the inequality for f(x,y)$\in$Z[x, y] irreducible over Q[x, y] and integer m

---

EXERCISE 2-20

Solve (integer solutions) the following equations and inequalities in Z[x,y]:

a) $x^2 + x y + y^2 = 19$

b) $abs(x^3 + x^2 y - 2 x y^2 - y^3) \leq 5$

c) $abs(x^5 + x^4 y - 4 x^3 y^2 - 3x^2 y^3 + 3x y^4 + y^5) \leq 10$

d) $x^3 + y^3 = 5$

a)

```
>> maple('with(numtheory)');
>> maple thue(x^2 + x*y + y^2 = 19,[x,y])
```

```
[x = 5, y = - 3], [x = - 2, y = - 3], [x = 2, y = - 5], [x = - 2, y = 5],
[x = - 5, y = 3], [x = 2, y = 3], [x = - 5, y = 2],
[x = - 3, y = - 2], [x = 5, y = - 2], [x = 3, y = 2],
[x = - 3, y = 5], [x = 3, y = - 5]
```

b)

```
>> maple thue(abs(x^3 + x^2*y-2*x*y^2-y^3) < = 5 [x, y])
```

```
[x = 0, y = 0], [x = 1, y = 0], [x = 1, y = 1], [x = 5, y = 4],
[x = - 5, y = - 4], [x = - 2, y = 1], [x = - 1, y = 0],
[x = - 1, y = 1], [x = - 1, y = 2], [x = - 1, y = - 1],
[x = 1, y = - 2], [x = 1, y = - 1], [x = - 4, y = 9], [x = 0, y = 1],
[x = 0, y = - 1], [x = 2, y = - 1], [x = 4, y = - 9,]
[x = - 9, y = 5], [x = 9, y = - 5]
```

c)

```
>> maple thue(abs(x^5 + x^4*y-4*x^3*y^2-3*x^2*y^3 + 3*x*y^4 + y^5) < = 10, [x, y])
```

$[x = 0, y = 0]$, $[x = 1, y = 0]$, $[x = 1, y = 1]$, $[x = -1, y = 1]$,
$[x = -2, y = 1]$, $[x = 0, y = 1]$, $[x = 0, y = -1]$,
$[x = -1, y = -1]$, $[x = -1, y = 0]$, $[x = 1, y = -1]$,
$[x = 2, y = -1]$

d)

```
>> maple thue(x^3 + y^3 =5,[x,y])
```

Error, (in thue) this binary form is not irreducible

EXERCISE 2-21

Solve the following Diophantine system in both homogeneous and inhomogeneous cases:

$$|e^{z1} + 2^{1/2}z_2 - s_1| \le 10^{-2}$$

$$|3^{1/3} z_1 + \pi z_2 - s_2| \le 10^{-4}$$

```
>> maple('with(numtheory)');
>> maple minkowski ({abs (exp(1)*z1 + 2^(1/2)*z2 - s1 ) <=10^(-2),
   abs (3^(1/3)*z1 + Pi*z2 - s2 ) <=10^(-4)}, {z1,z2},{s1,s2})
```

$[z1 = 7484]$, $[z2 = -2534]$, $[s1 = 16760]$, $[s2 = 2833]$

```
>> maple kronecker ({abs (exp(1)*z1 + 2^(1/2)*z2 - s1 ) <=10^(-2),
   abs (3^(1/3)*z1 + Pi*z2 - s2 ) <=10^(-4)}, {z1,z2},{s1,s2})
```

$[z1 = -1014]$, $[z2 = 5300]$, $[s1 = 4739]$, $[s2 = 15188]$

2.7 Number Systems

MATLAB allows you to work with number systems to any base, as long as the extended symbolic math *Toolbox* is available. It also allows you to express all kinds of numbers in different bases. The following functions are available:

maple('convert(decimal,base,n_base)') or dec2base(decimal,n_base) (base 10) converts the specified decimal number to the base n_base

base2dec(number,B) converts the given number in base B to decimal

maple('convert(decimal,binary)') or dec2bin(decimal) converts the specified decimal number to base 2 (binary)

maple('convert(decimal,octal)') converts the specified decimal number to base 8 (octal)

maple('convert(decimal,octal,n)') or dec2hex(decimal) converts to base 8 (octal) the specified decimal number with n digits of precision

maple('convert(decimal,hex)') converts the decimal number specified to base 16 (hexadecimal)

maple('convert(binary,decimal,binary)') or bin2dec (binary) converts the specified binary number to decimal

maple('convert(octal,decimal,octal)') converts the octal number to decimal

maple('convert(hexadecimal,decimal,hex)') or hex2dec (hexadecimal) converts the specified base 16 number to decimal

maple('convert([a,b,...,c],base,old_base,new_base)') converts the number whose digits in the old base are: c... ba, to the new base. The result is a list with the figures placed in the reverse order to the usual ordering

maple('convert(decimal,double,option)') converts a decimal number to a double-precision hexadecimal according to the given option (ibm, mips and vax)

maple('convert(hexad,double,maple,option)') converts the given double-precision hexadecimal number to a Maple format hexadecimal according to the given option (ibm, mips and vax)

EXERCISE 2-22

Express the decimal number 2342424 in base 2. Also express the decimal number 242345341 in base 16.

```
>> maple ('convert(2342424,binary)')
```

ans =

1000111011111000011000

```
>> maple('convert(242345341,hex)')
```

ans =

E71E57D

EXERCISE 2-23

Express the binary number 100101 in base 10, and express in base 10 the hexadecimal number ffffaa00. Find in base 10 the result of the operation of hexadecimal numbers fffaa2 + ff − 1.

```
>> maple ('convert(100101,decimal,binary)') or  base2dec('100101',2)
```

ans =

37

```
>> maple ('convert (FFFFAA0, decimal, hex)') or  base2dec ('FFFFAA0', 16)
```

ans =

268434080

```
>> maple ('convert (FFFAA2, decimal, hex) + convert(FF,decimal,hex) - 1')
```

ans =

16776096

```
>> base2dec ('FFFAA2', 16) + base2dec('FF',16)-1
```

ans =

   16776096

EXERCISE 2-24

Calculate in base 5 the results of the operation:

$a25aaff6_{16} + 6789aba_{12} + 1100221_8 + 35671_3 - 1250$

We first convert the base 12 number 6789aba to decimal:

```
>> base2dec('6789aba',12)
```

ans =

19840750

or we can also use the function convert:

```
>> maple('convert([10,11,10,9,8,7,6],base,12,10)')
```

ans =

[0, 5, 7, 0, 4, 8, 9, 1]

Let us not forget that this form of the function *convert* returns the result with the figures in the reverse order to the usual ordering.

We now transform the base 3 number 1100221 to decimal:

```
>> base2dec('1100221',3)
```

ans =

   997

We can also perform this operation as follows:

```
>> maple('convert([1,2,2,0,0,1,1],base,3,10)')
```

ans =

[7, 9, 9]

The number in base 10 is 997. Now we calculate the result of the entire operation in base 10:

```
>> maple ('convert(a25aaf6,decimal,hex) + 19840750 + convert(35671,decimal,octal) +
997-1250')
```

ans =

190096544

The same result is obtained directly as follows:

```
>> base2dec('a25aaf6',16) + base2dec('6789aba',12) + base2dec('35671',8) +
base2dec('1100221',3)-1250
```

ans =

   190096544

but we still need to convert this result to base 5:

```
>>  maple('convert([4,4,5,6,9,0,0,9,1],base,10,5)')
```

ans =

[4, 3, 1, 2, 4, 0, 1, 3, 1, 2, 4, 3]

Thus, the final result of the operation in base 5 is 342131042134.

This last step could also have been determined as follows:

>> dec2base (190096544,5)

ans =

342131042134

EXERCISE 2-25

In base 13, find the result of the following operation:

$(666551)_4 \ (aa199800a)_7 + (fffaaa125)_{11} / (33331 + 6)_{16}$

First of all, we convert all numbers to base 10:

>> maple('convert([1,5,5,6,6,6],base,7,10)')

ans =

[7, 8, 5, 7, 1, 1]

>> maple('convert([10,0,0,8,9,9,1,10,10],base,11,10)')

ans =

[7, 6, 9, 3, 2, 8, 1, 4, 3, 2]

>> maple ('convert (FFFAAA125, decimal, hex)')

ans =

68713881893

>> maple('convert([1,3,3,3,3],base,4,10)')

ans =

[1, 2, 0, 1]

Now we carry out the proposed calculations in base 10.

>> vpa ' 117587 * 2341823967 + 79 * 68713881893 /(1021+6)' 15

ans =

275373340490852

A more direct way of doing all of the above is:

```
>> base2dec('666551',7) * base2dec('aa199800a',11) + 79 * base2dec('fffaaa125',16) /
(base2dec ('33331', 4) + 6)
```

ans =

275373340490852

We now transform the result gained into base 13.

```
>> maple('convert([2,5,8,0,9,4,0,4,3,3,7,3,5,7,2],base,10,13)')
```

ans =

[6, 9, 4, 1, 12, 3, 6, 9, 7, 6, 8, 10, 11]

Thus, the final result in base 13 is the number BA867963C1496.

This last conversion can also be done as follows:

```
>> dec2base (275373340490852,13)
```

ans =

BA867963C1496

EXERCISE 2-26

Convert the decimal 125.7864 to binary and convert the results of the decimal operation 8796.43 + 0.6789 - 4.25 to octal.

```
>> maple('convert(125.7864, binary)')
```

ans =

1111101.110010010

```
>> vpa '8796.43+0.6789-4.25'
```

ans =

8792.8589

```
>> maple('convert(8792.8589, octal)')
```

ans =

21130.66760336645

CHAPTER 3

■ ■ ■

Real and Complex Numbers

3.1 Rational Numbers

A rational number is a number of the form p/q, where p and q are integers. That is, the rational numbers are those numbers that can be represented as the quotient of two integers. The way in which MATLAB treats rational numbers is different from the majority of calculators.

If we ask a calculator to calculate the sum *2/4 + 24/144*, most will return something like *0.6666667*, which is no more than an approximation of the result.

MATLAB can work with rational numbers in exact mode, so the result of arithmetic expressions involving rational numbers is always another rational number. To this end, it is necessary to activate the rational format with the command *format rat*. However, if the reader so wishes, MATLAB can also return decimal approximations of rational numbers, activating any other type of format (e.g. *format short* or *format long*). MATLAB evaluates rational expressions in exact mode as follows:

`>> format rat`

`>> 2/4 + 24/144`

ans =

2/3

By dealing with rational numbers exactly as ratios of integers, rounding errors are not introduced in calculations with fractions, which can become very serious, as evidenced by the theory of errors. Note that, once the rational format is enabled, when MATLAB is asked to add two rational numbers, it returns a rational number as a ratio of integers and thus represents it symbolically, as you can see in the following examples:

`>> (2/3-3/5) * 5/2`

ans =

1/6

`>> 2 + 2/5`

ans =

12/5

In the second example, the number 12/5 is exactly equivalent in value to 2.4, but MATLAB represents these numbers in different ways.

Once the rational format is enabled, operations with rational numbers will be exact until a different format is introduced, in which case we can also obtain decimal approximations.

A floating point or decimal number is interpreted as exact if the rational format has been enabled. If there is a number with a floating point expression, MATLAB will treat it as an exact expression and represent it as a rational number. If an irrational number appears in a rational expression, MATLAB will approximate it by a fraction and then work with it in rational form.

```
>> 1/2 + 2.4/144
```

ans =

31/60

```
>> .5/7 + pi
```

ans =

5626/1751

Another way to work with accurate results with rational numbers, without having to enable the *rat* format, is to use the command *simplify*. Using this command allows you to work with rational expressions exactly, even if the expressions contain irrational numbers. The use of this command requires that the numeric expressions be considered as symbolic, so you will need to prepend to all numeric expressions the command **sym**.

```
>> simplify(sym(2/5+3/4))
```

ans =

23/20

```
>> simplify(sym(2/5+3/4+pi))
```

ans =

2415951884441619/562949953421312

```
>> simplify(sym(2/5+3/4)+pi)
```

ans =

23/20 + pi

There are certain commands that can be used when working with rational numbers. Among the most important are the following:

> **simplify(sym(rational_expr))** completely simplifies the specified rational expression and gives the result as a rational number

> **[n,m] = numden(rational_expr)** gives the simplified numerator and denominator of the rational expression

> **maple('simplify(rational)')** simplifies the specified rational number

> **maple('normal(rational_expr)')** simplifies the specified rational expression

> **maple('convert(decimal,fraction)')** converts the decimal to a fraction

> **maple('convert(decimal,rational)')** converts the decimal to rational form

> **maple('denom(fraction)')** gives the denominator of the simplified fraction

> **maple('num(fraction)')** gives the numerator of the simplified fraction

Here are some examples:

```
>> simplify (sym(125/1500))
```

ans =

1/12

```
>> maple('simplify(125/1500)')
```

ans =

1/12

```
>> maple('normal(125/1500)')
```

ans =

1/12

```
>> [n,m]=numden(sym(125/1500))
```

n =

1

m =

12

```
>> maple('denom(125/1500)')
```

ans =

12

```
>> maple('numer(125/1500)')
```

ans =

1

```
>> maple('convert(125.1500,fraction)')
```

ans =

2503/20

```
>> maple('convert(125.1500,rational)')
```

ans =

2503/20

EXERCISE 3-1

Perform the following operations with rational numbers:

a) 3/5+2/5+7/5

b) 1/2+1/3+1/4+1/5+1/6

c) 1/2-1/3+1/4-1/5+1/6

d) (2/3-1/6)-(4/5+2+1/3)+(4-5/7)

e) ((1/5*4/7)/(4/3-2/5))/(6-(5/9-1/7)*5+1/4)

f) $((-1)^4 /(2/5)^3)^{-2}$ / $((-3/7)^2 -(2/5)^{-1})$

g) $[(2-1/5)^2 /(3-2/9)^{-1}]/[(6/7*5/4-(2/7)/(1/2))]^3$ /(1/2-1/3)

a)

```
>> format rat
>> 3/5+2/5+7/5
```

ans =

   12/5

b)

`>> 1/2+1/3+1/4+1/5+1/6`

ans =

   29/20

c)

`>> 1/2-1/3+1/4-1/5+1/6`

ans =

   23/60

d)

`>> (2/3-1/6)-(4/5+2+1/3)+(4-5/7)`

ans =

   137/210

e)

`>> (1/5*4/7/(4/3-2/5))/(6-(5/9-1/7)*5+1/4)`

ans =

   216/7385

f)

`>> ((-1)^4/(2/5)^3)^(-2)/((-3/7)^2-(2/5)^(-1))`

ans =

   -53/29972

g) ,

`>> (2-1/5)^2/(3-2/9)^(-1)/(6/7*5/4-(2/7)/(1/2))^3/(1/2-1/3)`

ans =

   432

Alternatively, the operations can be performed as follows:

```
>> simplify(sym(3/5+2/5+7/5))
```

ans =

   12/5

```
>> simplify(sym(1/2+1/3+1/4+1/5+1/6))
```

ans =

   29/20

```
>> simplify(sym(1/2-1/3+1/4-1/5+1/6))
```

ans =

   23/60

```
>> simplify(sym((2/3-1/6)-(4/5+2+1/3)+(4-5/7)))
```

ans =

   137/210

```
>> simplify(sym((1/5*4/7/(4/3-2/5))/(6-(5/9-1/7)*5+1/4)))
```

ans =

   216/7385

```
>> simplify(sym((-1)^4/(2/5)^3)^(-2)/((-3/7)^2-(2/5)^(-1)))
```

ans =

   53/29972

```
>> simplify(sym((2-1/5)^2/(3-2/9)^(-1)/(6/7*5/4-(2/7)/(1/2))^3/(1/2-1/3)))
```

ans =

   432

EXERCISE 3-2

Perform the following rational operations:

a) 3/a+2/a+7/a

b) 1/2a+1/3a+1/4a+1/5a+1/6a

c) 1/2a+1/3b+1/4a+1/5b+1/6c

To treat operations with expressions that contain the symbolic variable *a*, it is necessary to prepend the command **syms a** to declare the variable *a* as symbolic, and then use *simplify*. The commands *normal, maple* and *simplify* can also be used.

a)

```
>> syms a
>> simplify(3/a+2/a+7/a)
```

ans =

12/a

```
>> 3/a+2/a+7/a
```

ans =

12/a

```
>> maple('3/a+2/a+7/a')
```

ans =

12/a

b)

```
>> 1/(2*a)+1/(3*a)+1/(4*a)+1/(5*a)+1/(6*a)
```

ans =

29/20/a

c)

```
>> syms a b c
>> 1/(2*a)+1/(3*b)+1/(4*a)+1/(5*b)+1/(6*c)
```

ans =

1/60(45*b*c+32*a*c+10*a*b)/a/b/c*

EXERCISE 3-3

Simplify the following rational expressions as much as possible:

a) $(1-a^9)/(1-a^3)$

b) $1/2a+1/3a+1/4a+1/5a+1/6a$

c) $1/2a+1/3b+1/4a+1/5b+1/6c$

d) $(3a+2a+7a)/(a^3+a)$

e) $1/(1+a)+1/(1+a)^2+1/(1+a)^3$

f) $1+a/(a+b)+a^2/(a+b)^2$

a)

```
>> syms a
>> simplify((1-a^9)/(1-a^3))
```

ans =

a^6+a^3+1

```
>> maple('simplify((1-a^9)/(1-a^3))')
```

ans =

a^6+a^3+1

```
>> maple('normal((1-a^9)/(1-a^3))')
```

ans =

a^6+a^3+1

b)

```
>> simplify((1/2)*a+(1/3)*a+(1/4)*a+(1/5)*a+(1/6)*a)
```

ans =

*29/20*a*

c)

```
>> syms a b c
>> [n, d] = numden (1 /(2*a) + 1 /(3*b) + 1 /(4*a) + 1 /(5*b) + 1 /(6*c))
```

n =

*45 * b * c + 32 * a * c + 10 * a * b*

d =

*60 * a * b * c*

The result is an algebraic fraction whose numerator is *n* and whose denominator is *d*.

d)

```
>> simplify ((3*a+2*a+7*a) /(a^3+a))
```

ans =

12 /(a^2+1)

e)

```
>> maple ('normal (1 /(1+a) + 1 /(1+a) ^ 2 + 1 /(1+a) ^ 3)')
```

ans =

*(3 + 3 * a + a ^ 2) /(1+a) ^ 3*

f)

```
>> maple('simplify(1+a/(a+b)+a^2/(a+b)^2)')
```

ans =

*(3 * a ^ 2 + 3 * a * b + b ^ 2) / (a + b) ^ 2*

3.2 Continued Fractions

MATLAB enables you to work with continued fractions using the following commands. With the exception of the first and last commands, these can be found in Maple's *numtheory* library:

> **rat(r): returns the continued fraction of the rational number *r***

> **maple('cfrac (r)'): returns the continued fraction of the rational number *r***

> **maple('cfrac(polynomial)'): returns the continued fraction for each of the real roots of the given univariate polynomial**

maple('invcfrac (frac)'): converts the continued fraction *frac* to an irrational quadratic

maple('nthnumer(expr,n)'): gives the nth numerator of the continued fraction expr

maple('nthdenom(expr,n)'): gives the nth denominator of the continued fraction expr

maple('nthdconver(expr,n)'): gives the nth partial quotient of the continued fraction expr

maple('pdexpand(rational)'): gives the periodic expansion of the given rational number, i.e. it gives the sign, the positive integer part, the non-recurrent part and the periodic part

maple('convert(number,confrac,m)'): converts a number to a continued fraction with *m* partial quotients

Here are some examples:

```
>> rat(3/5)
```

ans =

```
1 + 1/(-3 + 1/(2))
```

```
>> maple('cfrac(3/5)')
```

ans =

```
1/(1+1/(1+1/2))
```

```
>> pretty(sym(maple('cfrac(3/5)')))
```

```
      1
-----------
        1
1 + -------
      1 + 1/2
```

```
>> pretty(sym(maple('cfrac(125.1500)')))
```

```
           1
125 + -----------
            1
      6 + -------
            1 + 1/2
```

```
>> maple('convert(125.1500, confrac, 4)')
```

ans =

```
[125, 6, 1, 2]
```

```
>> maple nthnumer([125, 6, 1, 2],3)
```

ans =

2503

```
>> maple nthdenom([125, 6, 1, 2],3)
```

ans =

20

EXERCISE 3-4

Express the following numbers as continued fractions:

a) 7/9

b) the roots of the polynomial $x^6 - x^5 - 6x^4 + 6x^3 + 8x^2 - 8x + 1$

c) the roots of the polynomial $- 117260219\, x^6 + 139540883\, x^5 + 17033080\, x^4 + 800302\, x^3 + 18628\, x^2\, x + 216 + 1$

d) 11/9999997

e) $31^{1/2}$

```
>> maple('with(numtheory)');
>> maple cfrac(7/9)
```

ans =

1/(1+1/(3+1/2))

```
>> pretty(sym(maple('cfrac(7/9)')))
```

```
     1
-----------
        1
1 + -------
     3 + 1/2
```

```
>> maple('cfracpol(x^6 - x^5 - 6*x^4 + 6*x^3 + 8*x^2 - 8*x + 1)')
```

ans =

```
[-2, 44, 1, 3, 3, 1, 1, 1, 3, 2, 3, ... ],
[-2, 1, 1, 6, 1, 7, 34, 1, 12, 1, 5, ...],
[0, 6, 1, 2, 4, 3, 1, 1, 3, 1, 63, ... ],
[0, 1, 2, 1, 2, 2, 16, 1, 1, 5, 11, ... ],
[1, 1, 1, 1, 7, 6, 10, 2, 29, 20, 1, ...],
[1, 1, 10, 3, 1, 13, 1, 1, 3, 1, 4, ... ]
```

```
>> maple('cfracpol( -117260219*x^6+139540883*x^5 + 17033080*x^4 + 800302*x^3
+18628*x^2+216*x+1)')
```

ans =

```
[-1, 1, 41, 7, 1, 7, 34, 1, 12, 1, 5, ...],
[-1, 1, 42, 1, 1, 6, 1, 2, 4, 3, 1, ... ],
[-1, 1, 42, 1, 1, 1, 2, 1, 2, 2, 16, ... ],
[-1, 1, 42, 1, 2, 1, 1, 1, 7, 6, 10, ... ],
[-1, 1, 42, 1, 2, 1, 10, 3, 1, 13, 1, ...],
[1, 3, 3, 1, 1, 1, 3, 2, 3, 4, 1, ...    ]
```

```
>> pretty(sym(maple('cfrac(11/9999997)')));
```

ans =

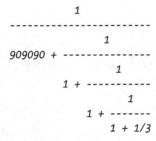

```
                    1
         -------------------------
                       1
         909090 + ---------------
                         1
              1 + -----------
                        1
              1 + -------
                   1 + 1/3
```

```
>> pretty(sym(maple('cfrac(31^(1/2))')));
```

ans =

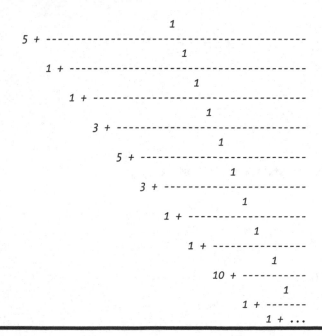

```
                          1
       5 + ---------------------------------------------
                             1
          1 + ----------------------------------------
                             1
             1 + ---------------------------------
                              1
               3 + -------------------------------
                               1
                 5 + --------------------------
                                1
                   3 + ------------------------
                                 1
                     1 + --------------------
                                  1
                       1 + ----------------
                                   1
                         10 + -----------
                                    1
                            1 + -------
                                 1 + ...
```

3.3 Irrational Numbers

Irrational numbers, because of their special nature, have always created difficulties in numerical calculations. The impossibility of representing an irrational accurately in numeric mode (using ten decimal digits, for example) is the cause of most of the problems. MATLAB can represent the results with greater accuracy or to any accuracy specified by the user. Nevertheless, by definition, an irrational number cannot be represented exactly as the ratio of two integers. If ordered to find the square root of 17, MATLAB will return 4.12310562561766. However, the result can be treated symbolically using the *maple* command, so that *sqrt[17]* will be represented by *17 ^(1/2)*:

```
>> sqrt(17)
```

ans =

   4.12310562561766

```
>> maple('sqrt(17)')
```

ans =

17 ^(1/2)

Note that if the square root of a floating point (decimal) number, e.g. $\sqrt{17.0}$, is requested, MATLAB always calculates an approximate result, even using the command *maple*.

```
>> maple ('sqrt (17.0)')
```

ans =

4.123105625617661

The main difficulty presented by the treatment of irrational numbers is the impossibility of representing them accurately, unless they are treated as symbolic constants, so that if it is asked to calculate the sum of the square root of 2 and the square root of 3 (using the function *sqrt*), MATLAB will return as a result *2^(1/2) + 3^(1/2)*, since this is the only way to accurately represent the sum (using the command *maple*). In all subsequent calculations involving *2^(1/2)* and *3^(1/2)* they will be operated on symbolically following the mathematical rules of calculation with radicals.

Of course we can also work with decimal approximations of irrational numbers, as we pointed out above. Among the commands used to work with irrational numbers, we have the following:

maple('radsimp(expr)') **simplifies the expression and, where necessary, rationalizes denominators**

maple('simplify(expr,radical)') **simplifies the given irrational expression using standard rules of radicals**

maple('simplify(expr,symbolic)') **simplifies the expression assuming all algebraic subexpressions are positive**

maple('combine(expr,radical)') **simplifies the given irrational expression and returns the result in radical form**

maple('combine(expr,radical,symbolic)') **simplifies the given irrational expression and returns the result in radical form, assuming all algebraic subexpressions are positive**

maple('combine(expr,power)') simplifies the given irrational expression returning the result in terms of powers

maple('normal(expr)') simplifies the given irrational expression

maple('readlib(radnormal): radnormal(irrational_expression)') simplifies expressions containing various levels of radicals

maple('readlib(radnormal): rationalize(irrational_expression)') rationalizes denominators

maple('simplify(irrat_expr)') simplifies the given irrational expression

EXERCISE 3-5

Perform the following operations with irrational numbers:

a) $3\sqrt{a} + 2\sqrt{a} - 5\sqrt{a} + 7\sqrt{a}$

b) $\sqrt{2} + 3\sqrt{2} - \sqrt{2}/2$

c) $4a^{1/3} - 3b^{1/3} - 5a^{1/3} - 2b^{1/3} + ma^{1/3}$

d) $\sqrt{432} + \sqrt{75} - \sqrt{363} - \sqrt{108}$

e) $\sqrt{3a}\ \sqrt{27a}$

f) $\sqrt{a}\ \sqrt[3]{a}$

g) $(3a^2\ b^5)^{1/3}\ (9a^3\ b^2)^{1/4}\ (3ab)^{1/6}$

h) $\sqrt{a\sqrt[5]{a}}$

a)

First, we use the command *simplify*:

```
>> syms a
>> simplify(3*sqrt(a) + 2*sqrt(a) - 5*sqrt(a) + 7*sqrt(a))
```

ans =

$7 * a \wedge (1/2)$

We can also use different variants of the *maple(simplify)*, *maple* and *maple(combine)* commands, which yields a completely simplified result:

```
>> maple('simplify(3*sqrt(a) + 2*sqrt(a) - 5*sqrt(a) + 7*sqrt(a))')
```

ans =

$7*a^{(1/2)}$

```
>> maple('simplify(3*sqrt(a) + 2*sqrt(a) - 5*sqrt(a) + 7*sqrt(a),radical)')
```

ans =

7*a^(1/2)

```
>> maple('combine(3*sqrt(a) + 2*sqrt(a) - 5*sqrt(a) + 7*sqrt(a),sqrt(a))')
```

ans =

7 * a ^(1/2)

b)

We can perform numerical operations directly in MATLAB, obtaining decimal results either to default accuracy or to a predefined accuracy:

```
>> sqrt (2) + 3 * sqrt (2) - sqrt (2) / 2
```

ans =

4.9497

We can consider the calculation as an algebraic expression, in which case the result obtained is not fully simplified:

```
>> sym(sqrt(2)+3*sqrt(2)-sqrt(2)/2)
```

ans =

sqrt(49/2)

We can apply the command *simplify* to completely simplify the result:

```
>> simplify(sym(sqrt(2)+3*sqrt(2)-sqrt(2)/2))
```

ans =

7/2 * 2 ^(1/2)

We can use different variants of the commands *maple(simplify)* and *maple(combine)*, in which case we also obtain a completely simplified result:

```
>> maple('simplify(sqrt(2)+3*sqrt(2)-sqrt(2)/2)')
```

ans =

7/2*2^(1/2)

```
>> maple('simplify(sqrt(2)+3*sqrt(2)-sqrt(2)/2,radical)')
```

ans =

*7/2*2^(1/2)*

```
>> maple('combine(sqrt(2)+3*sqrt(2)-sqrt(2)/2,power)')
```

ans =

*7/2*2^(1/2)*

c)

```
>> syms a b m
>> simplify(4*a^(1/3)- 3*b^(1/3)-5*a^(1/3)- 2*b^(1/3)+m*a^(1/3))
```

ans =

*-a^(1/3)-5*b^(1/3)+m*a^(1/3)*

```
>> maple('simplify(4*a^(1/3)- 3*b^(1/3)-5*a^(1/3)- 2*b^(1/3)+m*a^(1/3))')
```

ans =

*-a^(1/3)-5*b^(1/3)+m*a^(1/3)*

```
>> maple('simplify(4*a^(1/3)-3*b^(1/3)-5*a^(1/3)-2*b^(1/3)+m*a^(1/3),radical)')
```

ans =

*-a^(1/3)-5*b^(1/3)+m*a^(1/3)*

```
>> maple('combine(4*a^(1/3)-3*b^(1/3)-5*a^(1/3)- b^(1/3)+m*a^(1/3),radical)'))
```

ans =

*-a^(1/3)-5*b^(1/3)+m*a^(1/3)*

d)

If we consider the operation directly, we do not get the exact result:

```
>> sym(sqrt(432)+sqrt(75)-sqrt(363)-sqrt(108))
```

ans =

2 ^(-48)

If we use the command *maple('simplify')*, the exact result is obtained.

```
>> maple('simplify(sqrt(432)+sqrt(75)-sqrt(363)-sqrt(108))')
```

ans =

0

e)

```
>> maple('simplify(sqrt(3*a)*sqrt(27*a))')
```

ans =

*9 * a*

or also:

```
>> simplify(sym (sqrt(3*a) * sqrt(27*a)))
```

ans =

*9*a*

f)

```
>> simplify(a^(1/2)*a^(1/3))
```

ans =

a^(5/6)

g)

```
>> maple('simplify((3*a^2*b^5)^(1/3)*(9*a^3*b^2)^(1/4)*(3*a*b)^(1/6),symbolic)')
```

ans =

*3*a^(19/12)*b^(7/3)*

h)

```
>> maple('radsimp(sqrt(a*(a^(1/5))))')
```

ans =

a ^(3/5)

EXERCISE 3-6

Simplify the following irrational expressions by rationalizing the denominators:

a) $\dfrac{2}{\sqrt{2}}$ b) $\dfrac{\sqrt{2}}{\sqrt[3]{2}}$ c) $\dfrac{2}{\sqrt[3]{4}}$ d) $\dfrac{3}{\sqrt{3}}$ e) $\dfrac{a}{\sqrt{a}}$

In these cases of rationalization, the simple use of the command *simplify* solves the problem. You can also use the command *radsimp*.

a)

```
>> simplify (sym (2/sqrt (2)))
```

ans =

2^(1/2)

b)

```
>> maple('simplify( sqrt(2)/2^(1/3))')
```

ans =

2^(1/6)

c)

```
>> maple('simplify(2/4^(1/3))')
```

ans =

2^(1/3)

d)

```
>> simplify(sym(3/sqrt(3)))
```

ans =

3 ^(1/2)

e)

```
>> maple ('simplify(a/sqrt(a), radical)')
```

ans =

a ^(1/2)

EXERCISE 3-7

Simplify the following expression:

$$\sqrt{6-2\sqrt{2}-2\sqrt{3}+2\sqrt{6}}$$

```
>> maple('readlib(radnormal):radnormal(sqrt(6-2*sqrt(2)- 2*sqrt(3)+2*sqrt(6)))')
```

ans =

-1 + 2 ^(1/2) + 3 ^(1/2)

EXERCISE 3-8

Rationalize the following expressions:

$$\frac{1}{2+\sqrt{5}},\ \frac{1}{\sqrt{a}+\sqrt[3]{b}},\ \frac{1}{1+\sqrt{2}}+\frac{1}{1-\sqrt{2}},\ \frac{1}{\sqrt{1+\sqrt{2}}}+\frac{1}{\sqrt{1-\sqrt{2}}}$$

```
>> maple('readlib(rationalize):rationalize(1/(2+sqrt(5)))')
```

ans =

-2 + 5 ^(1/2)

$$-2+\sqrt{5}$$

```
>> maple('readlib(rationalize):rationalize( 1/(a^(1/2)+b^(1/3)) )')
```

ans =

(-b^(1/3)+a^(1/2))(a^2+a*b^(2/3)+b^(4/3))/(a^3-b^2)*

$$\frac{\left(a-\sqrt{ab}^{\,1/3}+b^{2/3}\right)\left(-a^{3/2}+b\right)}{a^3-b^2}$$

```
>> maple('readlib(rationalize):rationalize(1/(1+sqrt(2)) + 1/(1-sqrt(2)) )')
```

ans =

-2

```
>> maple('readlib(rationalize):rationalize( 1/sqrt(1+sqrt(2)) + 1/sqrt(1-sqrt(2)) )')
```

ans =

$-((1-2 \char`\^(1/2)) \char`\^(1/2) + (2 \char`\^(1/2) + 1) \char`\^(1/2)) * (1-2 \char`\^(1/2)) \char`\^(1/2) * (2 \char`\^(1/2) + 1) \char`\^(1/2)$

$$-\left(\sqrt{1-\sqrt{2}} + \sqrt{1+\sqrt{2}}\right)\sqrt{1+\sqrt{2}} + \sqrt{1-\sqrt{2}}$$

3.4 Algebraic Numbers

MATLAB can operate with algebraic numbers using two types of representations, one in the form of radicals and the other in terms of roots of polynomials (*RootOf(polynomial))*.

Using the command *convert*, MATLAB can convert a radical representation to a *RootOf* representation and vice versa, when possible.

The commands for working with algebraic numbers are as follows:

> **maple('convert(RootOf_expression,radical)')** converts a RootOf expression to a radical expression

> **maple('convert(radical_expression, RootOf)')** converts a radical expression to a RootOf expression

> **maple('simplify RootOf(expression)')** simplifies the RootOf expression

---

EXERCISE 3-9

---

a) Convert the following radical expressions to RootOf expressions:

i) $\sqrt{2}$

ii) $\sqrt[3]{1-\sqrt{2}}$

b) Perform the reverse conversions of (i) and (ii) above.

a)

i)

```
>> maple('convert(sqrt(2),RootOf)')
```

ans =

RootOf(_Z^2-2)

ii)

```
>> maple('convert((1-2^(1/2))^(1/3),RootOf)')
```

ans =

RootOf(_Z^3-1+RootOf(_Z^2-2))

b)

```
>> maple('convert(RootOf(_Z^2-2),radical)')
```

ans =

2^(1/2)

```
>> maple('convert(RootOf(_Z^3-1+RootOf(_Z^2-2)),radical)')
```

ans =

(1-2 ^(1/2)) ^(1/3)

3.5 Real Numbers

The disjoint union of the set of rational numbers and the set of irrational numbers is the set of real numbers. Included in the set of rational numbers is the set of integers, so all functions applicable to real numbers will also be valid for integers, rational and irrational numbers.

3.6 Common Functions with Real Arguments

MATLAB provides a full range of predefined functions, most of which are discussed later in this book. Within the group of functions with real arguments offered by MATLAB, the following are the most important:

Trigonometric functions	
Function	**Inverse**
sin(x)	asin(x)
cos(x)	acos(x)
tan(x)	atan(x)
csc(x)	acsc(x)
sec(x)	asec(x)
cot(x)	acot(x)
atan2(x) (inverse tangent in the fourth quadrant)	

(continued)

Hyperbolic functions	
Function	Inverse
sinh(x)	asinh(x)
cosh(x)	acosh(x)
tanh(x)	atanh(x)
csch(x)	acsch(x)
sech(x)	asech(x)
coth(x)	acoth(x)

Exponential and logarithmic functions

exp(x) exponential of x to base e (e ^ x)

log(x) logarithm of x to base e

log10(x) base 10 logarithm of x

log2(x) base 2 logarithm of x

pow2(x) power to base 2 of x

sqrt(x) square root of x

Specific functions of a numeric variable

abs(x) the absolute value of the real number x

floor(x) the greatest integer less than or equal to the real x

ceil(x) the lowest integer greater than or equal to the real x

round(x) the integer closest to the real x

fix(x) removes the decimal part of the real x

rem(a,b) gives the remainder of the division of a by b

sign(x) gives the sign of the real x (1 if x > 0, - 1 if x < 0)

First, we see how the function *round* rounds a real number:

```
>> round(2.574)
```

ans =

   3

```
>> round(2.4)
```

ans =

    2

```
>> round(sqrt(17))
```

ans =

    4

The function *ceil* is illustrated in the following two cases:

```
>> ceil (4.2)
```

ans =

    5

```
>> ceil (4.8)
```

ans =

    5

The *floor* function is illustrated in the following two examples:

```
>> floor (4.2)
```

ans =

    4

```
>> floor (4.8)
```

ans =

    4

The *fix* function simply removes the decimal part of a real number:

```
>> fix (5.789)
```

ans =

    5

3.7 Complex Numbers

Operations on complex numbers are well implemented in MATLAB. MATLAB follows the convention that *i* or *j* represents the key value in complex analysis, the *imaginary number* $\sqrt{-1}$. All the usual arithmetic operators can be applied to complex numbers, and there are also some specific functions which have complex arguments. Both the real and the imaginary part of a complex number can be a real number or a symbolic constant, and operations with them are always performed in exact mode, unless otherwise instructed or necessary, in which case an approximation of the result is returned. As the imaginary unit is represented by the symbol *i* or *j*, the complex numbers are expressed in the form *a+bi* or *a+bj*. Note that you don't need to use the product symbol (asterisk) before the imaginary unit:

```
>> (2-3i)*(1-i)/(-1+2i)
```

ans =

  -1.8000 + 1.4000i

```
>> format rat
>> (2-3i)*(1-i) /(-1+2i)
```

ans =
   -9/5 + 7/5i

3.8 Common Functions with Complex Arguments

MATLAB performs the usual arithmetic operations with complex numbers, but in addition, there are several features built into the program especially designed to work with complex variables.

The function *real(z)* returns the real part of the complex number z:

```
>> real(3 + 4i)
```

ans =

   3

The function *imag(z)* returns the imaginary part of z:

```
>> imag(3 + 4i)
```

ans =

   4

The function *conj(z)* returns the conjugate of z:

```
>> conj(3 + 4i)
```

ans =

   3 - 4i

The function *abs(z)* returns the modulus (absolute value) of z:

```
>> abs(3 + 4i)
```

ans =

   5

The function *angle(z)* returns the argument of z:

```
>> angle(3 + 4i)
```

ans =

   0.9273

In addition to these specific functions of a complex variable, there are many other functions that can also be applied to complex numbers.

For example, the function *round(z)* rounds both the real part and the imaginary part of z:

```
>> round(2.7-8.4i)
```

ans =

   3.0000 - 8.0000i

There are many more functions in MATLAB that work with complex numbers, including *sin, cos, exp, log*, etc. Some of the most important are presented in the following table:

Trigonometric functions	
Function	Inverse
sin(z)	asin(z)
cos(z)	acos(z)
tan(z)	atan(z)
csc(z)	acsc(z)
sec(z)	asec(z)
cot(z)	acot(z)
atan2(z) (inverse tangent in the fourth quadrant)	

(continued)

Hyperbolic functions

Function	Inverse
sinh(z)	asinh(z)
cosh(z)	acosh(z)
tanh(z)	atanh(z)
csch(z)	acsch(z)
sech(z)	asech(z)
coth(z)	acoth(z)

Exponential and logarithmic functions

exp(z) exponential of z to base e (e ^ Z)

log(z) base e logarithm of z

log10(z) base 10 logarithm of z

sqrt(z) square root of z

log2(z) base 2 logarithm of z

pow2(z) base 2 power of z

Specific functions for real and imaginary parts

floor(z) applies the function *floor*(z) to real(z) and imag(z)

ceil(z) applies the function *ceil*(z) to real(z) and imag(z)

round(z) applies the function *round*(z) to real(z) and imag(z)

fix(z) applies the function *fix*(z) to real(z) and imag(z)

Specific functions of a complex variable

abs(z) or maple('abs (z)'): modulus (absolute value) of z

angle(z) or maple('argument(z)'): argument of z

conj(z) or maple('conjugate (z)'): conjugate of z

real(z) or maple('Re(z)'): real part of z

imag(z) or maple('Im (z)'): imaginary part of z

It should be noted that, as every real number is a complex number (with zero imaginary part), all functions defined above are also valid for real variables.

A number of commands used to simplify and transform complex expressions also play an important role in working with complex numbers. These include the following:

expand(sym(expression)) simplifies the complex expression and usually gives the output in trigonometric or binary form

maple('evalc(expression)') simplifies the complex expression and usually gives the output in trigonometric or binary form

maple('simplify(expression,polar)') simplifies a complex expression in polar form

maple('simplify(expression,trig)') simplifies a complex expression in trigonometric form

maple('simplify(expression,power)') simplifies a complex expression with powers

maple('simplify(expression,radical)') simplifies a complex expression with radicals

maple('simplify(expression,sqrt)') simplifies a complex expression with square roots

maple('simplify (expression,ln)') simplifies a complex expression with logarithms

maple('simplify RootOf(expression)') simplifies a complex expression with algebraic numbers

maple('convert(expression,polar)') converts the expression to polar form

maple('convert(expression,exp)') converts the expression to exponential or binary form

maple('convert(expression,trig)') converts the expression to trigonometric or binary form

Here are some examples:
We convert 1 + i to polar form:

```
>> maple('convert(1+i,polar)')
```

ans =

*polar (2 ^(1/2), 1/4 * pi)*

We simplify the value of sqrt ((1+2*i) /(1-2*i)):

```
>> maple('evalc(sqrt((1+2*i)/(1-2*i)))')
```

ans =

*1/5 * 5 ^(1/2) + 2/5 * i * 5 ^(1/2)*

We convert the complex number $2 * cos(Pi/4) + 2 * I * sin(Pi/4)$ to binary form:

```
>> maple('convert(2*cos(Pi/4)+2*I*sin(Pi/4),trig)')
```

ans =
*2 ^(1/2) + I * 2 ^(1/2)*

We convert the complex number *3 * exp(Pi*I/4)* to trigonometric and polar form:

```
>> maple('convert(3*exp(Pi*I/4),trig)')
```

ans =

3*cosh(1/4*pi*I)+3*sinh(1/4*pi*I)

```
>> maple('convert(3*exp(Pi*I/4),polar)')
```

ans =

polar(3*exp(1/4*pi*Re(I)),argument(exp(1/4*pi*I)))

EXERCISE 3-10

Given the complex numbers X = 3 + 2i, Y = 3–2i and Z = i ^ 307, calculate X+Y+Z, X * Y * Z, x/y and y/z.

```
>> 3+2*i + 3-2*i - i^307
```

ans =

   6.0000 + 1.0000i

```
>> (3+2*i)*(3-2*i)*i^307
```

ans =

   0.0000 -13.0000i

```
>> (3+2*i)/(3-2*i)
```

ans =

   0.3846 + 0.9231i

```
>> (3-2*i)/i^307
```

ans =

   2.0000 + 3. 0000i

EXERCISE 3-11

Given the complex numbers X = 2 + 2i and Y = –3–3√3 i, calculate Y^3 and X^2/Y^{90}.

```
>> expand(sym(-3-3*sqrt(3)*i)^3)
```

ans =

216

```
>> maple('evalc((2+2*i)^2/(-3-3*sqrt(3)*i)^90)')
```

ans =

*1/1350586945294983814787399212987393606090501966076362410331422244995072 * i*

EXERCISE 3-12

Calculate the value of $\frac{i^8 - i^{-8}}{3 - 4i} + 1$.

```
>> (i^8-i^(-8))/(3-4*i) + 1
```

ans =

   1.0000 - 0.0000i

Alternatively we can write:

```
>> maple('simplify(evalc(i^8-i^(-8))/(3-4*i) + 1)')
```

ans =

1

EXERCISE 3-13

Calculate the modulus and the argument of each of the following complex numbers:

$$i^i, \ i^{3+i}, \ (i^i)^i, \ (1+i\sqrt{3})^{1-i}.$$

```
>> abs(i^i)
```

ans =

   0.2079

```
>> angle(i^i)
```

ans =

   0

```
>> abs(i^(3+i))
```

ans =

   0.2079

```
>> angle(i^(3+i))
```

ans =

  -1.5708

```
>> abs((i^i)^i)
```

ans =

   1

```
>> angle((i^i)^i)
```

ans =

  -1.5708

```
>> maple('simplify(evalc(abs((1+sqrt(3)*i)^(1-i))))')
```

ans =

2*exp(1/3*pi)

```
>> maple('simplify(evalc(argument((1+sqrt(3)*i)^(1-i)))')
```

ans =

*-log (2) + 1/3 * pi*

The moduli and arguments of the first three complex numbers have been obtained approximately. They can be calculated exactly as follows:

```
>> maple ('simplify(evalc(abs(i^i)))')
```

ans =

*exp(-1/2*pi)*

```
>> maple('simplify(evalc(argument(i^i)))')
```

ans =

0

```
>> maple('simplify(evalc(abs(i^(3+i))))')
```

ans =

*exp(-1/2*pi)*

```
>> maple('simplify(evalc(argument(i^(3+i))))')
```

ans =

*-1/2*pi*

```
>> maple('simplify(evalc(abs(i^(i^i))))')
```

ans =

1

```
>> maple('simplify(evalc(argument(i^(i^i))))')
```

ans =

*1/2 * exp(-1/2*pi) * pi*

EXERCISE 3-14

Solve the following equations:

a) cos(z) = 2

b) cos(z) = a, where a is a real number.

a)

>> maple ('evalc (solve (cos (z) = 2))')

ans =

*i * log (2 + 3 ^(1/2))*

b)

>> maple ('evalc (solve (cos (z) = a, z))')

ans =

*acos(1/2 * ((a+1) ^ 2) ^(1/2)-1/2 * ((a-1) ^ 2) ^(1/2)) + i * signum (a) * log(1/2 * ((a+1) ^ 2) ^(1/2) + 1/2 * ((a-1) ^ 2) ^(1/2) + ((1/2 * ((a+1) ^ 2) ^(1/2) + 1/2 * ((a-1) ^ 2) ^(1/2)) ^ 2-1) ^(1/2))*

EXERCISE 3-15

Solve the following equations:

a) $1+x+x^2+x^3+x^4+x^5 = 0$

b) $x^2+(6-i)x+8-4i = 0$

c) tan(z) = 3i/5

a)

>> solve('1+x+x^2+x^3+x^4+x^5 = 0')

ans =

```
[                -1]
[-1/2+1/2*i*3^(1/2)]
[-1/2-1/2*i*3^(1/2)]
[ 1/2+1/2*i*3^(1/2)]
[ 1/2-1/2*i*3^(1/2)]
```

b)

```
>> solve('x^2+(6-i)*x+8-4*i = 0')
```

ans =

```
[    -4]
[-2 + i]
```

c)

```
>> maple ('evalc(solve(tan (z) = 3 * i / 5))')
```

ans =

*(i * atanh(3/5))*

EXERCISE 3-16

Perform the following operations:

a) $i^{\sin(1+i)}$

b) $(2+Ln(i))^{1/i}$

c) $(1+i)^i$

d) $i^{Ln(1+i)}$

e) $(1+i*sqrt(3))^{1-i}$

a)

```
>> maple('evalc(i^(sin(1+i)))')
```

ans =

*exp (-1/2 * cos(1) * sin(1) * pi) * cos(1/2 * (1) * cosh(1) * pi) +
i * exp(-1/2 * cos(1) * sin(1) * pi) * sin(1/2 * (1) * cosh(1) * pi)*

To approximate the result, we use the command "***numeric***".

```
>> numeric(maple('simplify(evalc(i^(sin(1+i))))'))
```

ans =

  -0.1667 + 0.3290i

b)

```
>> maple('simplify(evalc((2+log(i))^(1/i)))')
```

ans =

*exp (atan(1/4*pi)) * cos(-log (2) + 1/2 * log(16+pi^2))-i * exp(atan(1/4*pi)) * sin(-log (2) + 1/2 * log(16+pi^2))*

We can find the approximate result in this case directly in MATLAB (since it contains no complex trigonometric expressions):

```
>> (2+log(i))^(1/i)
```

ans =

1.1581 - 1.5639i

c)

```
>> maple('simplify(evalc((1+i)^i))')
```

ans =

*exp(-1/4*pi) * cos(1/2 * log(2)) + i * exp(-1/4*pi) * sin(1/2 * log(2))*

Now we find the approximate result:

```
>> (1+i)^i
```

ans =

0.4288 + 0.1549i

d)

```
>> maple('simplify(evalc(i^log(1+i)))')
```

ans =

*exp(-1/8*pi^2) * cos (1/4 * log (2) * pi) + i * exp(-1/8*pi^2) * sin(1/4 * log(2) * pi)*

The approximate result is obtained directly:

```
>> i^log(1+i)
```

ans =

0.2491 + 0.1508i

e)

```
>> maple('simplify(evalc((1+i*sqrt(3))^(1-i)))')
```

ans =

2 * exp(1/3*pi) * cos(-log (2) + 1/3 * pi) + 2 * i * exp(1/3*pi) * sin(-log (2) + 1/3 * pi)

The approximate result is obtained directly:

```
>> (1+i*sqrt(3))^(1-i)
```

ans =

5.3458 + 1.9759i

EXERCISE 3-17

Find the following:

a) the fourth roots of -1 and 1

b) the fifth roots of $2 + 2i$ and $-1 + i\sqrt{3}$

c) the real part of tan(iLn((a+ib)/(a–ib)))

d) the imaginary part of $(2 + i)^{\cos(4-i)}$

a)

```
>> solve('x^4+1=0')
```

ans =

```
[   1/2* 2^(1/2) +1/2* i* 2^(1/2)]
[- 1/2* 2^(1/2) +1/2* i* 2^(1/2)]
[   1/2* 2^(1/2) -1/2* i* 2^(1/2)]
[- 1/2* 2^(1/2) -1/2* i* 2^(1/2)]
```

We can obtain the approximate result easily:

```
>> numeric(solve('x^4+1=0'))
```

ans =

```
 0.7071 + 0.7071i
-0.7071 + 0.7071i
 0.7071 - 0.7071i
-0.7071 - 0.7071i
```

```
>> solve('x^4-1=0')
```

ans =

```
[ 1]
[-1]
[ i]
[-i]
```

b)

```
>> solve('x^5-2-2*i=0')
```

ans =

```
[                                             (2+2*i)^(1/5)]
[ (1/4*5^(1/2)-1/4+1/4*i*2^(1/2)*(5+5^(1/2))^(1/2))*(2+2*i)^(1/5)]
[(-1/4*5^(1/2)-1/4+1/4*i*2^(1/2)*(5-5^(1/2))^(1/2))*(2+2*i)^(1/5)]
[(-1/4*5^(1/2)-1/4-1/4*i*2^(1/2)*(5-5^(1/2))^(1/2))*(2+2*i)^(1/5)]
[ (1/4*5^(1/2)-1/4-1/4*i*2^(1/2)*(5+5^(1/2))^(1/2))*(2+2*i)^(1/5)]
```

We now find the approximate result:

```
>> numeric(solve('x^5-2-2*i=0'))
```

ans =

```
  1.2160 + 0.1926i
  0.1926 + 1.2160i
 -1.0970 + 0.5589i
 -0.8706 - 0.8706i
  0.5589 - 1.0970i
```

c)

```
>> solve('x^5+1-sqrt(3)*i=0')
```

ans =

```
[                                             (-1+i*3^(1/2))^(1/5) ]
[ ( 1/4*5^(1/2)-1/4+1/4*i*2^(1/2)*(5+5^(1/2))^(1/2))*(-1+i*3^(1/2))^(1/5) ]
[ (-1/4*5^(1/2)-1/4+1/4*i*2^(1/2)*(5-5^(1/2))^(1/2))*(-1+i*3^(1/2))^(1/5) ]
[ (-1/4*5^(1/2)-1/4-1/4*i*2^(1/2)*(5-5^(1/2))^(1/2))*(-1+i*3^(1/2))^(1/5) ]
[ ( 1/4*5^(1/2)-1/4-1/4*i*2^(1/2)*(5+5^(1/2))^(1/2))*(-1+i*3-^(1/2))^(1/5)]
```

The approximate result is immediate:

```
>> numeric(solve('x^5+1-sqrt(3)*i=0'))
```

ans =

```
   1.0494 + 0.4672i
  -0.1201 + 1.1424i
  -1.1236 + 0.2388i
  -0.5743 - 0.9948i
   0.7686 - 0.8536i
```

d)

```
>> maple('simplify(evalc(Re(tan(i*log((a+i*b)/(a-i*b)))))))')
```

ans =

```
-2*a*b/(a^2-b^2)
```

e)

```
>> maple('simplify(evalc(Im((2+i)^cos(4-i))))')
```

ans =

```
5 ^ (1/2 * cos(4) * cosh(1)) * exp(-sin(4) * sin(1) * atan(1/2))
* sin(1/2 * sin(4) * sin(1) * log(5) + cos(4) * cosh(1) * atan(1/2))
```

Now we find the approximate result:

```
>> numeric(maple('evalc(Im((2+i)^cos(4-i)))'))
```

ans =

```
-0.6211
```

3.9 Divisibility in the Complex Field. The Ring of Gaussian Integers

Within the set C of complex numbers, the subset $G = \{z \in C \,/\, z = a + bi, a,b \in Z\}$ formed by all the complex numbers with integer real and imaginary parts is a ring, known as the ***ring of Gaussian integers***. Within this ring, divisibility can be studied in a similar manner to the study of divisibility in the ring of integers.

There are some functions in MATLAB that allow you to work in this ring, as long as the extended symbolic math *Toolbox* is available. Among them are the following:

> **maple('with(GaussInt)')** loads the Maple library *GaussInt* (required before using the commands specified below)
>
> **maple('GIfactor(z)')** factorizes the Gaussian integer z
>
> **maple('GIfactors(z)')** returns the prime factors of z and their orders

maple('GIfacset(z)') returns the set of prime factors of z

maple('GIdivisor(z)') returns the list of divisors of z in the first quadrant

maple('GIprime(z)') determines if the Gaussian integer z is prime

maple('GIphi(z)') returns the number of Gaussian integers in a reduced system modulo z

maple('GInorm(z)') returns the norm of z ($norm(a+bi) = a^2 + b^2$)

maple('GIbasis(z1,z2)') determines whether $z1$ and $z2$ form a Gaussian basis (i.e if for all Gaussian integers z, there exist integers p and q such that $z = pz1 + qz2$)

maple('GIcombine(a,b,c,d)') is the Gaussian integer n such that: $n=b(mod\,a)$ and $n=d(mod\,c)$ (a, b, c and d are Gaussian integers)

maple('GIquadres(z1,z2)') determines whether there exists a Gaussian integer m such that $m^2 = z1(mod\,z2)$

maple('GIorder(z1,z2)') returns the smallest positive integer n such that z1^n = $1(mod\,z2)$.

maple('GIquo(z1,z2)') gives the quotient $z1/z2$

maple('GIrem(z1,z2)') gives the remainder of the quotient $z1/z2$

maple('GIgcd(a,b,...c)') gives the Gaussian integer in the first quadrant nearest to the greatest common divisor of the Gaussian integers $a,b,...,c$

maple('GIlcm(a,b,...c)') gives the Gaussian integer in the first quadrant closest to the least common multiple of the Gaussian integers a,b,...,c

maple('GIissqr(z)') determines if z is the square of a Gaussian integer

maple('GIsqrt(z)') gives the Gaussian integer best approximating the square root of z

maple('GInearest(z)') gives the Gaussian integer nearest to the complex number z

maple('GIroots(complex_polynomial)') gives the Gaussian integer roots of a univariate polynomial with Gaussian integer coefficients

maple('GIchrem([n1,...,nx],[m1,...,mx])') gives the unique Gaussian integer G such that G(mod mi) = y, i = 1,..., x

maple('GIfacpoly(polynomial)') factorizes the polynomial over the Gaussian integers

maple('GIgcdex(a,b,c,d)') gives the Gaussian integer g located in the first quadrant which is the greatest common divisor of the Gaussian integers a and b, using Euclid's algorithm, returning c and d such that g = c * a + d * b

maple('GIhermite(M)') calculates the Gaussian integer Hermite normal form of the integer matrix M. This is an upper triangular matrix with a number of non-zero rows equal to the rank of the matrix M.

maple('GIhermite(M,A)') calculates the Gaussian integer Hermite normal form H of the integer matrix M and the matrix A such that H = A * M

maple('GInodiv(z)') gives the number of non-associated factors of the Gaussian integer z

maple('GInormal(z)') normalizes the Gaussian integer z

maple('GIsieve(z)') generates the list of all prime Gaussian integers with norm less than or equal to z^2 (0≤x<y)

maple('GIsmith(M)') returns the Smith normal form of the matrix M of Gaussian integers

maple('GIsmith(M,A,B)') returns the Smith normal form of the matrix M of Gaussian integers and the matrices A and B such that S = A * M * B

maple('GIsqrfree(z)') returns the square-free factorization of z, [u,[[p[1],e[1]],...,[p[m],e[m]]] where p[i] is a principal factor of z, e[i] is its multiplicity, gcd(p[i],p[j]) = 1 ∀i≠j, and u is a unit in the ring of Gaussian integers. The square-free factorization of z will be of the form: z = u * p[1]^e[1] * ... * p[m]^e[m].

maple('GIunitnormal(z)') normalizes the Gaussian integer z

Here are some examples:
We factorize the number 30 in the ring of Gaussian integers.

>> maple('with(GaussInt):GIfactor(30)')

ans =

(i) *(1+i) ^ 2 *(1+2*i) *(1-2*i) *(-3)

The prime factors of 30 in the ring of Gaussian integers are: -3 with multiplicity 1,-1-2i with multiplicity 1,-1 + 2i with multiplicity 1, 1 + i with multiplicity 2 and i with multiplicity 1.

You can also find the set of prime factors of 30 or the list of prime factors together with their orders of multiplicity.

>> maple('with(GaussInt):GIfacset(30)')

ans =

{-3, 1+i, -1+2*i, -1-2*i}

>> maple('with(GaussInt):GIfactors(30)')

ans =

[i, [[1 + i, 2], [- 1 + 2 * i, 1], [- 1-2 * i, 1], [1, - 3]]]

You can also determine if a Gaussian integer is prime or not.
The number 1 + i is prime in the ring of Gaussian integers:

>> maple('with(GaussInt):GIprime(1+i)')

ans =

true

EXERCISE 3-18

Solve the following equation in the ring of Gaussian integers:

$x^4 - 17*x^3 - 29*i*x^3 - 188*x^2 + 339*i*x^2 + 1682*x - 86*i*x - 1178 - 1244*i = 0$

```
>> maple('with(GaussInt):GIroots(x^4-17*x^3-29*i*x^3-188*x^2+339*i*x^2+
1682*x-86*i*x-1178-1244*i)')
```

ans =

[[5+8*i, 1], [1+i, 1], [7+11*i, 1], [4+9*i, 1]]

EXERCISE 3-19

Check if the number 1000 - 500i is prime. If not, find all of its divisors and decompose it into prime factors. Also find the closest Gaussian integer to the least common multiple and the greatest common divisor of 1000-500i, 100-50i and 10-5i. Finally, find the norm of 1000-500i.

```
>> maple('with(GaussInt)'); maple('GIprime(1000-500*i)')
```

ans˙ =

false

```
>> maple('with(GaussInt)');maple('GIdivisor(1000-500*i)')
```

ans =

{1, 2, 4, 5, 10, 20, 25, 50, 100, 125, 500, 500+1000*i, 1+i, 1+2*i, 250, 12+16*i, 13+9*i, 4+22*i, 14+2*i, 11+2*i, 4+8*i, 28+96*i, 9+13*i, 55+10*i, 6+2*i, 62+34*i, 20+40*i, 100+200*i, 60+80*i, 5+5*i, 45+65*i, 25+25*i, 125+125*i, 30+10*i, 150+50*i, 70+10*i, 750+250*i, 2+i, 2+2*i, 3+4*i, 2+11*i, 8+4*i, 8+44*i, 1+3*i, 7+i, 4+2*i, 6+8*i, 2+6*i, 26+18*i, 4+3*i, 7+24*i, 16+12*i, 44+8*i, 3+i, 1+7*i, 31+17*i, 5+10*i, 20+15*i, 2+4*i, 8+6*i, 22+4*i, 14+48*i, 2+14*i, 18+26*i, 10+5*i, 25+50*i, 100+75*i, 15+20*i, 50+25*i, 125+250*i, 80+60*i, 220+40*i, 40+20*i, 400+300*i, 200+100*i, 15+5*i, 5+35*i, 5+15*i, 75+25*i, 25+175*i, 35+5*i, 25+75*i, 375+125*i, 10+20*i, 40+30*i, 110+20*i, 20+10*i, 50+100*i, 200+150*i, 30+40*i, 100+50*i, 250+500*i, 10+10*i, 10+70*i, 90+130*i, 10+30*i, 50+50*i, 50+350*i, 50+150*i, 250+250*i}

```
>> maple('with(GaussInt)');maple('GIfactor(1000-500*i)')
```

ans =

(-i)*(1+i)^4*(-1+2*i)^3*(-1-2*i)^4

```
>> maple('with(GaussInt)');maple('GIgcd(1000-500*i,100-50*i,10-5*i)')
```

ans =

*5+10*i*

```
>> maple('with(GaussInt)');maple('GIlcm(1000-500*i,100-50*i,10-5*i)')
```

ans =

*500+1000*i*

```
>> maple('with(GaussInt)');maple('GInorm(1000-500*i)')
```

ans =

1250000

EXERCISE 3-20

Find the square-free factorization of the Gaussian integers 1574 + 368 * i and 3369067456 + 16670818364 * i

```
>> maple('with(GaussInt):GIsqrfree(1574+368*i)')
```

ans =

*[i, [[65+148*i, 1], [-1+3*i, 2]]]*

```
>> maple('with(GaussInt):GIsqrfree(3369067456 + 16670818364*i)')
```

ans =

*[i, [[-3-2*i, 1], [-7+2*i, 2], [1+i, 4], [5-2*i, 5], [1+4*i, 6]]]*

```
                        EXERCISE 3-21
```

Find the Smith normal form of the matrix H of Gaussian integers whose rows are the vectors [− 4 + 7 * i, 8 + 10 * i, − 6 − 8 * i], [− 5 + 7 * i, 6 − 6 * i, 5 * i] and [−10 + i, 1 - 3 * i, − 10 + 5 * i]. Find the corresponding transformation matrices. Also find the step reduced Hermite normal form of the matrix H and the corresponding transformation matrix.

```
>> maple('with(GaussInt):H:= array([[-4+7*i,8+10*i,-6-8*i],[-5+7*i,6-6*i,5*i],
[- 10+i,1-3*i,-10+5*i]])')
```

ans =

*H := matrix([[-4+7*i, 8+10*i, -6-8*i], [-5+7*i, 6-6*i, 5*i], [-10+i, 1-3*i, -10+5*i]])*

```
>> maple('with(GaussInt):GIsmith(H)')
```

ans =

*matrix([[1, 0, 0], [0, 1, 0], [0, 0, 1797+791*i]])*

The matrix is displayed in standard row and column format using *pretty*.

```
>> pretty(sym(maple('with(GaussInt):GIsmith(H)')))
```

```
[1    0         0     ]
[                     ]
[0    1         0     ]
[                     ]
[0    0    1797 + 791i]
```

```
>> pretty(sym(maple('with(GaussInt):GIsmith(H,A,B),eval(A),eval(B)')));
```

```
[1    0         0      ]
[                      ]
[0    1         0      ],
[                      ]
[0    0    1797 + 791i ]
```

```
[    1                -1                 0          ]
[                                                   ]
[-5521 - 954i      16188 - 11418i    1405 + 13698i ],
[                                                   ]
[ 7440 - 10079i     6598 + 43799i    -28787 - 10920i ]
```

```
[1    778 + 3519i    -3051937 + 837129i]
[                                       ]
[0        1             44 + 877i       ]
[                                       ]
[0    247 + 54i       -36491 + 218995i  ]
```

```
>> pretty(sym(maple('with(GaussInt):GIhermite(H,M),eval(M)')))
```

```
[1      0      679 - 58i]   [-14 + 25i    51 + 16i    -49 +  3i]
[              ]            [                                   ]
[0    1 + i    121 - 712i], [ 22 + 21i    30 - 48i    -10 + 51i]
[              ]            [                                   ]
[0      0      503 + 1294i]  [-57 - 13i    -2 + 109i   -34 - 94i]
```

Here we have defined a matrix simply by placing its rows between square brackets, separated by commas. As we will see later, this is a standard way to define arrays in MATLAB.

EXERCISE 3-22

Factorize the polynomial $x^4 - 17x^3 - 29ix^3 - 188x^2 + 339ix^2 + 1682x - 86ix - 1178 - 1244i$ in the ring of Gaussian integers. Also find its roots in the ring of Gaussian integers.

```
>> maple('with(GaussInt):GIfacpoly(x^4-17*x^3-29*I*x^3-188*x^2+339*I*x^2
+1682*x-86*I*x-1178-1244*I)')
```

ans =

```
[1, [[x-4-9*i, 1], [x-5-8*i, 1], [x-1-i, 1], [x-7-11*i, 1]]]
```

The factorization is: *(x-4-9i)(x-5-8i)(x-1-i)(x-7-11i)*. Now we find the roots, which must logically be $1 + i$, $4 + 9i$ and $11i\ 7 + 5 + 8i$, all with multiplicity 1.

```
>> maple('with(GaussInt):GIroots(x^4-17*x^3-29*i*x^3-188*x^2+339*i*x^2
+1682*x-86*i*x-1178-1244*i)')
```

ans =

```
[[4 + 9 * i, 1], [5 + 8 * i, 1], [1 + i, 1], [7 + 11 * i, 1]]
```

3.10 Approximation and Precision

The accuracy of the output of numerical operations with MATLAB can be relaxed using special approximation techniques, returning results to a certain degree of precision.

MATLAB represents results with accuracy, but even if internally you are always working with exact calculations to avoid rounding errors, you can enable different approximate representation formats, which sometimes facilitate the interpretation of results. The following commands can be used for numerical approximation:

format long: Delivers results to 16 significant decimal figures.

format short: Delivers results to 4 decimal places. This is MATLAB's default format.

format long e: Provides the results to 16 decimal figures more than the power of 10 required.

format short e: Provides the results to four decimal figures more than the power of 10 required.

format long g: Delivers results in optimal long format.

format short g: Delivers results in optimal short format.

format bank: Delivers results to 2 decimal places.

format rat: Offers an approximation of results in the form of a rational number

format +: Returns the sign of the results (+, - or 0).

format hex: Returns results in hexadecimal.

vpa 'operations' n: Provides the result of operations to *n* significant decimal figures.

numeric('expr'): Provides the value of the expression numerically approximated by the current active format.

digits(n): Returns results to n significant digits.

maple('evalf(expr)'): Evaluates the expression numerically up to an accuracy determined by *digits*.

maple('evalf(expr,m)'): Evaluates the expression to *m* digits without affecting the value of *digits*.

maple('value(expr)'): Evaluates symbolically or numerically the inert symbolic expression.

maple('evalhf(expr)'): Evaluates the numerical expression with double precision to the number of accurate digits specified by *digits*.

maple('evala(expr)'): Evaluates the expression algebraically.

maple('evalc(expr)'): Evaluates the complex expression with double-precision.

maple('evalr(expr)'): Evaluates an expression containing ranges of variables or inequalities or logical symbols.

maple('evalb(expr)'): Evaluates an expression, equation, Boolean expression or inequality that contains relational operators.

maple('eval(expr)'): Completely evaluates the expression.

maple('eval(expr, n)'): Evaluates the expression to *n* levels. This is often used to evaluate the results of the command *subs*.

maple('evaln(expr)'): Evaluates an expression to a name. This is equivalent to introducing quotes in the expression.

maple('fnormal(expr)'): Normalizes a floating point expression.

maple('fnormal(expr, n)'): Normalizes a floating point expression to *n* digits.

maple('fnormal(expr,n,m)'): Normalizes a floating point expression to *n* digits with an error tolerance given by *m*.

maple('Float(m,n)'): Gives the number m*10^n in floating-point form. The result can be of the form *integer.integer*, *integer*, *.integer* or any of these forms multiplied by $10^{exponent}$.

Here are some examples:

For each *format*, find a numerical approximation of √17:

```
>> sqrt(17)
```

ans =

    4.1231

```
>> format long; sqrt(17)
```

ans =

    4.12310562561766

```
>> format long e; sqrt(17)
```

ans =

    4.123105625617660e+000

```
>> format short e; sqrt(17)
```

ans =

   4.1231e+000

```
>> format long g; sqrt(17)
```

ans =

            4.12310562561766

```
>> format short g; sqrt(17)
```

ans =

        4.1231

```
>> format bank; sqrt(17)
```

ans =

            4.12

```
>> format hex; sqrt (17)
```

ans =

   40107e0f66afed07

Now we give some examples of the calculation of the value of *sqrt(17)* specifying the precision that we desire:

```
>> vpa 'sqrt(17)' 10
```

ans =

4.123105626

```
>> digits(15); maple('evalf(sqrt(17))')
```

ans =

4.12310562561766

```
>> digits(15); maple('evalhf(sqrt(17))')
```

ans =

4.123105625617661

```
>> digits (15); maple ('evala (sqrt (17))')
```

ans =

17 ^(1/2)

We find the decimal approximation of π to 100 digits of precision.

```
>> vpa 'pi' 100
```

ans =

3.1415926535897932384626433832795028841971693993751058209749445923078164062862089986280348253421 17068

```
>> digits(100); maple('evalf(pi)')
```

ans =

3.1415926535897932384626433832795028841971693993751058209749445923078164062862089986280348253421 17068

Now we convert the numbers $12345 * 10^{-4}$, $456 * 10^{-4}$ and $12345 * 10^{18} - 12345 * 10^{-18}$ to floating point format:

```
>> maple('Float(123456,-4)')
```

ans =

12.3456

```
>> maple('Float(456,-4)')
```

ans =

.456e-1

```
>> maple('Float(12345,18)')
```

ans =

. 12345e23

```
>> maple ('Float(12345, - 18) ')
```

ans =

. 12345e-13

We convert 1234598678 * 10^{-3} to a floating-point number:

```
>> maple ('Float(1234598678, - 3)')
```

ans =

1234598.678

We now consider the integral of x^4 between 0 and 1 as an inert function and then calculate its numerical value:

```
>> maple('Int(x^4,x=0..1)')
```

ans =

Int(x^4,x = 0 .. 1)

```
>> maple('value(Int(x^4,x=0..1))')
```

ans =

1/5

3.11 Types of Numbers and Expressions

In MATLAB, you can work with different types of numbers and expressions. It is possible to declare the corresponding type of each number or expression, as well as to check the type of a given number or expression. These types of numbers and expressions cover integers, real numbers and complex numbers, and are used in arguments of functions whose definition is preceded by the command *maple*.

Among the types of numbers in MATLAB we have the following:

integer: integer

negint: negative integer

posint: positive integer

nonnegint: nonnegative integer

even: even integer

odd: odd integer

prime: prime integer

rational: rational number

fractional: fraction

realcons: real constant

radical: radical number

radext: algebraic extension in terms of radicals

radnum: algebraic number in terms of radicals

radnumext: radical number exension

sqrt: number or expression in terms of square roots

square: perfect square expression or number

numeric: numeric expression

number: constant or constant expression

positive: positive number

negative: negative number

infinity: infinite number

nonneg: nonnegative number

algnum: algebraic number

algnumext: algebraic number extension

rootof: RootOf expression

complex: complex number or complex expression

complex(integer): complex number a+bi with *a* and *b* integer (possibly zero)

complex(rational): complex number a+bi with a and b rational

complex(float): complex number a+bi with *a* and *b* constant floating point

complex(numeric): complex number a+bi of any of the above forms

facint: integer in factored form

float: number or floating point expression

intersect: intersection

union: union

minus: difference

list: list expression

listlist: list of lists

set: set

relation: relational expression

boolean: boolean expression

logical: logical expression

vector: vector

array: array (vector or matrix)

matrix: matrix

scalar: scalar matrix

name: name

nothing: nothing (always returns false)

protected: name protected by Maple (not editable)

range: range

string: string

table: table

text: text

Having described the types of numbers and the most important numerical expressions that can be declared in MATLAB, we now summarize the commands that handle them:

type(expr, type): determines whether the number or expression *expr* is of the specified type

tymematch(expr, type): determines if the number or expression *expr* is of the specified type

whattype(expr): returns the type of the number or expression *expr*

func(parameter::type) determines the type of the parameter of the function *func*

Here are some examples:

```
>> maple('type ((3+2*i), complex)')
```

ans =

true

```
>> maple('type(257,prime)')
```

ans =

true

```
>> maple('whattype([1,2,3])')
```

ans =

list

```
>> maple('whattype({1,2,3})')
```

ans =

set

3.12 Random Numbers

The automatic generation of (pseudo) random numbers is a problem well handled by MATLAB.

MATLAB provides the function *rand* to generate uniformly distributed random numbers and the function *randn* to generate normally distributed random numbers. The following functions can be used to generate random floating point numbers:

rand: returns a random uniformly distributed decimal number in the interval *[0,1]*

rand(n): returns a matrix of size *n×n* whose elements are random uniformly distributed decimal number in the interval *[0,1]*

rand(m,n): returns a matrix of dimension *m×n* whose elements are random uniformly distributed decimal number in the interval *[0,1]*

rand(size(a)): returns a matrix of the same size as the matrix *a* and whose elements are random uniformly distributed decimal number in the interval *[0,1]*

rand('seed'): returns the current value of the uniform random number generator seed

rand('seed',n): sets the current value of the uniform random number generator seed to the value *n*

randn: returns a normally distributed random decimal number with mean *0* and variance *1*

randn(n): returns a matrix of size *n×n* whose elements are normally distributed random decimal numbers with mean *0* and variance *1*

maple('with(linalg):randmatrix(m,n)'): returns a matrix of dimension *m×n* whose elements are random integers between −99 and 99

maple('with(linalg):randmatrix(m,n,option)'): returns a matrix of dimension *m×n* whose elements are random integers between −99 and 99, and of the specified type in option, the possible options being *symmetric*, *antisymmetric*, *diagonal*, *identity* and *sparse*

maple('with(linalg):randvector(n)'): returns a vector of dimension *n* whose elements are random integers between –99 and 99

randn(m,n): returns a matrix of dimension *m*×*n* whose elements are normally distributed random decimal number with mean *0* and variance *1*

randn(size(A)): returns a matrix of the same size as the matrix A and whose elements are normally distributed random decimal number with mean *0* and variance *1*

randn ('seed'): returns the current value of the normal random number generator seed

randn('seed',n): sets the current value of the normal random number generator seed to the value *n*

Here are some examples:

```
>> [rand, rand (1), randn, randn (1)]
```

ans =

```
    0.8310    0.0346    1.1650    0.6268
```

```
>> [rand(2), randn(2)]
```

ans =

```
    0.0535    0.6711    0.0751   -0.6965
    0.5297    0.0077    0.3516    1.6961
```

```
>> [rand(4,3), randn(4,3)]
```

ans =

```
    0.6326 0.2470 0.6515 - 0.0562    0.4005    0.7286
    0.7564 0.9826 0.0727    0.5135 - 1.3414 - 2.3775
    0.9910 0.7227 0.6316    0.3967    0.3750 - 0.2738
    0.7534 0.8847 0.7562    1.1252 - 0.3229
```

```
>> maple with(linalg):randmatrix(3,3,symmetric)
```

ans =

```
matrix([[-85,-55,-35], [-55,-37, 97], [-35, 97, 50]])
```

CHAPTER 4

■ ■ ■

Numerical Variables, Vectors and Matrices

4.1 Variables

The concept of variable, like the concept of function, is essential when working with mathematical software. Obviously, the theoretical concept of a mathematical variable is fixed and independent of the software package, but how to implement and manage variables is very characteristic of each particular program. MATLAB allows you to define and manage variables, and store them in files, in a very simple way.

When extensive calculations are performed, it is convenient to give names to intermediate results. Each intermediate result is assigned to a variable to make it easier to use. For example, we can define the variable x and assign the value 5 to it in the following way:

```
>> x = 5

x =

    5
```

From now on, whenever the variable x appears it will be replaced by the value 5, and it will not change its value until it is redefined.

```
>> x ^ 2

ans =

    25
```

The variable x will not change until we explicitly assign another value to it.

```
>> x = 7 + 4

x =

    11
```

From this moment on, the variable x will take the value 11.

It is very important to stress that the value assigned to a variable will remain fixed until it is expressly changed or if the current MATLAB session is closed. It is common to forget the definitions given to variables during a MATLAB session, causing misleading errors when the variables are used later in the session. For this reason, it is convenient to be able to remove the assignment of a value to a variable. This operation is performed by using the command *clear*. It is also useful to recall the variables we have defined in the present session, which is done using the command *who*:

- The expression $x = value$ assigns the value *value* to the variable x.

- The command *clear* removes the value assigned to all variables.

- The command *clear x* removes the value assigned to the variable x.

- The command *clear x y* removes the value assigned to the variables x and y.

- The command *who* gives the names of all variables currently in memory (variables in the workspace).

- The command *whos* gives the names, sizes, number of items, bytes occupied, and the type of all variables currently in memory.

Here are some examples that use the variable handling commands defined above:

```
>> x = 7, y = 4 + i, z = sqrt (3)

x =

    7

y =

    4.0000 + 1. 0000i

z =

    1.7321

>> p=x+y+z

p =

    12.7321 + 1. 0000i

>> who

Your variables are:

ans     p       x       y       z

>> whos
```

Name	Size	Elements	Bytes	Density	Complex
ANS	1 by 1	1	8	Full	No
p	1 by 1	1	16	Full	Yes
x	1 by 1	1	8	Full	No
y	1 by 1	1	16	Full	Yes
z	1 by 1	1	8	Full	No

Grand total is 5 elements using 56 bytes

Now we are going to change the value of the variable *y*, and delete the variable *x*.

```
>> y = pi

y =

    3.1416

>> clear x;
>> whos
```

Name Size	Elements Bytes Density Complex

Name Size	Elements	Bytes	Density	Complex
ANS 1 by 1	1	8	Full	No
p 1 by 1	1	16	Full	Yes
y 1 by 1	1	8	Full	No
z 1 by 1	1	8	Full	No

Grand total is 4 elements using 40 bytes

We see that the variable *x* has disappeared and that the variable *y* has the new value assigned, but the variable *p* has not changed, despite having changed two of its components. ***For an expression that contains a variable whose value has been changed, to update its value it is necessary to rerun it:***

```
>> p=y+z

p =

    4.8736

>> whos
```

Name Size	Elements	Bytes	Density	Complex
ANS 1 by 1	1	8	Full	No
p 1 by 1	1	8	Full	No
y 1 by 1	1	8	Full	No
z 1 by 1	1	8	Full	No

Grand total is 4 elements using 32 bytes

Now all values are updated, including that of *p*.

As for the names that can be given to the variables, the only restriction is that they cannot start with a number or contain punctuation characters that are assigned a special meaning in MATLAB. It is also advisable to name variables with words that begin with lowercase letters, and in general with words completely in lowercase. This avoids collisions with MATLAB functions beginning with an uppercase letter. MATLAB is case sensitive. There can be any number of characters in the name of a variable, but MATLAB will handle only the first 19.

4.2 Variables and Special Constants

In many kinds of calculations we need to work with variables and special constants that the program has enabled. Here are some examples:

PI or maple('PI'): 3.1415926535897...

i or j or maple('i'): imaginary unit (square root of -1).

inf or maple('infinity'): infinity, returned for example when presented with 1/0.

NaN (*Not a Number*): indeterminate, returned for example when presented with 0/0.

realmin: the smallest usable positive real number.

realmax: the greatest usable positive real number.

finite(x): returns 1 if x is finite and zero otherwise.

isinf(x): returns 1 if x is infinity or -infinity, and zero otherwise.

isNaN(x): returns 1 if x is undetermined and zero otherwise.

isfinite(x): returns 1 if x is finite and zero otherwise.

ana: automatically creates a variable to represent the last unmapped processing result which has not been assigned to a variable.

eps: returns the distance from 1.0 to the next largest double-precision number. This is the default tolerance for floating-point operations (floating point relative accuracy). In current IEEE machines its value is $2 \wedge (-52)$.

isieee: returns 1 if the machine is IEEE and 0 otherwise.

computer: returns the type of the computer.

flops: returns the number of floating point operations that have been executed in a session (flops(0) resets the operations counter).

version: returns the current version of MATLAB.

why: returns a concise message.

cputime: returns CPU time in seconds used by MATLAB since the beginning of the session.

clock: returns a list consisting of the following 6 items: [year month day hour minutes seconds].

date: returns the current calendar date.

etime: returns the time elapsed between two *clock* type lists (defined above).

tic: enables a temporary counter in seconds that ends with the use of the variable *toc*.

toc: returns the elapsed time in seconds since the variable *tic* was activated.

LastErr: returns the last error message.

See: gives information about the program and its *Toolbox*.

Info: provides information about MATLAB.

subscribe to: gives information about the subscription to MATLAB.

whatsnew: provides information about new undocumented MATLAB features.

Here are some examples:

First we check if our computer is an IEEE machine, determine what type of computer it is, and find the current date and time:

>> **isieee**

ans =

　1

>> **computer**

ans =

PCWIN

>> **clock**

ans =

　1. 0e + 003 *

　　1.9950 0.0110 0.0140 0.0100 0.0150 0.0079

>> **date**

ans =

14-mar-99

Now we check the CPU time (in seconds) that has passed since the beginning of the MATLAB session, as well as the number of floating-point operations that have occurred during that time:

>> **cputime**

ans =

　23.5100

>> **flops**

ans =

　1180

EXERCISE 4-1

Calculate the time in seconds that the computer takes to return the irrational number π to 50 decimal places.

```
>> tic; vpa 'pi' 50; toc
```

elapsed_time =

   0.110000000000001

EXERCISE 4-2

Calculate the number of floating-point operations required to calculate the numerical value of the square root of the irrational number π to default accuracy. Consider the number π first as a numerical constant, and secondly, as a symbolic constant.

```
>> flops(0);numeric((pi)^(1/2));flops
```

ans =

   427

```
>> flops(0);numeric('(pi)^(1/2)');flops
```

ans =

   6

We see that much fewer floating-point operations are required when we consider π as a symbolic constant. The calculations are faster when we work in the symbolic field.

4.3 Symbolic and Numeric Variables

MATLAB deems as symbolic any algebraic expression whose variables have previously been defined as symbolic via the command **syms**. For example, if we want to treat as symbolic the expression $6ab + 3a^2 + 2ab$ in order to simplify it, we need to declare the two variables a and b as symbolic as shown below:

```
>> syms a b
>> simplify(6*a*b + 3*a^2 + 2*a*b)
```

ans =

*8 * a * b + 3 * a ^ 2*

The command *sym* can be used to transform a numeric expression into a symbolic expression. For example, if we want to simplify the numeric expression $2/5 + 6/10 + 8/20$, we first need to transform it into a symbolic expression via *sym(2/5+6/10+8/20)*, making the simplification as follows:

```
>> simplify (sym(2/5+6/10+8/20))
```

ans =

7/5

The variables contained in a symbolic expressions must be symbolic. Some commands for working with symbolic and numerical variables are described below:

syms x y z... t: makes the variables *x, y, z,..., t* **symbolic.**

syms x y z... t real: makes the variables *x, y, z,..., t* **symbolic with real values.**

syms x y z... t unreal: makes the variables *x, y, z,..., t* **symbolic with non-real values.**

syms: lists the symbolic variables in the workspace.

x = sym ('x'): *x* **becomes a symbolic variable (equivalent to** *syms x***).**

x = sym ('x', real): *x* **becomes a real symbolic variable.**

x = sym('x',unreal): *x* **becomes a symbolic non-real variable.**

S = sym(A): creates a symbolic variable S from A, where A can be a string, a scalar, an array, a numeric expression, etc.

S = sym(A,'option'): converts the array, scalar or numeric expression A to a symbolic variable S according to the specified option. The option can be 'f' for floating point, 'r' for rational, 'e' for error format and 'd' for decimal.

numeric(x): makes the variable or expression *x* **numeric with double precision.**

sym2poly(poly): converts the symbolic polynomial *poly* **to a vector whose components are its coefficients.**

poly2sym(vector): creates a symbolic polynomial whose coefficients are the components of the vector.

poly2sym(vector,'v'): converts a symbolic polynomial in the variable *v* **whose coefficients are the components of the vector.**

digits(d): gives symbolic variables to an accuracy of *d* **significant figures.**

digits: returns the current accuracy for symbolic variables.

vpa(expr): returns the numerical result of the expression to an accuracy determined by *digits*.

vpa(expr, n): returns the numerical result of the expression to *n* **significant figures.**

vpa('expr', n): returns the numerical result of the expression to *n* **significant figures.**

pretty(expr): returns the symbolic expression in the form of standard mathematical script.

EXERCISE 4-3

Solve the equation $ax^2 + bx + c = 0$ assuming that the variable is x. Solve it when the variables are a, b or c, respectively.

Since by default MATLAB considers x to be the only symbolic variable, to solve the equation in x we don't need to declare x as symbolic. We simply use the command *solve* as follows:

```
>> solve('a*x^2+b*x+c=0')
```

ans =

```
[1/2/a*(-b+(b^2-4*a*c)^(1/2))]
[1/2/a*(-b-(b^2-4*a*c)^(1/2))]
```

But to solve the equation with respect to the variables *a*, *b* or *c* respectively, it is necessary to first specify them as symbolic variables:

```
>> syms a
>> solve('a*x^2+b*x+c=0',a)
```

ans =

```
-(b*x+c)/x^2
```

```
>> syms b
>> solve('a*x^2+b*x+c=0',b)
```

ans =

```
-(a*x^2+c)/x
```

```
>> syms c
>> solve('a*x^2+b*x+c=0',c)
```

ans =

```
-a * x ^ 2-b * x
```

EXERCISE 4-4

Find the roots of the polynomial $x^4 - 8x^2 + 16 = 0$ obtaining the result to default accuracy, to 20 significant figures and with double-precision. Also generate the vector of coefficients associated with the polynomial.

```
>> p = solve('x^4-8*x^2-16=0')

p =

[ 2*(2^(1/2)+1)^(1/2)]
[-2*(2^(1/2)+1)^(1/2)]
[ 2*(1-2^(1/2))^(1/2)]
[-2*(1-2^(1/2))^(1/2)]

>> vpa(p)

ans =

[    3.1075479480600746146883179061262]
[   -3.1075479480600746146883179061262]
[  1.2871885058111652494708868748364*i]
[ -1.2871885058111652494708868748364*i]

>> numeric(p)

ans =

    3.1075
   -3.1075
        0 + 1.2872i
        0 - 1.2872i

>> vpa(p,20)

ans =

[    3.1075479480600746146]
[   -3.1075479480600746146]
[ 1.2871885058111652495*i]
[-1.2871885058111652495*i]

>>  syms x
>>  sym2poly(x^4-8*x^2-16)

ans =

    1   0   -8   0   -16
```

EXERCISE 4-5

Find the numerical value to default precision of the abscissa of the intersection point in the first quadrant of the curves y = sin(x) and y = cos(x). Find the symbolic solution. Find the abscissa to 12 significant figures.

```
>> p = numeric(solve('sin(x) = cos(x)'))
```

p =

    0.7854

```
>> q = sym(p)
```

q =

PI/4

```
>> digits(12);r=numeric(solve('sin(x)=cos(x)'))
```

r =

.785398163398

EXERCISE 4-6

Simplify the following expressions as much as possible:

1 / 2m - 1 / 3m + 1 / 4 m + 1 / 5m + 1 / 6m

1/2 - 1/3 + 1/4 + 1/5 + 1/6

```
>> syms m
>> simplify(1/(2*m) - 1/(3*m) + 1/(4*m) +1/(5*m) +1/(6*m))
```

ans =

47/60m

```
>> pretty(simplify(1/(2*m) - 1/(3*m) + 1/(4*m) +1/(5*m) +1/(6*m)))
```

                    47

                    60m

```
>> sym(1/2-1/3 + 1/4 +1/5 +1/6)
```

ans =

47/60

4.4 Vector Variables

A variable that represents a vector of length n can be defined in MATLAB in the following ways:

```
variable = [e1, e2, e3,..., en]
variable = [e1 e2 e3 ... en]
```

Therefore, to define a vector variable, simply insert the vector elements between brackets separated by commas or blank spaces.

When you apply most MATLAB commands and functions to a vector variable, the result obtained is that found by applying the command or function to each element of the vector:

```
>> vector1 = [1,3,5,2.3,1/2]
```

vector1 =

    1.0000 3.0000 5.0000 2.3000 0.5000

```
>> sin(vector1)
```

ans =

    0.8415 0.1411 - 0.9589 0.7457 0.4794

```
>> exp (vector1)
```

ans =

    2.7183 20.0855 148.4132 9.9742 1.6487

```
>> log (vector1)
```

ans =

    0 1.0986 1.6094 0.8329 - 0.6931

There are different ways of defining a vector variable without explicitly bracketing all its elements, separated by commas or blank spaces.

> variable = [first_element:last_element]: Defines the vector whose first and last elements are specified, and the intermediate elements differ by one unit.

> variable = [first_element:increase:last_element]: Defines the vector whose first and last elements are specified, and the intermediate elements differ by the amount specified by the increase.

> variable = linspace (first_element, last_element, n): Defines the vector whose first and last elements are specified, and which has in total n evenly spaced elements.

> variable = logspace (a,b,n): Defines the vector whose first and last elements are 10^a and 10^b, and which has in total n evenly logarithmically spaced elements.

Here are some examples:

>> **vector2 = [0:5:20]**

vector2 =

  0 5 10 15 20

We have obtained the numbers between 0 and 20 separated by 5 units.

>> **vector3 = [0:20]**

vector3 =

  Columns 1 through 12

    0   1   2   3   4   5   6   7   8   9 10 11

  Columns 13 through 21

   12 13 14 15 16 17 18 19 20

We have obtained the numbers between 0 and 20 separated by units.

>> **vector4 = linspace(0,10,11)**

vector4 =

   0 1 2 3 4 5 6 7 8 9 10

We have obtained the numbers between 0 and 10 separated by units.

>> **vector5 = linspace(0,20,6)**

vector5 =

  0 4 8 12 16 20

We have obtained 6 equally spaced numbers between 0 and 20.

>> **vector6 = logspace(0,2,6)**

vector6 =

  1.0000 2.5119 6.3096 15.8489 39.8107 100.0000

We have obtained 6 evenly logarithmically spaced numbers between 10^0 and 10^2.

We can also consider row and column vectors in MATLAB. A column vector is obtained by separating its elements by semicolons, or by transposing a row vector using a single apostrophe at the end of its definition.

```
>> a=[1;2;3;4]

a =

    1
    2
    3
    4

>> a=[1:4];b=a'

b =

    1
    2
    3
    4

>> c=(a')'

c =

    1   2   3   4
```

You can also select an element of a vector or a subset of elements.

x(n): returns the n-th element of the vector x.

x(a:b): returns the a-th through b-th elements of the vector x, both inclusive.

x(a:p:b): returns the a-th through b-th elements of the vector x, both inclusive, each separated from the next by p units (a < b).

x(b:-p:a): returns the b-th through a-th elements of the vector x, both inclusive, each separated from the next by p units and starting with the b-th (b > a).

Here are some examples:

```
>> x =(1:10)

x =

    1    2    3    4    5    6    7    8    9   10

>> x(6)

ans =

    6
```

We have obtained the sixth element of the vector *x*.

>> x(4:7)

ans =

   4 5 6 7

We have obtained the elements of the vector *x* located between the fourth and the seventh elements, both inclusive.

>> x(2:3:9)

ans =

   2 5 8

We have obtained the elements of the vector *x* located between the second and ninth elements, both inclusive, but separated from each other by three units.

>> x(9:-3:2)

ans =

   9 6 3

We have obtained the elements of the vector *x* located between the ninth and second elements, both inclusive, but separated from each other by three units and starting at the ninth.

Simple mathematical operations between scalars and vectors scale each element of the vector according to the defined operation, and simple operations between vectors are performed elementwise.

Below is a summary of these operations:

      a = {a1, a2,..., an}, b = {b1, b2,..., bn}, c = scalar

      a + c = [a1 + c, a2 + c,..., an + c]: sum of a scalar and a vector

      a * c = [a1 * c, a2 * c,..., an * c]: product of a scalar and a vector

      a + b = [a1 + b1, a2 + b2,... an + bn]: sum of two vectors

      a. * b = [a1 * b1, a2 * b2,... , an * bn]: product of two vectors

      a. / b = [a1/b1 a2/b2... an/bn]: right ratio of two vectors

      a. \ b = [a1\b1 a2\b2... an\bn]: left ratio of two vectors

      a. ^ c = [a1 ^ c, a2 ^ c,..., an ^ c]: scalar power of a vector

      c. ^ a = [c ^ a1, c ^ a2,... ,c ^ an]: vector power of a scalar

      a. ^ b = [a1 ^ b1, a2 ^ b2,... ,an ^ bn]: vector power of a vector

It must be borne in mind that the vectors must be of the same length, and that in the product, quotient, and power the first operand is followed by a point.

On the other hand, you can also set the vector variables to be symbolic using the command *syms*.

```
>> syms t
>> A=sym([sin(t),cos(t)])

A =

[sin (t), cos (t)]
```

EXERCISE 4-7

Given the vector variables a = [π, 2π, 3π, 4π, 5π] and b = [e, 2e, 3e, 4e, 5e] calculate c = sin (a) + b, d = cos (a), e = ln (b), f = c * d, g = c/d, h = d ^ 2, i = d ^ 2-e ^ 2 and j = 3d ^ 3-2e ^ 2.

```
>> a = [pi, 2 * pi, 3 * pi, 4 * pi, 5 * pi], b = [exp (1), 2 * exp (1), 3 * exp (1), 4 * exp (1), 5 * exp (1)], c=sin(a)+b,
d=cos(a), e=log(b), f=c.*d, g=c./d, h=d.^2, i=d.^2-e.^2, j = 3 * d. ^ 3-2 * e ^ 2

a =

    3.1416  6.2832  9.4248  12.5664  15.7080

b =

    2.7183  5.4366  8.1548  10.8731  13.5914

c =

    2.7183  5.4366  8.1548  10.8731  13.5914

d =

    -1    1    -1    1    -1

e =

    1.0000 1.6931 2.0986 2.3863 2.6094

f =

    -2.7183 5.4366 - 8.1548 10.8731 - 13.5914

g =

    -2.7183 5.4366 - 8.1548 10.8731 - 13.5914

h =

    1    1    1    1    1

i =

    0  - 1.8667 - 3.4042 - 4.6944 - 5.8092

j =

    -5.0000 - 2.7335 - 11.8083 - 8.3888 - 16.6183
```

4.5 Matrix Variables

MATLAB defines matrices by inserting in brackets all its row vectors separated by a semicolon. Vectors can be entered by separating their components by spaces or by commas, as we already know. For example, a 3 × 3 matrix variable can be entered in the following two ways:

$M = [a_{11} \ a_{12} \ a_{13};a_{21} \ a_{22} \ a_{23};a_{31} \ a_{32} \ a_{33}]$
$M = [a_{11}, \ a_{12} \ ,a_{13};a_{21}, \ a_{22}, \ a_{23};a_{31}, \ a_{32}, \ a_{33}]$

Similarly we can define a matrix of general dimension *(M×N)*. Once a matrix variable has been defined, MATLAB enables many ways to insert, extract, renumber, and generally manipulate its elements. The following list summarizes different ways to define matrix variables.

A(m,n) defines the (m, n)-th element of the matrix A (row m and column n)

A(a:b,c:d) defines the subarray of A formed between the a-th and the b-th rows and between the c-th and the d-th columns, inclusive

A(a:p:b,c:q:d) defines the subarray of A formed by every p-th row between the a-th and the b-th rows, inclusive, and every q-th column between the c-th and the d-th columns, inclusive

A([a b],[c d]) defines the subarray of A formed by the intersection of the a-th through b-th rows and c-th through d-th columns, inclusive

A([a b c...],[e f g...]) defines the subarray of A formed by the intersection of rows a, b, c,... and columns e, f, g,...

A(:,c:d) defines the subarray of A formed by all the rows in A and the c-th through to the d-th columns

A(:,[c d e ...]) defines the subarray of A formed by all the rows in A and columns c, d, e,...

A(a:b,:) defines the subarray of A formed by all the columns in A and the a-th through to the b-th rows

A([a b c...],:) defines the subarray of A formed by all the columns in A and rows a, b, c,...

A(a,:) defines the a-th row of the matrix A

A(:,b) defines the b-th column of the matrix A

A(:) defines a column vector whose elements are the columns of A placed in order below each other

A(:,:) this is equivalent to the entire matrix A

[A, B, C,...] defines the matrix formed by the matrices A, B, C,...

SA = [] clears the subarray of the matrix A, SA, and returns the remainder

diag(v) creates a diagonal matrix with the vector v in the diagonal

diag(A) extracts the diagonal of the matrix as a column vector

eye(n) creates the identity matrix of order n

eye(m,n) creates an m×n matrix with ones on the main diagonal and zeros elsewhere

zeros(m,n) creates the zero matrix of order m×n

ones(m,n) creates the matrix of order m×n with all its elements equal to 1

rand(m,n) creates a uniform random matrix of order m×n

randn(m,n) creates a normal random matrix of order m×n

flipud(A) returns the matrix whose rows are those of A but placed in reverse order (from top to bottom)

fliplr(A) returns the matrix whose columns are those of A but placed in reverse order (from left to right)

rot90(A) rotates the matrix A counterclockwise by 90 degrees

reshape(A,m,n) returns an m×n matrix formed by taking consecutive entries of A by columns

size(A) returns the order (size) of the matrix A

find(cond$_A$) returns all A items that meet a given condition

length(v) returns the length of the vector v

tril(A) returns the lower triangular part of the matrix A

triu(A) returns the upper triangular part of the matrix A

A' returns the transpose of the matrix A

inv(A) returns the inverse of the matrix A

Here are some examples:

We consider first the *2 × 3* matrix whose rows are the first six consecutive odd numbers:

```
>> A = [1 3 5; 7 9 11]
```

A =

```
1 3 5
7 9 11
```

Now we are going to change the *(2,3)-th* element, i.e. the last element of *A*, to zero:

```
>> A(2,3) = 0
```

A =

```
1 3 5
7 9 0
```

We now define the matrix *B* to be the transpose of *A*:

```
>> B = A'
```

B =

```
1 7
3 9
5 0
```

111

We now construct a matrix C, formed by attaching the identity matrix of order 3 to the right of the matrix B:

```
>> C = [B eye (3)]
```

C =

```
1   7   1   0   0
3   9   0   1   0
5   0   0   0   1
```

We are going to build a matrix D by extracting the odd columns of the matrix C, a matrix E formed by taking the intersection of the first two rows of C and its third and fifth columns, and a matrix F formed by taking the intersection of the first two rows and the last three columns of the matrix C:

```
>> D = C(:,1:2:5)
```

D =

```
1   1   0
3   0   0
5   0   1
```

```
>> E = C([1 2],[3 5])
```

E =

```
1   0
0   0
```

```
>> F = C([1 2],3:5)
```

F =

```
1   0   0
0   1   0
```

Now we build the diagonal matrix G such that the elements of the main diagonal are the same as those of the main diagonal of D:

```
>> G = diag(diag(D))
```

G =

```
1   0   0
0   0   0
0   0   1
```

We then build the matrix *H*, formed by taking the intersection of the first and third rows of *C* and its second, third and fifth columns:

```
>> H = C([1 3],[2 3 5])
```

H =

```
7 1 0
0 0 1
```

Now we build an array *I* formed by the identity matrix of order *5 × 4*, appending the zero matrix of the same order to its right and to the right of that, the unit matrix, again of the same order. Then we extract the first row of *I* and, finally, form the matrix *J* comprising the odd rows and even columns of *I* and calculate its order (size).

```
>> I = [eye(5,4) zeros(5,4) ones(5,4)]
```

ans =

```
1   0   0   0   0   0   0   0   1   1   1   1
0   1   0   0   0   0   0   0   1   1   1   1
0   0   1   0   0   0   0   0   1   1   1   1
0   0   0   1   0   0   0   0   1   1   1   1
0   0   0   0   0   0   0   0   1   1   1   1
```

```
>> I(1,:)
```

ans =

```
1   0   0   0   0   0   0   0   1   1   1   1
```

```
>> J = I(1:2:5,2:2:12)
```

J =

```
0   0   0   0   1   1
0   0   0   0   1   1
0   0   0   0   1   1
```

```
>> size(J)
```

ans =

```
3 6
```

113

We now construct a random matrix K of order 3×4, reverse the order of the rows of K, reverse the order of the columns of K and then perform both operations simultaneously. Finally, we find the matrix L of order 4×3 whose columns are obtained by taking the elements of K sequentially by columns.

```
>> K = rand(3,4)
```

K =

```
0.5269    0.4160    0.7622    0.7361
0.0920    0.7012    0.2625    0.3282
0.6539    0.9103    0.0475    0.6326
```

```
>> K(3:-1:1,:)
```

ans =

```
0.6539    0.9103    0.0475    0.6326
0.0920    0.7012    0.2625    0.3282
0.5269    0.4160    0.7622    0.7361
```

```
>> K(:,4:-1:1)
```

ans =

```
0.7361    0.7622    0.4160    0.5269
0.3282    0.2625    0.7012    0.0920
0.6326    0.0475    0.9103    0.6539
```

```
>> K(3:-1:1,4:-1:1)
```

ans =

```
0.6326    0.0475    0.9103    0.6539
0.3282    0.2625    0.7012    0.0920
0.7361    0.7622    0.4160    0.5269
```

```
>> L = reshape(K,4,3)
```

L =

```
0.5269 0.7012 0.0475
0.0920 0.9103 0.7361
0.6539 0.7622 0.3282
0.4160 0.2625 0.6326
```

EXERCISE 4-8

Given the square matrix of order 3 whose entries are the first nine natural numbers, find its inverse, its transpose and its diagonal. Transform it into a lower triangular matrix and an upper triangular matrix and rotate it by 90 degrees counterclockwise. Find the sum of the elements in the first row and the sum of the diagonal elements. Extract the subarray whose diagonal is formed by the elements at $_{11}$ and $_{22}$ and also remove the subarray whose diagonal elements are at $_{11}$ and $_{33}$.

```
>> M = [1,2,3;4,5,6;7,8,9]

M =

    1    2    3
    4    5    6
    7    8    9

>> A = inv(M)
```

Warning: Matrix is close to singular or badly scaled.

Results may be inaccurate. RCOND = 2.937385e-018

```
A =

  1. 0e + 016 *

    0.3152 -0.6304  0.3152
   -0.6304  1.2609 -0.6304
    0.3152 -0.6304  0.3152

>> B = M'

B =

    1 4 7
    2 5 8
    3 6 9

>> V = diag(M)

V =

    1
    5
    9
```

```
>> TI=tril(M)

TI =

      1      0      0
      4      5      0
      7      8      9

>> TS=triu(M)

TS =

      1      2      3
      0      5      6
      0      0      9

>> TR=rot90(M)

TR =

      3      6      9
      2      5      8
      1      4      7

>> s=M(1,1)+M(1,2)+M(1,3)

s =

      6

>> sd=M(1,1)+M(2,2)+M(3,3)

sd =

     15

>> SM=M(1:2,1:2)

SM =

      1      2
      4      5

>> SM1=M([1 3],[1 3])

SM1 =

     1 3
     7 9
```

The most important matrix operations are summarized below:

A + B, A-B, A * B: addition, subtraction and product of matrices

$A\backslash B = inv(A) * B$ if A is square.

$A\backslash B$ is the solution of the system $AX = B$ in the sense of least-squares if A is not square

B coincides with $(A' \backslash B')'$

A ⁿ coincides with A * A * A *... * A n times (n scalar)

p ^ performs the calculation only if p is a scalar

Here are some examples:

```
>> A = [1, 3, 5; pi exp(pi) sin(1); i 2 * i 1 + i]

A =

   1.0000   3.0000  5.0000
   3.1416   2.7183  0.0000
   1.0000i  2.0000i 1.0000 + 1.0000i
```

We have defined a complex matrix. Next we will calculate its inverse, its square and its square root:

```
>> B=inv(A)

B =

    0.0711 - 0.2874i  0.5810 - 0.0806i  0.5407 + 0.8963i
   -0.0822 + 0.3322i -0.3036 + 0.0932i -0.6249 - 1.0359i
    0.2351 - 0.1418i  0.0659 - 0.0398i  0.2668 + 0.4423i
```

```
>> C=A^2

C =

   10.425 +       5i  72.422 +      10i  12.524 +           5i
   75.84 + 0.84147i  544.92 + 1.6829i   36.022 +     0.84147i
      -1 + 8.2832i       -2 + 51.281i        0 +      8.6829i
```

```
>> A^(1/2)

ans =

    0.7181 + 0.3784i 0.6691 - 0.6583i 2.0360 - 1.1395i
    1.2547 - 0.3193i 1.6690 + 0.3804i -0.5550 + 0.8311i
   -0.1046 + 0.1852i 0.1152 + 0.5870i 1.2790 + 0.2869i
```

Now we check that the product of the matrix *A* with its inverse is the identity matrix of order 3:

```
>> A*B
```

ans =

```
1.0000 + 0.0000i 0.0000 + 0.0000i 0.0000 + 0.0000i
0.0000 + 0.0000i 1.0000 + 0.0000i 0.0000 + 0.0000i
0.0000 + 0.0000i 0.0000 + 0.0000i 1.0000 + 0.0000i
```

Now we find the exponential of *A* with bases 2 and - 2:

```
>> 2^A
```

ans =

```
1.0e+07 *

 0.0218 + 0.0057i    0.1569 + 0.0384i    0.0106 + 0.0031i
 0.1673 + 0.0176i    1.2036 + 0.1080i    0.0816 + 0.0110i
-0.0024 + 0.0157i   -0.0156 + 0.1131i   -0.0014 + 0.0076i
```

```
>> (-2)^A
```

ans =

```
1.0e+06 *

 0.0585 - 0.1313i    0.4059 - 0.9492i    0.0305 - 0.0634i
 0.2852 - 1.0365i    1.9345 - 7.4766i    0.1545 - 0.5029i
 0.0965 + 0.0316i    0.6969 + 0.2161i    0.0468 + 0.0168i
```

So far, we have always worked with numeric matrices. To work with **symbolic matrices**, we simply define the variables to be symbolic using the command **syms**.

```
>>  syms t
>>  A=sym([sin(t),cos(t);tan(t),exp(t)])
```

A =

```
[sin(t), cos(t)]
[tan(t), exp(t)]
```

```
>> b = inv (A)
```

b =

```
[-exp (t) / (-sin (t) * exp (t) + cos (t) * tan (t)), cos (t) / (-sin (t) * exp (t) +
cos (t) * tan (t))]
[tan (t) / (-sin (t) * exp (t) + cos (t) * tan (t)), - sin (t) / (-sin (t) * exp (t) +
cos (t) * tan (t))]
```

4.6 Character Variables

MATLAB is a powerful numerical calculation program, but it is also a versatile character variable (i.e. text) manipulator. A character variable (or chain) is simply a string of characters contained within single quotes that MATLAB interprets as a vector form. For example:

```
>> c = 'string'

c =

character string
```

We have thus defined the character variable *c*. Among the MATLAB commands that handle character variables we have the following:

abs('character_string') returns the array of ASCII characters equivalent to each character in the string

setstr(numeric_vector) returns the string of ASCII characters that are equivalent to the elements of the vector

str2mat(t1,t2,t3,...) returns the matrix whose rows are the strings t1, t2, t3,..., respectively

str2num('string') converts the string to its exact numeric value used by MATLAB

num2str(number) returns the exact number in its equivalent string with fixed precision

int2str(integer) converts the integer to a string

sprintf('format', a) converts a numeric array into a string in the specified format

sscanf('string', 'format') converts a string to a numeric value in the specified format

dec2hex(integer) converts a decimal integer into its equivalent string in hexadecimal

hex2dec('string_hex') converts a hexadecimal string into its integer equivalent

hex2num('string_hex') converts a hexadecimal string into the equivalent IEEE floating point number

lower('string') converts a string to lowercase

upper('string') converts a string to uppercase

strcmp(s1,s2) compares the strings s1 and s2 and returns 1 if they are equal and 0 otherwise

strcmp(s1,s2,n) compares the strings s1 and s2 and returns 1 if their first n characters are equal and 0 otherwise

strrep(c,'exp1', 'exp2') replaces exp1 by exp2 in the chain c

findstr(c, 'exp') finds where exp is in the chain c

isstr(expression) returns 1 if the expression is a string and 0 otherwise

ischar(expression) returns 1 if the expression is a string and 0 otherwise

strjust(string) right justifies the string

119

blanks(n) generates a string of n spaces

deblank(string) removes blank spaces from the right of the string

eval(expression) executes the expression, even if it is a string

disp('string') displays the string (or array) as written, and continues the MATLAB process

input('string') displays the string on the screen and waits for a key press to continue

Here are some examples:

```
>> eval ('4 * atan(1)')
```

ans =

   3.1416

This shows how MATLAB numerically evaluates the contents of a string (according to the program's standard interpretation of the syntax).

```
>> hex2dec ('3ffe56e')
```

ans =

   67102062

 MATLAB has converted a hexadecimal string to a decimal string.

```
>> dec2hex (1345679001)
```

ans =

   50356E99

The program has converted a decimal string to a hexadecimal string.

```
>> sprintf('%f',[1+sqrt(5)/2,pi])
```

ans =

 2.118034 3.141593

The exact numerical components of a vector have been converted to a string (to default precision).

```
>> sscanf('121.00012','%f')
```

ans =

  121.0001

A numeric string has been passed to exact numerical format (with default precision). Later we will see which alternative formats are possible.

```
>> num2str(pi)
```

ans =

3.142

The exact number *p* has been approximated to default precision and converted to a string.

```
>> str2num('15/14')
```

ans =

   1.0714

A string representing a rational number has been approximated to default precision and converted to a string.

```
>> setstr(32:126)
```

ans =

*!"#$% &' () * +, -. / 0123456789:; < = >? @ABCDEFGHIJKLMNOPQRSTUVWXYZ [\] ^*
_'abcdefghijklmnopqrstuvwxyz {|}~

The ASCII characters associated with whole numbers between 32 and 126 have been generated.

```
>> abs('{]}><#¡¿?ºª')
```

ans =

   123 93 125 62 60 35 161 191 63 186 170

The integers corresponding to the given ASCII characters have been generated.

```
>> lower('ABCDefgHIJ')
```

ans =

abcdefghij

The given string has been converted to lowercase text.

```
>> upper('abcd eFGHi jKlMn')
```

ans =

ABCD EFGHI JKLMN

The given string has been converted to uppercase text.

```
>> str2mat(' The world ',' The country ',' Daily 16 ', ' ABC ')
```

ans =

```
The world
The country
Daily 16
ABC
```

The chains given as arguments of the command *str2mat* have been converted into rows of an array.

```
>> disp('This text will appear on the screen')
```

This text will appear on the screen

The argument of the command *disp* is displayed on screen.

```
>> c = 'this is a good example';
>> strrep(c, 'good', 'bad')
```

ans =

this is a bad example

The string *good* has been replaced by the string *bad* in the string c.

```
>> findstr(c, 'is')
```

ans =

```
     3 6
```

The positions of the first character of the string *is* in *c* are given.

4.7 Operators

MATLAB features arithmetic, logical, relational, conditional and structural operators.

4.7.1 Arithmetic Operators

There are two types of arithmetic operators in MATLAB: matrix arithmetic operators, which are governed by the rules of linear algebra, and arithmetic operators on vectors, which are performed elementwise. The operators involved, which we have already seen, are summarized below.

+	**Sum of scalars, vectors or matrices**
-	**Subtraction of scalars, vectors, or matrices**
*	**Product of scalar or matrix**
.*	**Product of scalar or vector**

\ $A \backslash B = inv\ (A) * B$, where A and B are matrices

.\ $A. \backslash B = [B(i,j) / A\ (i, j)]$ where A and B vectors ($dim\ (A) = dim\ (B)$)

/   Quotient, or $B/A = B * inv\ (A)$, where A and B are matrices

./ $A ./ B = [A(i,j)/B\ (i, j)]$, where A and B are vectors [$dim\ (A) = dim\ (B)$]

^   Power of a scalar or matrix (Mp)

.^   Power of vectors ($A.\ ^\wedge\ B = [A(i,j)B\ (i, j)]$, for vectors A and B)

EXERCISE 4-9

Where X = [1 2 3] and Y = [4 5 6], calculate X + Y, X-Y, X * Y, X'* Y, X * Y', X.*Y, X.' * Y, X.*Y', 2 * X, 2.*X, X/Y, Y\X, X. / Y, Y\X, 2/X, 2. / X, 2\Y, 2. \Y, X ^ Y, X. ^ Y, X ^ 2, X^ 2, 2 ^ X and 2. ^ X.

```
>> X = [1,2,3]; Y = [4,5,6]; a = X + Y, b = X-Y, c = X * Y, d = 2. * X, e = 2/X, f = 2. \Y, g
= X. / Y,
  h =. \X, i = x ^ 2, j = 2. ^ X, k = x. ^ Y

a =

    5  7  9

b =

   -3   -3   -3

c =

    4  10  18

d =

    2   4   6

e =

   2.0000  1.0000  0.6667

f =

   2.0000  2.5000  3,0000

g =

   0.2500  0.4000  0.5000

h =

   0.2500  0.4000  0.5000
```

```
i =

    1 4 9

j =

    2 4 8

k =

    1 32 729
```

The above operations are all valid since in all cases the variable operands are of the same dimension, so the operations are successfully carried out element by element. For the sum and the difference there is no distinction between vectors and matrices, as the operations are identical in both cases.

```
>> X = [1,2,3]; Y = [4,5,6]; l = X'* Y, m = X * Y ', n = 2 * X, o = X / Y, p = Y\X
```

```
l =

     4    5    6
     8   10   12
    12   15   18

m =

    32

n =

    2 4 6

o  =

    0.4156

p =

    0              0              0
    0              0              0
    0.1667         0.3333         0.5000
```

All of the above matrix operations are well defined since the dimensions of the operands are compatible in every case. We must not forget that a vector is a particular case of matrix, but to operate with it in matrix form (not element by element), it is necessary to respect the rules of dimensionality for matrix operations. For example, the vector operations *X.' * Y* and *X.*Y'* make no sense, since they involve vectors of different dimensions. Similarly, the matrix operations *X * Y, 2/X, 2\Y, X ^ 2, 2 ^ X* and *X ^ Y* make no sense, again because of a conflict of dimensions in the arrays.

4.7.2 Relational Operators

MATLAB also provides relational operators. Relational operators perform element by element comparisons between two matrices and return an array of the same size whose elements are one if the corresponding relationship is true, or zero if the corresponding relation is false. The relational operators can also compare scalars with vectors or matrices, in which case the scalar is compared to all the elements of the array. Below is a summary of these operators.

<   **less than (for complex numbers this applies only to the real parts)**

< =   **less than or equal (only applies to real parts of complex numbers)**

>   **greater than (only applies to real parts of complex numbers)**

> =   **greater than or equal (only applies to real parts of complex numbers)**

x == y   **equality (also applies to complex numbers)**

x ~ = y   **inequality (also applies to complex numbers)**

Here are some examples:

```
>> X = 5 * ones(3,3); X > = [1 2 3; 4 5 6 ; 7 8 9]

ans =

   1 1 1
   1 1 0
   0 0 0
```

The elements of the array *X* which are greater than or equal to the corresponding element of the matrix *[1 2 3; 4 5 6; 7 8 9]* are given the value 1 in the response matrix. The rest of the elements are assigned the value 0 (the result of the operation would have been the same if we had compared the scalar 5 to the matrix *[1 2 3; 4 5 6; 7 8 9]* using the expression *X = 5; X > = [1 2 3; 4 5 6; 7 8 9]*).

Next we see another example that combines an arithmetic operation with a relational operation:

```
>> A = 1:9, B = 9-A, Y = A > 4, Z = B-(A>2)

A =

   1   2   3   4   5   6   7   8   9

B =

   8   7   6   5   4   3   2   1   0

Y =

   0   0   0   0   1   1   1   1   1

Z =

   8   7   5   4   3   2   1   0   -1
```

The values of *Y* equal to 1 correspond to elements of *A* larger than 4. The *Z* values result from subtracting 1 from the corresponding elements of *B* if the corresponding element of *A* is greater than 2, or 0 if the corresponding element of *A* is less than or equal to 2.

4.7.3 Logical Operators

MATLAB provides symbols to denote logical operators. The logical operators shown below offer a way to combine or negate relational expressions.

~ A	**logical negation (*NOT*) or the complement of *A***
A & B	**logical conjunction (*AND*) or the intersection of *A* and *B***
A | B	**logical disjunction (*OR*) or the union of *A* and *B***
xor(A,B)	**exclusive or (*XOR*) or the symmetric difference of *A* and *B* (gives 1 if *A* or *B*, but not both, are 1)**

Here are some examples:

```
>> A = 1:9; P =(A>2) &(A<6)

P =

   0   0   1   1   1   0   0   0   0
```

Returns 1 when A is greater than 2 and less than 6, and returns 0 otherwise.

```
>> A=[1 1 2 2 3 4 5 6 7 8 9],P=(A>=1)&(A<6),xor(A,P)

A =

   1   1   2   2   3   4   5   6   7   8   9
P =

   1   1   1   1   1   1   1   0   0   0   0

ans =

   0   0   0   0   0   0   0   1   1   1   1
```

Returns 1 when *A* or *P*, but not both, have the value 1.

4.8 Logic Functions

MATLAB implements logical functions whose output can take the value true (1) or false (0). The following list summarizes the most important logical functions.

exist(A) checks if the variable or function exists (returns 0 if A does not exist and a number between 1 and 5, depending on the type, if it does exist)

any(V) returns 0 if all elements of the vector V are null and returns 1 if some element of V is non-zero

any(A) returns 0 for each column of the matrix A with all null elements and returns 1 for each column of the matrix A which has non-null elements

all(V) returns 1 if all the elements of the vector V are non-null and returns 0 if some element of V is null

all(A) returns 1 for each column of the matrix A with all non-null elements and returns 0 for each column of the matrix A with at least one null element

find(V) returns the places (or indices) occupied by the non-null elements of the vector V

isNaN(V) returns 1 for the elements of V that are indeterminate and returns 0 for those that are not

isinf(V) returns 1 for the elements of V that are infinite and returns 0 for those that are not

isfinite(V) returns 1 for the elements of V that are finite and returns 0 for those that are not

isempty(A) returns 1 if A is an empty array and returns 0 otherwise (an empty array is an array such that one of its dimensions is 0)

issparse(A) returns 1 if A is a sparse matrix and returns 0 otherwise

isreal(V) returns 1 if all the elements of V are real and returns 0 otherwise

isprime(V) returns 1 for all elements of V that are prime and returns 0 for all elements of V that are not prime

islogical(V) returns 1 if V is a logical vector and 0 otherwise

isnumeric(V) returns 1 if V is a numeric vector and 0 otherwise

ishold returns 1 if the properties of the current graph are retained for the next graph and only new elements will be added and 0 otherwise

isieee returns 1 if the computer is capable of IEEE standard operations

isstr(S) returns 1 if S is a string and 0 otherwise

ischart(S) returns 1 if S is a string and 0 otherwise

isglobal(A) returns 1 if A is a global variable and 0 otherwise

isletter(S) returns 1 if S is a letter of the alphabet and 0 otherwise

isequal(A,B) returns 1 if the matrices or vectors A and B are equal, and 0 otherwise

ismember(V,W) returns 1 for every element of V which is in W and 0 for every element V that is not in W

Here are some examples:

```
>> isinf ([pi NaN Inf - Inf])
```

ans =

```
    0    0    1    1
```

```
>> any([pi NaN Inf -Inf])
```

ans =

```
    1
```

```
>> ismember([1,2,3,5],[8,12,1,3,56,5])
```

ans =

```
     1     0     1     1
```

```
>> A=[2,0,1]; B=[4,0,2];
>> isequal(2*A,B)
```

ans =

```
     1
```

```
>> V=[-10,5,3,12,0];
>> isprime(V)
```

ans =

```
     0     1     1     0     0
```

```
>> isnumeric(V)
```

ans =

```
     1
```

```
>> all(V)
```

ans =

```
     0
```

```
>> any(V)
```

ans =

```
     1
```

```
>> C=[0 2 3;0 1 2 ;0 4 6],D=[0 0 0 0;4 3 1 2;6 0 0 4]
>> any(C),all(C),any(D),all(D)
```

ans =

```
     0 1 1
```

ans =

```
     0 1 1
```

ans =

```
     1 1 1 1
```

ans =

```
     0 0 0 0
```

4.9 Elementary Functions that Support Complex Matrix Arguments

- **Trigonometric**

sin (z)	sine function
sinh (z)	hyperbolic sine function
asin (z)	arc sine function
asinh (z)	hyperbolic arc sine function
cos (z)	cosine function
cosh (z)	hyperbolic cosine function
acos (z)	arc cosine function
acosh (z)	hyperbolic arc cosine function
tan (z)	tangent function
tanh (z)	hyperbolic tangent function
atan (z)	arc tangent function
atan2 (z)	arc tangent function in the fourth quadrant
atanh (z)	hyperbolic arc tangent function
sec (z)	secant function
sech (z)	hyperbolic secant function
asec (z)	arc secant function
asech (z)	hyperbolic arc secant function
csc (z)	cosecant function
csch (z)	hyperbolic cosecant function
acsc (z)	arc cosecant function
acsch (z)	hyperbolic arc cosecant function
cot (z)	cotangent function
coth (z)	hyperbolic cotangent function
acot (z)	arc cotangent function
acoth (z)	hyperbolic arc cotangent function

- **Exponential**

exp (z)	base *e* exponential function
log (z)	Naperian logarithm
log10 (z)	base 10 logarithm
sqrt (z)	square root function

(continued)

- **Complex**

abs (z)	modulus or absolute value
angle (z)	argument
conj (z)	complex conjugate
imag (z)	imaginary part
real (z)	real part

- **Numerical**

fix (z)	removes the decimal part
floor (z)	rounds decimals to the nearest lower integer
ceil (z)	round decimals to the nearest greater integer
round (z)	performs the common rounding of decimal
rem (z1, z2)	remainder of the division of *z1* by *z2*
sign (z)	sign function

- **Matrix**

expm (Z)	matrix exponential function by default
expm1 (Z)	matrix exponential function in *M-file*
expm2 (Z)	matrix exponential function via Taylor series
expm3 (Z)	matrix exponential function via eigenvalues
logm (Z)	matrix logarithm
sqrtm (Z)	matrix square root
funm(Z, 'function')	applies the function to the matrix Z

Here are some examples:

```
>> A = [1 2 3; 4 5 6; 7 8 9]

A =

    1    2    3
    4    5    6
    7    8    9

>> sin(A)

ans =

   0.8415   0.9093   0.1411
  -0.7568  -0.9589  -0.2794
   0.6570   0.9894   0.4121
```

```
>> B=[1+i 2+i;3+i,4+i]

B =

   1.0000 + 1.0000i 2.0000 + 1.0000i
   3.0000 + 1.0000i 4.0000 + 1.0000i

>> sin(B)

ans =

   1.2985 + 0.6350i   1.4031 - 0.4891i
   0.2178 - 1.1634i  -1.1678 - 0.7682i

>> exp(A)

ans =

  1. 0e + 003 *

    0.0027 0.0074 0.0201
    0.0546 0.1484 0.4034
    1.0966 2.9810 8.1031

>> exp(B)

ans =

    1.4687 + 2.2874i    3.9923 + 6.2177i
   10.8523 +16.9014i   29.4995 +45.9428i

>> log(B)

ans =

   0.3466 + 0.7854i   0.8047 + 0.4636i
   1.1513 + 0.3218i   1.4166 + 0.2450i

>> sqrt(B)

ans =

   1.0987 + 0.4551i   1.4553 + 0.3436i
   1.7553 + 0.2848i   2.0153 + 0.2481i
```

The exponential functions, square root and logarithm used above apply to the array elementwise and have nothing to do with the matrix exponential and logarithmic functions that are used below.

>> expm(B)

ans =

  1.0e+002 *

  -0.3071 + 0.4625i   -0.3583 + 0.6939i
  -0.3629 + 1.0431i   -0.3207 + 1.5102i

>> logm(A)

ans =

  -5.6588 + 2.7896i   12.5041 - 0.4325i   -5.6325 - 0.5129i
  12.8139 - 0.7970i -23.3307 + 2.1623i   13.1237 - 1.1616i
  -5.0129 - 1.2421i   13.4334 - 1.5262i   -4.4196 + 1.3313i

>> abs(B)

ans =

    1.4142   2.2361
    3.1623   4.1231

>> imag(B)

ans =

    1   1
    1   1

>> fix(sin(B))

ans =

  1.0000   1.0000
  0 - 1.0000i   -1.0000

>> ceil(log(A))

ans =

    0   1   2
    2   2   2
    2   3   3

```
>> sign(B)
```

ans =

```
  0.7071 + 0.7071i    0.8944 + 0.4472i
  0.9487 + 0.3162i    0.9701 + 0.2425i
```

```
>> rem(A,3*ones(3))
```

ans =

```
  1    2    0
  1    2    0
  1    2    0
```

```
>> funm(B,'sinh')
```

ans =

```
 -15.8616 +23.2384i -17.6536 +34.7072i
 -17.7736 +52.1208i -16.2216 +75.4791i
```

The result of the last function is equivalent to *sinh(B)*, but the algorithm used is different.

4.10 Elementary Functions that Support Complex Vector Arguments

max(V) The maximum component of V. (max is calculated for complex vectors as the complex number with the largest complex modulus (magnitude), computed with max(abs(V)). Then it computes the largest phase angle with max(angle(x)), if necessary.)

min(V) The minimum component of V. (min is calculated for complex vectors as the complex number with the smallest complex modulus (magnitude), computed with min(abs(A)). Then it computes the smallest phase angle with min(angle(x)), if necessary.)

mean(V) Average of the components of V.

median(V) Median of the components of V.

std(V) Standard deviation of the components of V.

sort(V) Sorts the components of V in ascending order. For complex entries the order is by absolute value and argument.

sum(V) Returns the sum of the components of V.

prod(V) Returns the product of the components of V, so, for example, n! = prod(1:n).

cumsum(V) Gives the cumulative sums of the components of V.

cumprod(V) Gives the cumulative products of the components of V.

diff(V) Gives the vector of first differences of V (V_t - V_{t-1}).

gradient(V) Gives the gradient of V.

del2(V) Gives the Laplacian of V (5-point discrete).

fft(V) Gives the discrete Fourier transform of V.

fft2(V) Gives the two-dimensional discrete Fourier transform of V.

ifft(V) Gives the inverse discrete Fourier transform of V.

ifft2(V) Gives the inverse two-dimensional discrete Fourier transform of V.

These functions also support a complex matrix as an argument, in which case the result is a vector of column vectors whose components are the results of applying the function to each column of the matrix.

Here are some examples:

```
>> V = 1:5, W = [1-i 2i 2 + 3i]

V =

    1    2    3    4    5

W =

  1.0000 - 1.0000i      0 + 2.0000i   2.0000 + 3.0000i

>> diff(V)

ans =

    1    1    1    1

>> diff(W)

ans =

 -1.0000 + 3.0000i   2.0000 + 1.0000i

>> cumprod(V)

ans =

    1    2    6    24    120

>> cumsum(W)

ans =

  1.0000 - 1.0000i   1.0000 + 1.0000i   3.0000 + 4.0000i

>> mean(W)

ans =

  1.0000 + 1.3333i

>> std(V)

ans =

  1.5811
```

>> sort(W)

ans =

1.0000 - 1.0000i   0 + 2.0000i   2.0000 + 3.0000i

>> sum(W)

ans =

3.0000 + 4.0000i

>> prod(V)

ans =

120

>> gradient(W)

ans =

-1.0000 + 3.0000i   0.5000 + 2.0000i   2.0000 + 1.0000i

>> del2(W)

ans =

0   1.5000 - 1.0000i   0

>> fft(W)

ans =

3.0000 + 4.0000i   -0.8660 - 1.7679i   0.8660 - 5.2321i

>> ifft(W)

ans =

1.0000 + 1.3333i   0.2887 - 1.7440i   -0.2887 - 0.5893i

>> fft2(W)

ans =

3.0000 + 4.0000i   - 0.8660 - 1.7679i   0.8660 - 5.2321i

4.11 Vector Functions of Several Variables

Functions of one or several variables are defined via the command *maple* as follows:

maple('f: = x - > f (x)') or maple f: = x - > f (x): defines the function *f(x)*

maple('f:=(x,y,z...))(- > f(x,y,z...)'): defines the function *f(x,y,z,..)*

maple('f:=(x,y,z...))(- > (f1 (x, y...), f2(x,y..),...)'): defines the vector function (*f1(x,y,..),* *f2(x,y,..),....)*

To find the value of the function *(x, y, z) - >f(x,y,z...)* at the point *(a, b, c,...)* the expression **maple ('f(a,b,c,...)')** is used.

We find the value of the vector function *f:=(x,y,..)-> (f1(x,y,..), f2(x,y,..),...)* at the point *(a, b,...)* by using the expression **maple ('f(a,b,..)')**.

The function $f(x,y) = 2x + y$ is defined in the following way:

```
>> maple ('f:=(x,y) - > 2 * x + y ');
```

$f(2,3)$ and $f(a,b)$ are calculated as follows:

```
>> maple('f(2,3)')
```

ans =

7

```
>> maple('f(a,b)')
```

ans =

*2 * a + b*

EXERCISE 4-10

Given the function h defined by: h(x,y) = (cos(x²-y²), sin(x²-y²)), calculate h(1,2), h(-Pi,Pi) and h(cos(a²), cos(1-a²)).

As *h* is a vector function of two variables, we use the command *maple*:

```
>> maple ('h:=(x,y) - > (cos(x^2-y^2), sin(x^2-y^2))');
>> maple ('A = h (1, 2), B = h(-pi,pi), C = h (cos(a^2), cos(1-a^2))')
```

ans =

A = (cos(3),-sin(3)), B = (1, 0),
C = (cos(cos(a^2) ^ 2-cos(-1+a^2) ^ 2), sin(cos(a^2) ^ 2-cos(-1+a^2) ^ 2))

4.12 Functions of One Variable

Functions of one variable are a special case of functions of several variables, but they can also be defined in MATLAB via the command *f = 'function'*.

To find the value of the function *f* at a point, you use the command **subs**, whose syntax is as follows:

subs(f, a) applies the function *f* at the point *a*

subs (f, a, b) assigns the value of the function at the point *a* to the variable *b*

Let's see how to define the function $f(x) = x \wedge 2$:

```
>> f ='x ^ 2'

f =

x ^ 2
```

Now we calculate the values $f(4)$, $f(a+1)$ and $f(3x+x^2)$:

```
>> syms a x
>>  A=subs(f,4),B=subs(f,a+1),C=subs(f,3*x+x^2)

A =

16

B =

(a+1) ^ 2

C =

(3 * x + x ^ 2) ^ 2
```

It should also be borne in mind that if we use the command *maple*, the special constants π , e, i, and ∞ are defined as *maple('Pi')*, *maple('exp(1)')*, *maple('i')* and *maple('infinity')* respectively.

EXERCISE 4-11

Define the functions f (x) = x^2, g (x) = $x^{1/2}$ and h (x) = x + sin (x). Calculate f (2), g(4) and h (a-b^2).

```
>> f ='x ^ 2'; g = 'x ^(1/2)'; h = 'x+sin (x)';
```

```
>> syms a b
>> a=subs(f,2),b=subs(g,4),c=subs(h,'a-b^2')
```

a =

4

b =

4 ^(1/2)

c =

a-b ^ 2 + sin(a-b^2)

We could also have done the following:

```
>> maple('f:=x->x^2: g:=x->sqrt(x):h:=x->x+sin(x)');
>> maple('f(2),g(4),h(a-b^2)')
```

ans =

4, 2, a-b^2 + sin(a-b^2)

CHAPTER 5

■ ■ ■

Vectors and Matrices

5.1 Vectors and Matrices

We have already seen how vectors and matrices are represented in MATLAB in the chapter dedicated to variables, however we shall recall the notation.

Consider the matrix

$$A = (A_{ij}) = \begin{pmatrix} a_{11} & a_{12} & a_{13} & \ldots & a_{1n} \\ a_{21} & a_{22} & a_{23} & \ldots & a_{2n} \\ a_{31} & a_{32} & a_{33} & \ldots & a_{3n} \\ \ldots & \ldots & \ldots & \ldots & \ldots \\ a_{m1} & a_{m2} & a_{m3} & \ldots & a_{mn} \end{pmatrix},$$

$$i = 1,2,3,\ldots,m \quad j = 1,2,3,\ldots,n.$$

You can enter this in MATLAB in the following ways:

       A=[a11,a12,...,a1n ; a21,a22,...,a2n ; ... ; am1,am2,...,amn]

       A=[a11 a12 ... a1n ; a21 a22 ... a2n ; ... ; am1 am2 ... amn]

       A=maple('array([[a11,..,a1n],[a21,..,a2n],..,[am1,..,amn]])')

       A=maple('matrix(m,n,[a11,..,a1n,a21,..,a2n,..,am1,..,amn])')

       A=maple('matrix([[a11,..,a1n],[a21,..,a2n],..,[am1,..,amn]])')

On the other hand, a vector $V = (v1, v2, \ldots, vn)$ is introduced as a special case of a matrix with a single row (i.e. a matrix of dimension $1 \times n$) in the following form:

       V = [v1, v2,..., vn]

       V = [v1 v2... vn]

       V = maple ('vector([v1, v2,..., vn])')

       V = maple ('vector(n,[v1, v2,..., vn])')

       V=maple('array([v1, v2, ..., vn])')

5.2 Operations with Numeric Matrices

MATLAB supports the most common matrix algebra operations (sum, difference, product, scalar product), provided the dimensionality conditions hold.

The common MATLAB matrix commands are summarized below.

A + B sum of matrices *A* and *B*

A - B difference of the matrices *A* and *B* (*A* minus *B*)

c * M product of the scalar *c* and the matrix *M*

A * B product of the matrices *A* and *B*

A ^ p matrix *A* raised to the power of the scalar *p*

p ^ A scalar *p* raised to the power of the matrix *A*

expm1 (A) e^A calculated via Padé approximants

expm2 (A) e^A calculated via Taylor series

expm3 (A) e^A calculated via eigenvalues and eigenvectors

logm(A) (Napierian logarithm of the matrix A)

sqrtm (A) square root of the matrix *A*

funm (A, 'function') applies the function to the matrix *A*

transpose (A) or **A'** transpose of the matrix *A*

inv (A) inverse of the square matrix *A* (A^{-1})

det (A) determinant of the square matrix *A*

rank (A) range of the matrix *A*

trace (A) sum of the elements of the diagonal of *A*

svd (A) gives the vector V of singular values of *A*. The singular values of *A* are the square roots of the eigenvalues of the symmetric matrix *A'A*.

[U, S, V] = svd (A) gives the diagonal matrix *S* of singular values of *A* (ordered from largest to smallest), and the matrices *U* and *V* such that A= *U * S * V'*.

cond (A) gives the condition number of the matrix *A* (the ratio between the largest and the smallest singular values of *A*)

rcond (A) the reciprocal condition number of the matrix *A*

norm (A) the standard or 2-norm of *A* (the largest singular value of *A*)

norm(A,1) the 1-norm of A (the maximum column magnitude, where the column magnitude of a column is the sum of the absolute values of its elements)

norm(A,inf) the infinity norm of *A* (the maximum row magnitude, where the row magnitude of a row is the sum of the absolute values of its elements)

norm(A,'fro') the Frobenius norm of *A*, defined by *sqrt (sum (diag(A'A)))*

Z = null (A) gives an orthonormal basis for the null space of A obtained from the singular value decomposition, i.e. *AZ* has negligible elements, *size(Z,2)* is the nullity of A, and *Z'Z = I.*

Q = orth (A) returns an orthonormal basis for the range of *A, Q'Q=I.* The columns of *Q* are vectors which span the range of *A.* The number of columns in *Q* is equal to the rank of *A.*

subspace (A, B) finds the angle between two subspaces specified by the columns of *A* and *B.* If *A* and *B* are column vectors of unit length, this is the same as *acos(abs(A'*B)).*

rref(A) produces the reduced row echelon form of *A* using Gauss-Jordan elimination with partial pivoting. The number of non-zero rows of *rref (A)* is the rank of *A.*

Here are some examples:

We consider the matrix $M = [1/3,1/4,1/5; 1/4,1/5,1/6; 1/5,1/6,1/7]$, and find its transpose, its inverse, its determinant, its range, its trace, its singular values, its condition number, its norm, M^3, e^M, *log (M)* and *sqrt (M)*:

```
>> M = [1/3,1/4,1/5; 1/4,1/5,1/6; 1/5,1/6,1/7]

M =

    0.3333  0.2500  0.2000
    0.2500  0.2000  0.1667
    0.2000  0.1667  0.1429

>> transpose = M'

transpose =

    0.3333  0.2500  0.2000
    0.2500  0.2000  0.1667
    0.2000  0.1667  0.1429

>> inverse = inv(M)

inverse =

  1. 0e + 003 *

    0.3000  -0.9000   0.6300
   -0.9000   2.8800  -2.1000
    0.6300  -2.1000   1.5750
```

To verify that the inverse has been calculated, we multiply it by *M* and check that the result is the identity matrix of order 3:

```
>> M * inv(M)

ans =

    1.0000  0.0000  0.0000
    0.0000  1.0000  0.0000
    0.0000  0.0000  1.0000
```

```
>> determinantM = det(M)
```

determinantM =

  2. 6455e-006

```
>> rankM=rank(M)
```

rankM =

     3

```
>> traceM=trace(M)
```

traceM =

   0.6762

```
>> vsingular = svd(M)
```

vsingular =

   0.6571
   0.0189
   0.0002

```
>> condition = cond(M)
```

condition =

  3. 0886e + 003

For the calculation of the norm, we find the standard norm, the 1-norm, the infinity norm and the Frobenius norm:

```
>> norm(M)
```

ans =

   0.6571

```
>> norm(M,1)
```

ans =

   0.7833

```
>> norm(M,inf)
```

ans =

   0.7833

```
>> norm(M,'fro')
```

ans =

   0.6573

```
>> M^3
```

ans =

   0.1403   0.1096   0.0901
   0.1096   0.0856   0.0704
   0.0901   0.0704   0.0578

```
>> logm(M)
```

ans =

   -2.4766   2.2200   0.5021
    2.2200   -5.6421   2.8954
    0.5021   2.8954   -4.7240

```
>> sqrtm(M)
```

ans =

   0.4631 0.2832 0.1966
   0.2832 0.2654 0.2221
   0.1966 0.2221 0.2342

The variants using eigenvalues, Padé approximants and Taylor series will be used to calculate e^M:

```
>> expm(M)
```

ans =

   1.4679   0.3550   0.2863
   0.3550   1.2821   0.2342
   0.2863   0.2342   1.1984

```
>> expm1(M)
```

ans =

   1.4679   0.3550   0.2863
   0.3550   1.2821   0.2342
   0.2863   0.2342   1.1984

```
>> expm2(M)
```

ans =

```
    1.4679    0.3550    0.2863
    0.3550    1.2821    0.2342
    0.2863    0.2342    1.1984
```

```
>> expm3(M)
```

As we see, the exponential matrix coincides using all methods.

EXERCISE 5-1

Given the three matrices

$$A=\begin{bmatrix}1 & 1 & 0\\0 & 1 & 1\\0 & 0 & 1\end{bmatrix}, \quad B=\begin{bmatrix}i & 1-i & 2+i\\0 & -1 & 3-i\\0 & 0 & -i\end{bmatrix}, \quad C=\begin{bmatrix}1 & 1 & 1\\0 & i\sqrt{2} & -i\sqrt{2}\\1 & -1 & -1\end{bmatrix}$$

calculate AB - BA, $A^2 + B^2 + C^2$, ABC, sqrt(A) + sqrt(B) + sqrt(C), $e^A(e^B+e^C)$ and find the rank, inverse, trace, determinant, condition number and singular values of A, B and C.

```
>> A=[1 1 0;0 1 1;0 0 1]; B=[i 1-i 2+i;0 -1 3-i;0 0 -i];
   C=[1 1 1; 0 sqrt(2)*i -sqrt(2)*i;1 -1 -1];
```

```
>> M1=A*B-B*A
```

M1 =

```
    0          -1.0000 - 1.0000i    2.0000
    0               0               1.0000 - 1.0000i
    0               0                    0
```

```
>> M2=A^2+B^2+C^2
```

M2 =

```
    2.0000              2.0000 + 3.4142i    3.0000 - 5.4142i
         0 - 1.4142i    0.0000 + 1.4142i    0.0000 - 0.5858i
         0              2.0000 - 1.4142i    2.0000 + 1.4142i
```

```
>> M3=A*B*C
```

M3 =

```
    5.0000 + 1.0000i   -3.5858 + 1.0000i   -6.4142 + 1.0000i
    3.0000 - 2.0000i   -3.0000 + 0.5858i   -3.0000 + 3.4142i
         0 - 1.0000i         0 + 1.0000i         0 + 1.0000i
```

```
>> M4=sqrtm(A)+sqrtm(B)-sqrtm(C)
```

M4 =

```
   0.6356 + 0.8361i   -0.3250 - 0.8204i   3.0734 + 1.2896i
   0.1582 - 0.1521i    0.0896 + 0.5702i   3.3029 - 1.8025i
  -0.3740 - 0.2654i    0.7472 + 0.3370i   1.2255 + 0.1048i
```

```
>> M5=expm(A)*(expm(B)+expm(C))
```

M5 =

```
  14.1906 - 0.0822i   5.4400 + 4.2724i   17.9169 - 9.5842i
   4.5854 - 1.4972i   0.6830 + 2.1575i    8.5597 - 7.6573i
   3.5528 + 0.3560i   0.1008 - 0.7488i    3.2433 - 1.8406i
```

```
>> ranks=[rank(A) rank(B) rank(C)]
```

ranks =

```
     3     3     3
```

```
>> vsingular=[svd(A),svd(B),svd(C)]
```

vsingular =

```
    1.8019    4.2130    2.0000
    1.2470    1.4917    2.0000
    0.4450    0.1591    1.4142
```

```
>> traces=[trace(A) trace(B) trace(C)]
```

traces =

```
    3.0000             -1.0000              0 + 1.4142i
```

```
>> inv(A)
```

ans =

```
     1    -1     1
     0     1    -1
     0     0     1
```

```
>> inv(B)
```

ans =

```
    0 - 1.0000i  -1.0000 - 1.0000i  -4.0000 + 3.0000i
    0              -1.0000           1.0000 + 3.0000i
    0               0                0 + 1.0000i
```

```
>> inv(C)
```

ans =

```
   0.5000      0                0.5000
   0.2500      0 - 0.3536i     -0.2500
   0.2500      0 + 0.3536i     -0.2500
```

```
>> determinants = [det(A) det (B) det (C)]
```

determinants =

```
   1.0000 - 1.0000 0 - 5. 6569i
```

```
>> conditions = [cond(A) cond (B) cond(C)]
```

conditions =

```
   4.0489 26.4765 1.4142
```

EXERCISE 5-2

Consider the following matrix:

$$M = \begin{bmatrix} 1/3 & 1/4 & 1/5 \\ 1/4 & 1/5 & 1/6 \\ 1/5 & 1/6 & 1/7 \end{bmatrix}$$

Find its transpose, its inverse, its determinant, its rank, its trace, its singular values, its condition number, its norm and M^3, regarded as a symbolic matrix.

```
>> M = sym('[1/3,1/4,1/5; 1/4,1/5,1/6; 1/5,1/6,1/7]')
```

M =

```
[1/3,1/4,1/5]
[1/4,1/5,1/6]
[1/5,1/6,1/7]
```

```
>> Mtranspose = transpose(M)
```

Mtranspose =

```
[1/3, 1/4, 1/5]
[1/4, 1/5, 1/6]
[1/5, 1/6, 1/7]
```

```
>> Minverse = inv(M)
```

Minverse =

```
[ 300,  -900,   630]
[-900,  2880, -2100]
[ 630, -2100,  1575]
```

```
>> Mdeterminant=det(M)
```

Mdeterminant =

1/378000

```
>> Mrank=rank(M)
```

Mrank =

3

```
>> Mtrace=trace(M)
```

Mtrace =

71/105

```
>> numeric(svd(M))
```

ans =

```
  0.6571
  0.0002 - 0.0000i
  0.0189 + 0.0000i
```

```
>> norm = maple('norm([[1/3,1/4,1/5],[1/4,1/5,1/6],[1/5,1/6,1/7]])')
```

norm =

47/60

```
>> sympow(M,3)
```

ans =

```
[10603/75600,      1227/11200,   26477/294000]
[1227/11200,     10783/126000,  74461/1058400]
[26477/294000,   74461/1058400,   8927/154350]
```

Now we find the norms and condition number of *M* as a numeric matrix:

```
>> [norm(numeric(M)),norm(numeric(M),1),cond(numeric(M),inf),
cond(numeric(M),'fro'),normest(numeric(M))]
```

ans =

  1.0e+003 *

0.0008   4.6060   3.0900   0.0007   0.8

```
>> [cond(numeric(M),1),cond(numeric(M),2),cond(numeric(M),'fro'),
condest(numeric(M))]
```

ans =

  1.0e+003 *

    4.6060   3.0886   3.0900   4.6060

EXERCISE 5-3

Define a square matrix A of dimension 5 whose elements are given by A(i,j) = $i^3 - j^2$. Extract the submatrix of A formed by rows 2 to 4 and columns 3 to 4. Delete rows 2 to 4 of the matrix A, as well as column 5. Exchange the first and last rows of the matrix A. Exchange the first and last columns of the matrix A. Insert a column of 1s to the right of the matrix A. Insert a column of 1s to the left of the matrix A. Insert two rows of 1s at the top of the matrix A. Perform the same operation at the bottom.

First, we generate the matrix *A* as follows:

```
>> A=sym(maple('matrix(5,5,(i,j)-> i^3-j^2)'))
```

A =

```
[   0,   -3,   -8,  -15,  -24]
[   7,    4,   -1,   -8,  -17]
[  26,   23,   18,   11,    2]
[  63,   60,   55,   48,   39]
[ 124,  121,  116,  109,  100]
```

```
>> maple('A:=matrix(5,5,(i,j)-> i^3-j^2)');
>> sym(maple('submatrix(A,2..4,3..4)'))
```

ans =

```
[ -1,  -8]
[ 18,  11]
[ 55,  48]
```

```
>> sym(maple('delrows(A,2..4)'))
```

ans =

```
[   0,  -3,  -8, -15, -24]
[ 124, 121, 116, 109, 100]
```

```
>> sym(maple('delcols(A,5..5)'))
```

ans =

```
[   0,  -3,  -8, -15]
[   7,   4,  -1,  -8]
[  26,  23,  18,  11]
[  63,  60,  55,  48]
[ 124, 121, 116, 109]
```

```
>> pretty(sym(maple('swapcol(A,1,5),swaprow(A,1,5)')))
```

```
[-24     -3      -8     -15      0]  [124    121    116    109    100]
[                                 ]  [                                ]
[-17      4      -1      -8      7]  [  7      4     -1     -8    -17]
[                                 ]  [                                ]
[  2     23      18      11     26],  [ 26     23     18     11      2]
[                                 ]  [                                ]
[ 39     60      55      48     63]  [ 63     60     55     48     39]
[                                 ]  [                                ]
[100    121     116     109    124]  [  0     -3     -8    -15    -24]
```

```
>> maple('B:=array([1,1,1,1,1])');
>> pretty(sym(maple('augment(A,B),augment(B,A)')));
```

```
[  0     -3     -8    -15    -24     1]  [1      0     -3     -8    -15    -24]
[                                      ]  [                                   ]
[  7      4     -1     -8    -17     1]  [1      7      4     -1     -8    -17]
[                                      ]  [                                   ]
[ 26     23     18     11      2     1],  [1     26     23     18     11      2]
[                                      ]  [                                   ]
[ 63     60     55     48     39     1]  [1     63     60     55     48     39]
[                                      ]  [                                   ]
[124    121    116    109    100     1]  [1    124    121    116    109    100]
```

```
>> maple('C:=array([[1,1,1,1,1],[1,1,1,1,1]])');
>> pretty(sym(maple('stack(C,A),stack(A,C)')));
```

```
[  1     1     1     1     1]  [  0    -3    -8   -15   -24]
[                          ]  [                          ]
[  1     1     1     1     1]  [  7     4    -1    -8   -17]
[                          ]  [                          ]
[  0    -3    -8   -15   -24]  [ 26    23    18    11     2]
[                          ]  [                          ]
[  7     4    -1    -8   -17], [ 63    60    55    48    39]
[                          ]  [                          ]
[ 26    23    18    11     2]  [124   121   116   109   100]
[                          ]  [                          ]
[ 63    60    55    48    39]  [  1     1     1     1     1]
[                          ]  [                          ]
[124   121   116   109   100]  [  1     1     1     1     1]
```

5.3 Eigenvalues and Eigenvectors

MATLAB enables commands that allow you to work with eigenvalues and eigenvectors of a square matrix. For *numeric matrices*, we have the following:

eig(A) Finds the eigenvalues of the square matrix *A*.

[V, D] = eig(A) Returns the diagonal matrix *D* of eigenvalues of *A*, and a matrix *V* whose columns are the corresponding eigenvectors, so that *A * V = V * D*.

eig(A,B) Returns a vector with the generalized eigenvalues of the square matrices *A* and *B*. The generalized eigenvalues of *A* and *B* are the roots of the polynomial in *l: det (l * B - A)*.

[V, D] = eig(A, B) returns the diagonal matrix *D* of generalized eigenvalues of *A* and *B* and a matrix *V* whose columns are the corresponding eigenvectors, so that *A * V = B * V * D*.

[AA, BB, Q, Z, V] = qz(A, B)

Calculates the upper triangular matrices *AA* and *BB* and matrices *Q* and *Z* such that *Q * A * Z = Q* and *AA * B * Z = BB*, and gives the matrix *V* of generalized eigenvectors of *A* and *B*, so that *A * V * diag (BB) = B * V * diag (AA)*.

[T, B] = balance(A) Returns a similarity transformation *T* such that *B = T\A*T*, and *B* has, as closely as possible, approximately equal row and column norms. The matrix *B* is called the balanced matrix of *A*.

balance(A) Computes the balanced matrix *B* of *A*. This is used to approximate the eigenvalues of *A* when they are difficult to estimate. We have *eig (A) = eig (balance (A))*.

[V, D] = cdf2rdf (V, D) If the eigensystem *[V,D]= eig(X)* has complex eigenvalues appearing in complex-conjugate pairs, *cdf2rdf* transforms the system so *D* is in real diagonal form, with 2×2 real blocks along the diagonal replacing the original complex pairs. The eigenvectors are transformed so that *X = V*D/V* continues to hold.

[U, T] = schur (A) Returns a matrix T and a unitary matrix U such that $A = U * T * U'$ and $U'* U = eye\ (U)$. If A is complex, T is an upper triangular matrix with the eigenvalues of A on its diagonal. If A is real, T has the eigenvalues of A on its diagonal, and the corresponding complex eigenvalues correspond to the 2×2 diagonal blocks of T.

schur(A) Returns only the matrix T of the above decomposition.

[U, T] = rsf2csf (U, T) Converts the real Schur form to the complex form.

[H, P] = hess(A) Returns the unitary matrix P and Hessenberg matrix H such that $A = P * H * P'$ and $P'* P = eye\ (size\ (P))$.

hess(A) Returns the Hessenberg matrix of A.

poly(A) Returns the characteristic polynomial of the matrix A.

poly(V) Returns a vector whose components are the coefficients of the polynomial whose roots are the elements of the vector V.

vander(C) Returns the Vandermonde matrix A such that its j-th column is $A(:,j) = C \wedge (n-j)$.

EXERCISE 5-4

Consider the matrix:

$$M = \begin{bmatrix} 1 & -1 & 3 \\ -1 & i & -1-2i \\ i & 1 & i-2 \end{bmatrix}$$

Compute its eigenvalues and eigenvectors, the balanced matrix with its eigenvalues, and its characteristic polynomial.

```
>> M=[1,-1,3;-1,i,-1-2i;i,1,i-2];
>> [V,D] = eig(M)

V =

   0.9129              0.1826 + 0.5477i  -0.1826 + 0.3651i
  -0.2739 - 0.0913i    0.5477 - 0.1826i   0.3651 - 0.7303i
  -0.0913 + 0.2739i   -0.1826 - 0.5477i   0.1826 - 0.3651i

D =

   1.0000 + 1.0000i  0                  0
   0                 -2.0000 + 1.0000i  0
   0                  0                  0
```

We see that the eigenvalues of *M* are *1 + i*, *-2 + i* and *0*, and the eigenvectors are the columns of the matrix *V*. We now calculate the balanced matrix of *M* and verify that its eigenvalues coincide with those of *M*:

```
>> balance(M)
```

ans =

```
    1.0000           -1.0000            1.5000
   -1.0000            0 + 1.0000i      -0.5000 - 1.0000i
    0 + 2.0000i       2.0000           -2.0000 + 1.0000i
```

```
>> eig(balance(M))
```

ans =

```
 1.0000 + 1.0000i
-2.0000 + 1.0000i
 0
```

We now calculate the characteristic of polynomial of *M*:

```
>> p=poly(M)
```

p =

```
    1.0000    1.0000 - 2.0000i   -3.0000 - 1.0000i     0
```

```
>> vpa(poly2sym(p))
```

ans =

x^3+x^2-2.*i*x^2-3.*x-1.*i*x

Thus, the characteristic polynomial is $x^3 + x^2 - 2ix^2 - 3x - ix$.

EXERCISE 5-5

Consider the square matrix A of order 5 whose (i,j)th element is given by 1/(i+j-1/2). Compute the eigenvalues, eigenvectors, characteristic polynomial, minimum polynomial, characteristic matrix and singular values of A. Also find the vector of condition numbers of the eigenvalues and analyze whether A is positive definite, negative definite or positive or negative semidefinite.

MATLAB enables you to define this type of symbolic matrix in the general form:

```
>> A=sym(maple('matrix(5,5,(i,j)-> 1/(i+j-1/2))'))
```

A =

```
[ 2/3,  2/5,  2/7,  2/9, 2/11]
[ 2/5,  2/7,  2/9, 2/11, 2/13]
[ 2/7,  2/9, 2/11, 2/13, 2/15]
[ 2/9, 2/11, 2/13, 2/15, 2/17]
[2/11, 2/13, 2/15, 2/17, 2/19]
```

```
>> [V, E] = eig (A)
```

V =

```
[ -.1612e-1, -.6740e-2,   .3578,   2.482,  -288.7]
[    .2084,    .1400,  -2.513,  -15.01,   2298.]
[   -.7456,   -.6391,   3.482,   20.13,  -3755.]
[        1,        1,       1,       1,      1]
[   -.4499,   -.5011,  -2.476,  -8.914,   1903.]
```

E =

```
[ 2/55*.4005e-4,           0,            0,            0,          0]
[           0, 2/55* .3991e-2,            0,            0,          0]
[           0,           0, 2/55* .1629,            0,          0]
[           0,           0,            0, 2/55* 3.420,          0]
[           0,           0,            0,            0, 2/55* 34.16]
```

As is well known, the eigenvectors are the columns of the matrix V and the eigenvalues are the elements of the diagonal of the matrix E.

```
>> pretty(simple(poly(A)))
```

```
 5    10042  4   362807509088   3    268537284608     2
x  - ----- x  + ------------- x  - --------------- x
      7315       2228304933855       285965799844725

          22809860374528           4359738368
    + -------------------- x - ------------------------
       169975437532179654375    177624332221127738821875
```

We can approximate the above output as follows:

```
>> pretty(simple(vpa(poly(A))))
```

$$
x^5 -1.373\ x^4 +.1628\ x^3 -.0009391\ x^2 +.1342*10^{-6}\ x -.1934*10^{-12}
$$

The singular values are calculated in the following way:

```
>> pretty(simple(svd(A)))
```

$$
\begin{bmatrix}
.1456*10^{-5} \\
.0001451 \\
.005923 \\
.1244 \\
1.242
\end{bmatrix}
$$

The minimal polynomial and the characteristic matrix are calculated in the following way:

```
>> pretty(simple(sym(maple('minpoly(matrix(5,5,(i,j)-> 1/(i+j-1/2)),x)'))))
```

$$
-\ \frac{34359738368}{17762433222112773882 1875}\ +\ \frac{22809860374528}{169975437532179654375}\ x\ -\ \frac{268537284608}{285965799844725}\ x^2
$$

$$
+\ \frac{362807509088}{2228304933855}\ x^3\ -\ \frac{10042}{7315}\ x^4\ +\ x^5
$$

```
>> pretty(simple(sym(vpa(maple('minpoly(matrix(5,5,(i,j)->1/(i+j-1/2)),x)')))))
```

$$
-.1934\ 10^{-12}\ +\ .1342\ 10^{-6}\ x\ -\ .0009391\ x^2\ +\ .1628\ x^3\ -\ 1.373\ x^4\ +\ x^5
$$

```
>> pretty(simple(sym(maple('charmat(matrix(5,5,(i,j)-> 1/(i+j-1/2)),x)'))))
```

```
      [                                                    -2    ]
      [x - 2/3      -2/5          -2/7         -2/9         --    ]
      [                                                     11    ]
      [                                                           ]
      [                                         -2          -2    ]
      [ -2/5       x - 2/7        -2/9          --          --    ]
      [                                         11          13    ]
      [                                                           ]
      [                                         -2          -2    ]
      [ -2/7        -2/9        x - 2/11         --          --    ]
      [                                         13          15    ]
      [                                                           ]
      [             -2           -2                         -2    ]
      [ -2/9        --           --          x - 2/15        --    ]
      [             11           13                         17    ]
      [                                                           ]
      [ -2          -2           -2           -2                  ]
      [ --          --           --           --         x - 2/19]
      [ 11          13           15           17                  ]
```

The vector of condition numbers of the eigenvalues is calculated as follows:

```
>> condeig(numeric(A))
```

ans =

```
    1.0000
    1.0000
    1.0000
    1.0000
    1.0000
```

In a more complete way, we can calculate the matrix *V* whose columns are the eigenvectors of *A*, the diagonal matrix *D* whose diagonal elements are the eigenvalues of *A*, and the vector *S* of condition numbers of the eigenvalues of *A*, by using the command:

```
>> [V,D,s] = condeig(numeric(A))
```

V =

```
    0.0102     0.0697     0.2756    -0.6523     0.7026
   -0.1430    -0.4815    -0.7052     0.1593     0.4744
    0.5396     0.6251    -0.2064     0.3790     0.3629
   -0.7526     0.2922     0.2523     0.4442     0.2954
    0.3490    -0.5359     0.5661     0.4563     0.2496
```

D =

0.0000	0	0	0	0
0	0.0001	0	0	0
0	0	0.0059	0	0
0	0	0	0.1244	0
0	0	0	0	1.2423

S =

    1.0000
    1.0000
    1.0000
    1.0000
    1.0000

Using the command *definite*, we find that the matrix A is positive definite:

```
>> maple('definite(matrix(5,5,(i,j)-> 1/(i+j-1/2)),positive_def)')
```

ans =

true

5.4 Matrix Decomposition

MATLAB enables commands that allow you to decompose a matrix as a product of orthogonal matrices and diagonal matrices.

We have already seen how the command *[U, S, V] = svd (A)* returns a diagonal matrix S of singular values of A (in decreasing order of magnitude), and orthogonal matrices U and V such that $= U * S * V'$.

We have also seen that you can obtain the Jordan decomposition of a square matrix A via the command *[V, J] = jordan (A)*, which returns the Jordan canonical matrix J of A with the eigenvalues of A on its diagonal and the similarity transform V whose columns are the eigenvectors of A, so that $V^{-1} * A * V = J$.

On the other hand, we have also seen that you can obtain a decomposition of a square matrix A via the command schur, *[U, T] = schur(A)*, which returns an array T and an orthogonal matrix U such that $A = U * T * U'$ and $U'* U = eye$ (U). If A is complex, T is an upper triangular matrix with the eigenvalues of A on its diagonal. For real A, the matrix T has real eigenvalues of A on its diagonal and complex eigenvalues in 2×2 diagonal blocks in T.

We can also find the Hessenberg decomposition of the matrix A via the command *[H, P] = hess (A)*, which gives the orthogonal matrix P and Hessenberg matrix H such that $A = P * H * P'$ and $P'* P = eye (size (P))$.

In addition, MATLAB has a number of other commands for the numeric and symbolic decomposition of a matrix. They include the following:

> **[L, U] = lu (A) Decomposes the matrix A as the product $A = L * U$ (an LU decomposition), where U is an upper triangular matrix and L is a permutation of a lower triangular matrix.**
>
> **[L, U, P] = lu(A) Returns the lower triangular matrix L, the upper triangular matrix U and the permutation matrix P such that $P *A = L * U$.**
>
> **R = chol(A) Returns the upper triangular matrix R such that $R'* R = A$ (a Cholesky decomposition), where A is positive. If A is not positive, an error is returned.**

[Q, R] =qr (A) Returns the upper triangular matrix R **of the same dimension as** A**, and the orthogonal matrix** Q **such that** $A = Q * R$ **(a QR decomposition). This decomposition can be applied to non-square matrices.**

[Q, R, E] = qr(A) Returns the upper triangular matrix R **of the same dimension as** A**, the matrix permutation** E **and the orthogonal matrix** Q **such that** $A * E = Q * R$**.**

X = pinv(A) Returns the matrix X **(the pseudo-inverse of** A**), of the same dimension as** A' **such that** $A * X * A = A$ **and** $X * A * X = X$**, where** $A * X$ **and** $X * A$ **are hermitian.**

In addition, the commands listed below allow the decomposition of both numeric and symbolic matrices. All of these commands must be preceded by the command *maple*.

LUdecomp(A,P='p',L='l',U='u',U1='u1',R='r') decomposes the matrix A **into the product** $A = evalm(P\&*L\&*U)$ **(LU decomposition), where U is an upper triangular matrix, L is a lower triangular matrix and P is a pivot factor. In addition,** $U = evalm(U1\&*R)$ **with** $U1$ **upper triangular and R a row reduced factor, so that** $A = evalm(P\&*L\&*U1*R)$**.**

cholesky(A) returns the lower triangular matrix R **such that** $A = evalm(R\&*R')$ **(Cholesky decomposition of** A**).** A **must be positive definite.**

QRdecomp(A,Q='q') returns the upper triangular matrix R **of the same dimension as** A**, and the orthonormal matrix** Q **such that** $A = evalm(Q\&*R)$ **(QR decomposition of** A**).**

companion(poly,var) gives the matrix C **associated with the given monic polynomial in the specified variable. If** $poly = a0 + a1x +...+ x^n$**,** $C(i,n)=-coeff(poli,var,i-1)$**,** $i=1...n$**,** $C(i,i-1)=1$**,** $i=2...n$**, and** $C(i, j) = 0$ **for the rest of the elements in the matrix.**

frobenius(A) or ratform(A) returns the canonical Frobenius form F **of the matrix** A**.** F **is a block diagonal matrix** $(F = diag(C1,C2,...,Cn))$**, where the** Ci **are the companion matrices associated to polynomials** $p1, p2,..., pk$ **such that** pi **divides** p_{i-1}**,** $i = 2... K$**.**

frobenius(A,'P') assigns to P **the transformation matrix corresponding to the Frobenius form of the matrix** A**, so that evalm** $(P^{-1} \& * A \& * P) = F$**.**

smith(A,var) computes the Smith normal form of a matrix with univariate polynomial entries in var over the integers.

smith(A,var,U,V) in addition returns the matrices U **and** V **such that** $S = evalm(U\&*A\&*V)$**.**

ismith(A,var) gives the diagonal matrix corresponding to the Smith normal form S **of the square matrix** A **of polynomials in the variable** *var*.

ismith(A,var,U,V) in addition returns the matrices U **and** V **such that** $S =evalm(U\&*A\&*V)$**.**

hermite(A,var) computes the Hermite normal form (reduced row echelon form) of a matrix A **of univariate polynomials in var.**

hermite(A,var,U) in addition returns the matrix U **such that** $H = evalm(U\&*A)$**.**

ihermite(A,var) computes the Hermite normal form (reduced row echelon form) of a matrix A **of univariate polynomials in var over the integers.**

ihermite(A,var,U) in addition returns the matrix U **such that** $H = evalm(U\&*A)$**.**

gaussjord (A) returns an upper triangular matrix corresponding to the row reduced (Gauss-Jordan) echelon form of the matrix A**. This is used to facilitate the solution of systems of linear equations whose coefficient matrix is the matrix** A**.**

gaussjord (A, j) returns the j-th column of the above matrix.

gaussjord(A,r,d) gives the row reduced echelon form of the matrix A, assigns to the variable r the rank of A and to the variable d the determinant of *submatrix(A,1..r,1..r)*. This subarray is used for solving systems of linear equations whose coefficient matrix is A.

gausselim(A) performs Gaussian elimination with row pivoting on A, returning the reduced matrix. This is used to facilitate the solution of systems of linear equations whose coefficient matrix is the matrix A.

gausselim(A, j) returns the j-th column of the row reduced matrix of A.

gausselim(A,r,d) returns the row reduced matrix of A, assigns the variable r to the rank of A, and the variable d to the determinant of *submatrix(A, 1..r,1..r)*. This subarray is used for solving systems of linear equations whose coefficient matrix is A.

backsub(A) returns the vector x such that $A * x = V$, where V is the last column of the matrix A. If A is the result of applying forward Gaussian elimination to the augmented matrix of a system of linear equations (via gausselim or gaussjord, for example), backsub completes the solution by back substitution.

backsub(A, V) returns the vector x such that $A * x = V$.

backsub(A,V,t) returns the vector x such that $A * x = V$, where the parameter t is used for a possible family of parametric solutions of the system.

forwardsub(A,V) returns the vector x such that $A * x = V$. If A is the result of applying Gaussian elimination to the matrix of a system of linear equations (via LUdecomp, for example), forwardsub completes the solution by forward substitution.

forwardsub(A,V,t) returns the matrix X such that $A * X = V$, where the parameter t is used for a possible family of parametric solutions of the system.

forwardsub (A) returns the vector x such that $A * x = V$, where V is the last column of A.

forwardsub(A,B) returns the matrix X such that $A * X = B$.

geneqns(A,[x1,...,xn]) generates a system of linear equations in the given variables, equating each to zero, where the coefficients are determined by the matrix A.

geneqns(A,[x1,...,xn],V) generates a system of linear equations in the given variables, where the right-hand sides of the equations are determined by the vector V and the coefficients are determined by the matrix A.

genmatrix([equation1,...,equationm],[x1,...,xn]) generates the matrix corresponding to the given linear equations with respect to the specified variables.

genmatrix([equation1,...,equationm],[x1,...,xn],flag) generates the matrix corresponding to the given linear equations with respect to the specified variables, including as the last column of the matrix the right-hand sides of the equations.

genmatrix([equation1,...,equationm],[x1,..,xn],name) generates the matrix corresponding to the given linear equations with respect to the specified variables, and assigns a name to the vector that contains the right-hand sides of the equations.

EXERCISE 5-6

Consider the 3×3 matrix A whose rows are given by the vectors (1,5,-2), (-7,3,1) and (2,2,-2). Find the Schur, LU, QR, Cholesky, Hessenberg and singular value decompositions of A. Verify the results. Also find the pseudoinverse of A.

First, we find the Schur decomposition, checking that the result is correct:

```
>> A = [1,5,-2; -7,3,1; 2,2,-2];
>> [U, T] = schur (A)

U =

    -0.0530   -0.8892   -0.4544
    -0.9910   -0.0093    0.1337
     0.1231   -0.4573    0.8807


T =

     2.4475   -5.7952   -4.6361
     5.7628    0.3689    2.4332
          0         0   -0.8163
```

Now, we check that $U * T * U' = A$ and that $U * U' = eye (3)$:

```
>> [U * T * U', U * U']

ans =
     1.0000    5.0000   -2.0000      1.0000    0.0000    0.0000
    -7.0000    3.0000    1.0000      0.0000    1.0000    0.0000
     2.0000    2.0000   -2.0000      0.0000    0.0000    1.0000
```

Now, we find the LU, QR, Cholesky, Hessenberg and singular value decompositions, checking the results in each case:

```
>> [L, U, P] = lu (A)

L =

     1.0000         0         0
    -0.1429    1.0000         0          Lower triangular matrix
    -0.2857    0.5263    1.0000


U =

    -7.0000    3.0000    1.0000
          0    5.4286   -1.8571          Upper triangular matrix
          0         0   -0.7368
```

P =

```
    0    1    0
    1    0    0
    0    0    1
```

>> [P * A, L * U]

ans =

```
   -7    3    1    -7    3    1
    1    5   -2     1    5   -2        we have that P*A=L*U
    2    2   -2     2    2   -2
```

>> [Q, R, E] = qr (A)

Q =

```
  -0.1361 - 0.8785 - 0.4579
   0.9526 - 0.2430   0.1831
  -0.2722 - 0.4112   0.8700
```

R =

```
  -7.3485 1.6330 1.7691
   0      -5.9442 2.3366   Upper triangular matrix
   0       0      -0.6410
```

E =
```
    1 0 0
    0 1 0
    0 0 1
```

>> [A * E, Q * R]

ans =

```
   1.0000 5.0000 -2.0000   1.0000 5.0000 -2.0000
  -7.0000 3.0000  1.0000  -7.0000 3.0000  1.0000
   2.0000 2.0000 -2.0000   2.0000 2.0000 -2.0000
```

Then, A * E = Q * R.

>> R = chol(A)

??? Error using ==> chol
Matrix must be positive definite.

We obtain an error message because the matrix is not positive definite.

`>> [P,H] = hess(A)`

P =

```
    1.0000  0        0
    0      -0.9615  0.2747
    0       0.2747  0.9615
```

H =

```
    1.0000  -5.3571  -0.5494
    7.2801   1.8302  -2.0943
    0       -3.0943  -0.8302
```

`>> [P*H*P', P'*P]`

ans =

```
    1.0000  5.0000  -2.0000  1.0000  0       0
   -7.0000  3.0000   1.0000  0       1.0000  0
    2.0000  2.0000  -2.0000  0       0       1.0000
```

Then, PHP'= A and P'P = I.

`>> [U, S, V] = svd (A)`

U =

```
   -0.1034  -0.8623   0.4957
   -0.9808   0.0056  -0.1949
    0.1653  -0.5064  -0.8463
```

S =

```
    7.8306  0        0
    0       6.2735   0        diagonal matrix
    0       0        0.5700
```

V =

```
    0.9058  -0.3051  0.2940
   -0.3996  -0.8460  0.3530
   -0.1411   0.4372  0.8882
```

```
>> U * S * V'
```

ans =

```
   1.0000  5.0000 -2.0000
  -7.0000  3.0000  1.0000  therefore USV'= A
   2.0000  2.0000 -2.0000
```

Now, we calculate the pseudoinverse of A:

```
>> X = pinv (A)
```

X =

```
   0.2857 -0.2143 -0.3929
   0.4286 -0.0714 -0.4643
   0.7143 -0.2857 -1.3571
```

```
>> [A * X * A, X * A * X]
```

ans =

```
   1.0000  5.0000 -2.0000 0.2857 -0.2143 -0.3929
  -7.0000  3.0000  1.0000 0.4286 -0.0714 -0.4643
   2.0000  2.0000 -2.0000 0.7143 -0.2857 -1.3571
```

Thus, we have *AXA* = *A* and *XAX* = *X*.

EXERCISE 5-7

Consider the square matrix of order 5 whose (i,j)th element is defined by $A_{ij} = 1 /(i+j-1/2)$. Calculate its Jordan form (and check the result). Find its LU, QR, Frobenius, Smith and Hermite decompositions, calculating the matrices involved and verifying that they do indeed yield the original matrix.

```
>> A=sym(maple('matrix(5,5,(i,j)-> i+j-1/2)'))
```

A =

```
[3/2,  5/2,  7/2,  9/2,  11/2]
[5/2,  7/2,  9/2,  11/2, 13/2]
[7/2,  9/2,  11/2, 13/2, 15/2]
[9/2,  11/2, 13/2, 15/2, 17/2]
[11/2, 13/2, 15/2, 17/2, 19/2]
```

```
>> [V, J] = Jordan (A);
>> pretty(sym(V))

        [                    1/2                  1/2      22   19]
        [8/9, 9/170 17 + 3/10, 9/170 3/17 +  3/10, --,  --]
        [                                          45   45]
        [                                                   ]
        [-71            1/2           1/2    -7          ]
        [---, - 2/85 17 + 1/5, 2/85 17 + 1/5,---, - 2/9]
        [90                                 18          ]
        [                                                   ]
        [-67           1/2            1/2    -49  -14]
        [---, 1/170 17 + 1/10, -1/170 17 + 1/10, ----, ---]
        [90                                   90   45 ]
        [                                                   ]
        [               1/2          1/2                   ]
        [3/10, 3/85 17, - 3/85 17,  3/10, - 2/5]
        [                                             ]
        [31     11   1/2             11  ½         -13  -23]
        [-- ,  --- 17   - 1/10 ,   - --- 17   - 1/10 ,  -- , --]
        [90    170                  170            90   45]
```

```
>> pretty(sym(J))

        [0              0            0          0   0]
        [                                            ]
        [              1/2                           ]
        [0 55/4 + 15/4 17             0          0   0]
        [                                            ]
        [                            1/2             ]
        [0            0       55/4-15/4 17       0   0]
        [                                            ]
        [0            0              0          0   0]
        [                                            ]
        [0            0              0          0   0]
```

```
>> pretty(simple(sym(symmul(symmul(V,J),inv(V)))))

            [3/2   5/2   7/2   9/2   11/2]
            [5/2   7/2   9/2   11/2  13/2]
            [7/2   9/2   11/2  13/2  15/2]
            [9/2   11/2  13/2  15/2  17/2]
            [13/2  11/2  15/2  17/2  19/2]
```

We have calculated the transformation matrix *V* and the diagonal matrix (the Jordan form) *J* of *A*. We have also proven that $V * J * V^{-1} = A$. We now calculate the LU decomposition matrix of *A* and the matrices involved, checking the result. Since symbolic matrices are involved, we will use the *maple* command.

```
>> maple('A:=matrix(5,5,(i,j)-> i+j-1/2)');
>> pretty (sym (maple ('LUdecomp(A,P=p,L=l,U=u,U1=u1,R=r)')))
```

$$
\begin{bmatrix}
3/2 & 5/2 & 7/2 & 9/2 & 11/2 \\
0 & -2/3 & -4/3 & -2 & -8/3 \\
0 & 0 & 0 & 0 & 0 \\
0 & 0 & 0 & 0 & 0 \\
0 & 0 & 0 & 0 & 0
\end{bmatrix}
$$

```
>> pretty(sym(maple('print(p,l)')))
```

$$
\begin{bmatrix}
1 & 0 & 0 & 0 & 0 \\
0 & 1 & 0 & 0 & 0 \\
0 & 0 & 1 & 0 & 0 \\
0 & 0 & 0 & 1 & 0 \\
0 & 0 & 0 & 0 & 1
\end{bmatrix},
\begin{bmatrix}
1 & 0 & 0 & 0 & 0 \\
5/3 & 1 & 0 & 0 & 0 \\
7/3 & 2 & 1 & 0 & 0 \\
3 & 3 & 0 & 1 & 0 \\
11/3 & 4 & 0 & 0 & 1
\end{bmatrix}
$$

```
>> pretty(sym(maple('print(u1,r)')))
```

$$
\begin{bmatrix}
3/2 & 5/2 & 0 & 0 & 0 \\
0 & -2/3 & 0 & 0 & 0 \\
0 & 0 & 1 & 0 & 0 \\
0 & 0 & 0 & 1 & 0 \\
0 & 0 & 0 & 0 & 1
\end{bmatrix},
\begin{bmatrix}
1 & 0 & -1 & -2 & -3 \\
0 & 1 & 2 & 3 & 4 \\
0 & 0 & 0 & 0 & 0 \\
0 & 0 & 0 & 0 & 0 \\
0 & 0 & 0 & 0 & 0
\end{bmatrix}
$$

```
>> pretty (sym (maple ('evalm(p&*l&*u1&*r), evalm(p&*l&*u)')))
```

$$
\begin{bmatrix}
3/2 & 5/2 & 7/2 & 9/2 & 11/2 \\
5/2 & 7/2 & 9/2 & 11/2 & 13/2 \\
7/2 & 9/2 & 11/2 & 13/2 & 15/2 \\
9/2 & 11/2 & 13/2 & 17/2 & 15/2 \\
13/2 & 11/2 & 15/2 & 17/2 & 19/2
\end{bmatrix},
\begin{bmatrix}
3/2 & 5/2 & 7/2 & 9/2 & 11/2 \\
5/2 & 7/2 & 9/2 & 11/2 & 13/2 \\
7/2 & 9/2 & 11/2 & 13/2 & 15/2 \\
9/2 & 11/2 & 13/2 & 17/2 & 15/2 \\
13/2 & 11/2 & 15/2 & 17/2 & 19/2
\end{bmatrix}
$$

We see that $p * l * u1 * r = A$ and that $p * l * u = A$. We will now calculate the QR decomposition of A and the matrices involved, checking the result.

>> **pretty(sym(maple('print(R)')))**

```
[          1/2 71      1/2          85      1/2          33      1/2 113      1/2]
[1/2 285,  --- 285,         --- 285,         --- 285,      --- 285     ]
[           114                  114                38              114         ]
[                                                                              ]
[                    1/2                1/2                1/2            1/2]
[0,        2/57 570,       4/57 570,        2/19 570,      8/57 570    ]
[                                                                              ]
[0 ,           0 ,             0 ,              0 ,               0]
[                                                                              ]
[0 ,           0 ,             0 ,              0 ,               0]
[                                                                              ]
[0 ,           0 ,             0 ,              0 ,               0]
```

>> **pretty(sym(maple('print(q)')))**

```
[          1/2          1/2          1/2                                   ]
[1/95 285,    3/95 570,    1/5/10,          0,                         0]

[          1/2 11      1/2          1/2          1/2                       ]
[1/57 285,      --- 570,  - 1/5 10,    1/10 30,                       0]
[              570                                                         ]

[          1/2          1/2          1/2          1/2                 1/2 ]
[7/285 285, 2/285 570,      - 1/10, - 2/15 30,              1/6 6     ]

[          1/2          1/2                       1/2                 1/2 ]
[3/95 285, - 1/190 570,        0, - 1/30 30,          - 1/3 6        ]

[ 11       1/2          1/2          1/2          1/2                 1/2]
[--- 285 , - 1/57 570,    1/10/10,   1/15 30,              1/6 6     ]
[285                                                                      ]
```

>> **pretty(sym(maple('evalm(q&*R)')))**

```
[3/2   5/2   7/2   9/2   11/2]
[                            ]
[5/2   7/2   9/2  11/2  13/2]
[                            ]
[7/2   9/2  11/2  13/2  15/2]
[                            ]
[9/2  11/2  13/2  17/2  15/2]
[                            ]
[13/2 11/2  15/2  17/2  19/2]
```

We see that $q * R = A$. Next we find the Smith decomposition of the matrix A and the matrices involved, checking the result.

```
>> pretty(sym(maple('smith(A,X,U,V)')))
```

```
                [1 0 0 0 0]
                [         ]
                [0 1 0 0 0]
                [         ]
                [0 0 0 0 0]
                [         ]
                [0 0 0 0 0]
                [         ]
                [0 0 0 0 0]
```

```
>> pretty(sym(maple('print(U,V)')))
```

```
                                   [      -13        ]
   [0    0    0    0     2/11]     [1    ---   1   2  3]
   [                        ]      [      11         ]
   [0    0    0    11/2  - 9/2]    [                 ]
   [                        ]      [0     1   -2  -3 -4]
   [-1   2   -1    0      0 ],      [                 ]
   [                        ]      [0     0    1   0  0]
   [ 0   1   -2    1      0 ]      [                 ]
   [                        ]      [0     0    0   1  0]
   [ 0   0    1   -2      1 ]      [                 ]
                                   [0     0    0   0  1]
```

```
>> pretty(sym(maple('evalm(U&*A&*V)')))
```

```
                [1 0 0 0 0]
                [         ]
                [0 1 0 0 0]
                [         ]
                [0 0 0 0 0]
                [         ]
                [0 0 0 0 0]
                [         ]
                [0 0 0 0 0]
```

We see that $U * A * V = Smith\ matrix$. Next we calculate the Hermite decomposition of the matrix A and find the matrices involved.

```
>> pretty(sym(maple('H:=hermite(A,x,V); V:=evalm(V)')))
>> pretty(sym(maple('print(H,V)')))
```

```
[1    0    -1    -2    -3]    [-7/2    5/2     0    0    0]
[                        ]    [                          ]
[0    1     2     3     4]    [5/2   - 3/2     0    0    0]
[                        ]    [                          ]
[0    0     0     0     0],   [ 2      -4      2    0    0]
[                        ]    [                          ]
[0    0     0     0     0]    [ 4      -6      0    2    0]
[                        ]    [                          ]
[0    0     0     0     0]    [ 6      -8      0    0    2]
```

```
>> pretty(sym(maple('evalm(V&*A)')))
```

```
[1    0    -1    -2    -3]
[                        ]
[0    1     2     3     4]
[                        ]
[0    0     0     0     0]
[                        ]
[0    0     0     0     0]
[                        ]
[0    0     0     0     0]
```

We see that $V*A = H$. Finally, we calculate the Frobenius decomposition of A and find the matrices involved, checking the result.

```
>> pretty(sym(maple('F:=frobenius(A,P); P:=evalm(P)')))
>> pretty(sym(maple('print(F,P)')))
```

```
                                    [ 67                22      19 ]
                                    [ --    3/2   285/4  --      -- ]
                                    [ 45                45      45 ]
                                    [                             ]
[0    0    0    0    0]             [ -7                -7      ]
[                    ]             [ --    5/2   355/4  --    -2/9]
[1    0   50    0    0]             [ 18                18      ]
[                    ]             [                             ]
[0    1  55/2    0    0],          [-49                -49    -14 ]
[                    ]             [---    7/2   425/4  ---    --- ]
[0    0    0    0    0]             [90                 90     45 ]
[                    ]             [                             ]
[0    0    0    0    0]             [3/10   9/2   495/4  3/10   -2/5]
                                    [                             ]
                                    [ 13                13      23 ]
                                    [ --    11/2  565/4  --      -- ]
                                    [ 90                90     45 ]
```

```
>> pretty(sym(maple('evalm(P^(-1)&*A&*P)')))
```

$$
\begin{bmatrix}
0 & 0 & 0 & 0 & 0 \\
1 & 0 & 50 & 0 & 0 \\
55/2 & 1 & 0 & 0 & 0 \\
0 & 0 & 0 & 0 & 0 \\
0 & 0 & 0 & 0 & 0
\end{bmatrix}
$$

We have shown that $P^{-1} * A * P = F$.

EXERCISE 5-8

Consider the 3×3 matrix A whose rows are given by the vectors (1,5,-2), (-7,3,1) and (2,2,-2). If V is the vector of ones, solve the system L * x = V based on the LU decomposition of A. Solve the system G * x = V, where G is obtained from A via Gaussian elimination. Solve the system J * x = V where J is the Jordan form of A. Represent the matrix system in the form of equations, and find the Hermite and Smith decompositions of A.

First, we define the matrix *A* and the vector *V* using the *maple* command as follows:

```
>> maple ('A: = matrix(3,3,[1,5,-2,-7,3,1,2,2,-2]);) V: = array ([1,1,1])');
```

Then we find the LU decomposition of *A*, solving the system *L*x = V* using the command *backsub*.

```
>> pretty(sym(maple('L:=LUdecomp(A)')))
>> pretty(sym(maple('backsub(L,V)')))
```

$$
\begin{bmatrix}
\dfrac{253}{532} & -\dfrac{233}{532} & -\dfrac{19}{14}
\end{bmatrix}
$$

We have solved the system *L * x = V*, which can be expressed in the form of equations with the command *geneqns* as follows:

```
>> pretty(sym(maple('geneqns(L,[x1,x2,x3],V)')))
```

$$
\{x_1 + 5\,x_2 - 2\,x_3 = 1,\ 38\,x_2 - 13\,x_3 = 1,\ -\frac{14}{19}\,x_3 = 1\}
$$

Now we solve the system $G * x = V$ where G is obtained from A by Gaussian elimination.

```
>> pretty(sym(maple('G:=gausselim(A)')))
>> pretty(sym(maple('backsub(G,V)')))
```

$$
\begin{array}{lcr}
[79 & -11 &] \\
[-- & --- & -2/7] \\
[56 & 56 &]
\end{array}
$$

The system of equations is found as follows:

```
>> pretty(sym(maple('geneqns(G,[x1,x2,x3],V)')))
```

$$\{x\ 1 + 5\ x\ 2 - 2\ x\ 3 = 1,\ 8\ x\ 2 + 2\ x\ 3 = 1,\ -7/2\ x\ 3 = 1\}$$

Now, we solve the system $J * x = V$ where J is the canonical Jordan form of A. We use the command *forwardsub*.

```
>> pretty(sym(maple('J:=gaussjord(A)')))
>> pretty(sym(maple('forwardsub(J,V)')))
```

$$[1\ 1\ 1]$$

Finally, we find the Smith and Hermite matrices associated with A.

```
>> pretty(sym(maple('ihermite(A,x)')))
```

$$
\begin{array}{lll}
[1 & 1 & 6] \\
[0 & 2 & 3] \\
[0 & 0 & 14]
\end{array}
$$

```
>> pretty(sym(maple('ismith(A)')))
```

$$
\begin{array}{lll}
[1 & 0 & 0] \\
[0 & 1 & 0] \\
[0 & 0 & 28]
\end{array}
$$

5.5 Similar Matrices and Diagonalization

Two matrices A and B of dimensions $(M \times N)$ are equivalent if there exist two invertible matrices U and V such that $A = UBV$. The MATLAB command $[U, S, V] = svd\ (A)$ calculates a diagonal matrix S which is equivalent to A.

Two square matrices A and B of order n are said to be congruent if there is an invertible matrix P such that $A = P^tBP$.

The MATLAB command $[U, T] = schur\ (A)$ calculates a matrix T which is congruent with A.

Congruence implies equivalence, and two congruent matrices must always have the same rank.

Two square matrices of order n, A and B, are similar if there is an invertible matrix P such that $A = PBP^{-1}$.

Two similar matrices are equivalent.

A matrix A is diagonalizable if it is similar to a diagonal matrix D, that is, if there is an invertible matrix P such that $A = PDP^{-1}$.

The process of calculating the diagonal matrix D and the matrix P is called diagonalization of A.

Given a square matrix of real numbers A of order n, if all the eigenvalues of A are real and distinct, then A is diagonalizable. The matrix D will have the eigenvalues of A as the diagonal elements. The matrix P has as columns the eigenvectors of A corresponding to these eigenvalues.

If the matrix A has an eigenvalue with multiplicity r greater than 1, then it is diagonalizable if and only if the kernel of the matrix $A - r * I_n$ has dimension equal to the degree of multiplicity of the eigenvalue r.

The MATLAB command $[V, J] = jordan (A)$ diagonalizes the matrix A by calculating the diagonal matrix J and the matrix V such that $A=VJV_{-1}$.

EXERCISE 5-9

Diagonalize the symmetric matrix whose rows are the vectors:

(3, -1, 0), (-1, 2, -1), (0, -1, 3).

Check the result and confirm that the eigenvalues of the initial matrix are the elements of the diagonal matrix obtained.

We calculate the diagonal matrix J similar to A, which will have the eigenvalues of A on its diagonal, and the transformation matrix V. To do this, we use the command $[V, J] = jordan (A)$:

```
>> A = [3, 0, - 1, - 1, 2, - 1; 0, - 1, 3]

A =

    3  -1   0
   -1  -2  -1
    0  -3  -1

>> [V, J] = jordan (A)

V =

[1/6,  1/2, 1/3]
[1/3,   0,  -1/3]
[1/6, -1/2, 1/3]

J =

[1, 0, 0]
[0, 3, 0]
[0, 0, 4]
```

We now confirm that the diagonal matrix J has the eigenvalues of A on its diagonal:

```
>> eigensys (A)

ans =

[1]
[3]
[4]
```

The matrices *A* and *J* are similar because there a matrix *V* satisfying the equation $V^1 * A * V = J$:

```
>> symmul(symmul(inv(V),A),V)
```

ans =

```
[1, 0, 0]
[0, 3, 0]
[0, 0, 4]
```

5.6 Sparse Matrices

A matrix is called sparse if it has sufficiently many zero elements that one can take advantage of. Sparse matrix algorithms do not store most null elements in memory, so when working on matrix processing with sparse matrices one gains time and efficiency. There are specialized commands that can be used to deal with sparse matrices. Some of these commands are listed below.

S = sparse (i, j, s, m, n, nzmax), i = vector, j = vector, s = vector. Creates a sparse matrix *S* of dimension *m×n* with space for *nzmax* non-zero elements given by *s*. The vector *i* contains the i-input components of the non-null elements and the vector *j* contains the corresponding j-input components.

S=sparse(i,j,s,m,n) creates the sparse matrix *S* using *nzmax=length(s)*.

S = sparse(i,j,s) creates a sparse matrix *S* with *m = max (i)* and *n = max (j)*.

S = sparse (A) converts the matrix *A* into sparse form.

A = full (S) converts the sparse matrix *S* into full matrix form *A*.

S = spconvert (D) converts an external ASCII file read with name *D* into a sparse matrix *S*.

(i, j) = find (A) returns the row and column indices of the non-zero entries of the matrix *A*.

B = spdiags (A, d) builds a sparse matrix by extracting the diagonal elements of *A* specified by the vector *d*.

S = speye (m, n) creates the sparse *m×n* matrix with ones on the main diagonal.

S = speye (n) creates the sparse square identity matrix of order *n*.

R = sprandn (S) generates a random sparse matrix with non-zero values normally distributed in (0,1) with the same structure as the sparse matrix S.

R = sprandsym (S) generates a sparse random symmetric matrix with non-zero entries normally distributed in (0,1) whose lower diagonal triangle has the same structure as S.

r = sprank (S) gives the structural rank of the sparse matrix S.

n = nnz (S) gives the number of non-zero elements in the sparse matrix S.

k = nzmax (S) returns the amount of storage occupied by the non-zero elements in the sparse matrix S. If S is a full matrix then *nzmax (S) = prod (size (S))*.

s=spalloc(m,n,nzmax) creates space in memory for a sparse matrix of dimension *m×n*.

R = spones(S) replaces the zero entries of the sparse matrix S with ones.

n = condest(S) computes a lower bound for the 1-norm condition number of a square matrix S.

m = normest(S) returns an estimate of the 2-norm of the matrix S.

issparse(A) returns 1 if the matrix *A* is sparse, and 0 otherwise.

Here are some examples:

```
>> sparse([1,1,2,2,3,4],[4,2,3,1,2,3],[-7,12,25,1,-6,8],4,4,10)
```

ans =

```
(2,1) 1
(1,2) 12
(3,2) -6
(2,3) 25
(4,3) 8
(1,4) -7
```

Now we convert this sparse matrix into complete form:

```
>> full(ans)
```

ans =

```
0  12  0  -7
1   0 25   0
0  -6  0   0
0   0  8   0
```

Now we define a sparse matrix whose full form is a diagonal matrix:

```
sparse(1:5,1:5,-6)
```

ans =

```
(1,1)      -6
(2,2)      -6
(3,3)      -6
(4,4)      -6
(5,5)      -6
```

```
>> full(ans)
```

ans =

```
-6   0   0   0   0
 0  -6   0   0   0
 0   0  -6   0   0
 0   0   0  -6   0
 0   0   0   0  -6
```

5.7 Special Matrices

MATLAB provides commands to define certain special types of matrices. These include the following:

H = hadamard(n): Returns the Hadamard matrix of order n, a matrix with values 1 or –1 such that $H'^* H = n * eye(n)$.

hankel(V): Returns the square Hankel matrix whose first column is the vector V and whose elements are zero below the first anti-diagonal. The matrix $hankel(C,R)$ has first column vector C and last row vector R.

hilb(n): Returns the Hilbert matrix of order n, a matrix whose ij-th element is $1/(i+j-1)$.

invhilb(n): Returns the inverse of the Hilbert matrix of order n.

magic(n): Returns a magic square of order n. Its elements are integers from 1 to n^2 with equal sums of rows and columns.

pascal(n): Returns the Pascal matrix of order n (symmetric, positive definite with integer entries taken from Pascal's triangle).

rosser: Returns the Rosser matrix, an 8×8 matrix with a double eigenvalue, three nearly equal eigenvalues, dominant eigenvalues of the opposite sign, a zero eigenvalue and a small non-zero eigenvalue.

toeplitz(C,R): Returns a Toeplitz matrix (not symmetric, with the vector C in the first column and R as the first row vector).

vander(C): Returns a Vandermonde matrix whose penultimate column is the vector C. In addition, $A(:,j) = C \wedge (n-j)$.

wilkinson(n): Returns the Wilkinson matrix of order n (symmetric tridiagonal with pairs of eigenvalues close but not the same).

compan(P): Returns the corresponding companion matrix whose first row is -P(2:n)/P(1), where P is a vector of polynomial coefficients.

maple('hadamard (n)'): Returns the Hadamard matrix of order n, a matrix with values 1 or - 1 such that $H'^* H = n * eye(n)$.

maple ('hilbert (n)'): Returns the Hilbert matrix of order n, a matrix whose ij-th element is $1/(i+j-1)$.

maple ('hilbert(n,exp)'): Returns the matrix of order n with ij-th entry equal to $1/(i+j-exp)$.

maple('bezout(poly1,poly2,x)'): Constructs the Bézout matrix of the given polynomials in x, with dimension $max(m,n)$, where $m = degree (poly1)$ and $n = degree (poly2)$. The determinant of this matrix is the resultant of the two polynomials $(resultant(poly1,poly2,x))$.

maple('sylvester(p1,p2,x)'): Constructs the Sylvester matrix of the given polynomials in x, with dimension $n+m$, where $m = degree(p1)$ and $n = degree(p2)$. The determinant of this matrix is the resultant of the two polynomials.

maple ('fibonacci (n)'): Returns the nth Fibonacci matrix F(n) whose size is the sum of the dimensions of F (n-1) and F (n-2).

maple('toeplitz([ex1,...,exn])'): Returns the symmetric Toeplitz matrix whose elements are the specified expressions.

maple('vandermonde([expr1,..., exprn])'): Returns the Vandermonde matrix whose ij-th element is $expri^{j-1}$.

maple ('wronskian(V,x)'): Returns the Wronskian matrix of the vector V =(f1,...,fn) with respect to the variable x. The ij-th element is $diff(fj, x\$(i-1))$.

maple ('jacobian([expr1,...,exprm],[x1,..., xn])'): Returns the $m \times n$ Jacobian matrix with ij-th element $diff(expri,xj)$.

maple('hessian(exp,[x1,...,xn])'): Returns the $m \times n$ Hessian matrix with ij-th element $diff(exp, xi,xj)$.

EXERCISE 5-10

Find the eigenvalues of the Wilkinson matrix of order 8, a magic square of order 8 and the Rosser matrix.

```
>> [eig(wilkinson(8)), eig(rosser), eig(magic(8))]
```

ans =

1. 0e + 003 *

```
 0.0042   1.0000   0.2600
 0.0043   1.0000   0.0518
 0.0028   1.0200  -0.0518
 0.0026   1.0200   0.0000
 0.0017   1.0199   0.0000 + 0.0000i
 0,0011   0.0001   0.0000 - 0.0000i
 0.0002   0.0000   0.0000 + 0.0000i
-0.0010  -1.0200   0.0000 - 0.0000i
```

Observe that the Wilkinson matrix has pairs of eigenvalues which are close, but not equal. The Rosser matrix has a double eigenvalue, three nearly equal eigenvalues, dominant eigenvalues of the opposite sign, a zero eigenvalue and a small non-zero eigenvalue.

EXERCISE 5-11

Find the Smith and Hermite forms of the inverse of the Hilbert matrix of order 2 in the variable x. Also find the corresponding transformation matrices.

```
>> maple('with(linalg):H:= inverse(hilbert(2,x))');
>> pretty(simple(sym(maple('H'))))
```

$$
\begin{bmatrix}
-(-3 + x)^2 (-2 + x) & (-3 + x) (-2 + x) (-4 + x) \\
(-3 + x) (-2 + x) (-4 + x) & -(-3 + x)^2 (-4 + x)
\end{bmatrix}
$$

```
>> maple ('B: = smith(H,x,U,V);)U: = eval (U); V: = eval (V)');
>> pretty(simple(sym(maple('B'))))
```

$$
\begin{bmatrix}
-3 + x & 0 \\
0 & (- 2 + x) (x^2 - 7 x + 12)
\end{bmatrix}
$$

```
>> pretty(simple(sym(maple('U'))))
```

$$
\begin{bmatrix}
-1 & -1 \\
10 - 13/2 x + x^2 & - 13/2 x + 9 + x^2
\end{bmatrix}
$$

```
>> pretty(simple(sym(maple('V'))))
```

$$
\begin{bmatrix}
-7/2 + x & - 4 + x \\
-3/2 + x & - 2 + x
\end{bmatrix}
$$

```
>> maple('HM:=hermite(H,x,Q);Q:=evalm(Q)');
>> pretty(simple(sym(maple('HM'))))
```

$$
\begin{bmatrix}
x^2 - 5 x + 6 & 0 \\
0 & x^2 - 7 x + 12
\end{bmatrix}
$$

```
>> pretty(simple(sym(maple('Q'))))
```

$$
\begin{bmatrix}
- x + 3 & - x + 2 \\
- x + 4 & - x + 3
\end{bmatrix}
$$

EXERCISE 5-12

Verify that the functions x, x^2 and x^3 are linearly independent.

```
>> maple('v:=[x,x^2,x^3]:w:=wronskian(v,x)');
>> pretty(simple(sym(maple('w'))))
```

$$\begin{bmatrix} x & x^2 & x^3 \\ 1 & 2x & 3x^2 \\ 0 & 2 & 6x \end{bmatrix}$$

```
>> pretty(simple(sym(maple('det(w)'))))
```

$$2x^3$$

Since the determinant of the Wronskian is non-zero, the functions are linearly independent.

EXERCISE 5-13

Find the Jacobian matrix and the Jacobian determinant of the transformation:

```
x = e " sin (v), y = e " cos (v).
>> pretty(sym(maple('jacobian(vector([exp(u) * sin(v), exp(u) * cos(v)]), [u, v])')))
```

$$\begin{bmatrix} exp\ (u)\ sin\ (u) & exp\ (u)\ cos\ (v) \\ exp\ (u)\ cos\ (v) & -\ exp\ (u)\ sin\ (v) \end{bmatrix}$$

```
>> pretty(simple(sym(maple('det(")'))))
```

$$-exp\ (u)^2$$

EXERCISE 5-14

Find the Bézout and Sylvester matrices B and T for the functions $p = a + bx + cx^2$ and $q = d + ex + fx^2$. Verify that the determinants of B and T coincide with the resultant of p and q.

```
>> maple('p:=a+b*x+c*x^2; q:= d+e*x+f*x^2; B:=bezout(p, q, x); T:=sylvester(p, q, x)')
>> pretty(sym(maple('B')))
```

$$\begin{bmatrix} dc - af & db - ae \\ & \\ ec - bf & dc - af \end{bmatrix}$$

```
>> pretty(sym(maple('T')))
```

$$\begin{bmatrix} c & b & a & 0 \\ 0 & c & b & a \\ f & e & d & 0 \\ 0 & f & e & d \end{bmatrix}$$

```
>> pretty(sym(maple('det(B)'))),pretty(sym(maple('det(T)'))),
pretty(sym(maple('resultant(p,q,x)')))
```

$$d^2c^2 - 2dcaf + a^2f^2 - dbyc + db^2f + aec^2 - aebf$$

$$d^2c^2 - 2dcaf + a^2f^2 - dbyc + db^2f + aec^2 - aebf$$

$$d^2c^2 - 2dcaf + a^2f^2 - dbyc + db^2f + aec^2 - aebf$$

CHAPTER 6

■ ■ ■

Functions

6.1 Custom Defined Functions

We already know that MATLAB has a wide variety of functions that can be used in everyday work with the program. But, in addition, MATLAB also offers the possibility of custom defined functions. The most common way to define a function is to write its definition to a text file, called an M-file, which will be permanent and will therefore enable the function to be used whenever required.

The second way to define a function is to use the relation between MATLAB and Maple, provided you have the symbolic math *Toolbox* installed. In this case, functions of a variable can also be directly defined.

6.2 Functions and M-files

MATLAB is usually used in *command mode* (or *interactive mode*), in which case a command is written in a single line in the Command Window and is immediately processed. But MATLAB also allows the implementation of sets of commands in *batch* mode, in which case a sequence of commands can be submitted which were previously written in a file. This file (M-file) must be stored on disk with the extension ".*m*" in the MATLAB subdirectory, using any ASCII editor or by selecting *M-file New* from the *File* menu in the top menu bar, which opens a text editor that will allow you to write command lines and save the file with a given name. Selecting *M-File Open* from the *File* menu in the top menu bar allows you to edit any pre-existing M-file.

To run an M-file simply type its name (without extension) in interactive mode into the Command Window and press *Enter*. MATLAB sequentially interprets all commands and statements of the M-file line by line and executes them. Normally the literal commands that MATLAB is performing do not appear on screen, except when the command *echo on* is active and only the results of successive executions of the interpreted commands are displayed. Work in batch mode is useful when automating large scale tedious processes which, if done manually, would be prone to mistakes. You can enter explanatory text and comments into M-files by starting each line of the comment with the symbol %. The *help* command can be used to display comments made in a particular M-file.

MATLAB provides certain commands which are frequently used in M-file scripts. Among them are the following:

echo on: View on-screen commands of an M-file script while it is running.

echo off: Hides on-screen commands of an M-file script (this is the default setting).

pause: Interrupts the execution of an M-file until the user presses a key to continue.

keyboard: Interrupts the execution of an M-file and passes the control to the keyboard so that the user can perform other tasks. The execution of the M-file can be resumed by typing the return command into the Command Window and pressing Enter.

return: Resumes execution of an M-file after an outage.

break: Prematurely exits a loop.

clc: Clears the Command Window.

home: Hides the cursor.

more on: Enables paging of the MATLAB Command Window output.

more off: Disables paging of the MATLAB Command Window output.

more(N): Sets page size to N lines.

menu: Offers a choice between various types of menu for user input.

When you define a function using an M-file, the above commands can be used if necessary.

The command *function* allows you to define functions in MATLAB, making it one of the most useful applications of M-files. The syntax of this command is as follows:

function output_parameters = function_name (input_parameters)
the function body

Once the function has been defined, it is stored in an M-file for later use. It is also useful to enter some explanatory text in the syntax of the function (using %), which can be accessed later by using the *help* command.

When there is more than one output parameter, they are placed between square brackets and separated by commas. If there is more than one input parameter, they are separated by commas. The body of the function is the syntax that defines it, and should include commands or instructions that assign values to output parameters. Each command or instruction of the body often appears in a line that ends either with a comma or, when variables are being defined, by a semicolon (in order to avoid duplication of outputs when executing the function). The function is stored in the M-file named *function_name.m*.

Let us define the function $fun1(x) = x \wedge 3 - 2x + cos(x)$, creating the corresponding *M-file* named *fun1.m* by using the syntax:

```
function p = fun1(x)
% Definition of a simple function
p = x ^ 3 - 2 * x + cos(x);
```

To define this function in MATLAB select *M-file New* from the *File* menu in the top menu bar (or click the button ◻ in the MATLAB tool bar). This opens the *MATLAB Editor/Debugger* text editor that will allow us to insert command lines defining the function, as shown in Figure 6-1.

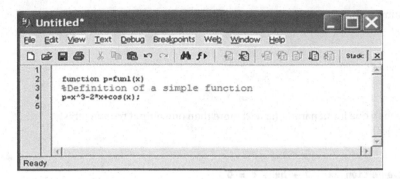

Figure 6-1.

To permanently save this code in MATLAB select the *Save* option from the *File* menu at the top of the MATLAB Editor/Debugger. This opens the Save dialog of Figure 6-2, which we use to save our function with the desired name and in the subdirectory indicated as a path in the file name field. Alternatively you can click on the button 🔲 or select Save and run from the Debug menu. Functions should be saved using a file name equal to the name of the function and in MATLAB's default work subdirectory C: \MATLAB6p1\work.

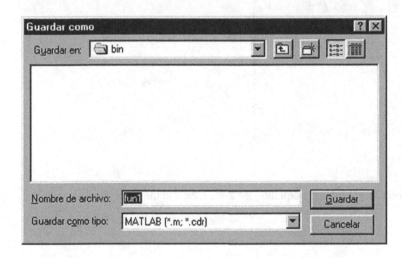

Figure 6-2.

Once a function has been defined and saved in an M-file, it can be used from the Command Window. For example, to find the value of the function at $3\pi-2$ we write in the Command Window:

>> fun1(pi)

ans =

23.7231

For help on the previous function (assuming that comments were added to the M-file that defines it) you use the command *help*, as follows:

```
>> help fun1(x)
```

 A simple function definition

The definition of a function with more than one input parameter and more than one output parameter is illustrated in the following example (Figure 6-3):

```
function [x1,x2]=equation2(a,b,c)
% This function solves the quadratic equation ax ^ 2 + bx + c = 0
% whose coefficients are a, b and c (input parameters)
% and whose solutions are x 1 and x 2 (output parameters)
d=b^2-4*a*c;
x1=(-b+sqrt(d))/(2*a);
x 2 = (-b-sqrt (d)) /(2*a);
```

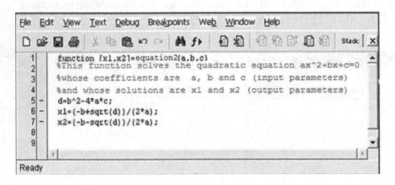

Figure 6-3.

The saved *M-file* with the name *equation2.m* will solve the equation $x \wedge 2 - 6x + 2 = 0$ in the following way:

```
>> [p,q]=equation2(1,-6,2)
```

 p =

   5.6458

 q =

   0.3542

We can also ask for help about the function *equation2*.

```
>> help equation2
```

 This function solves the quadratic equation ax ^ 2 + bx + c = 0
 whose coefficients are a, b and c (input parameters)
 and whose solutions are x1 and x2 (output parameters)

We can also evaluate a function defined in an M-file using the command *feval*, whose syntax is as follows:

`feval('F', arg1, arg1,..., argn)` **evaluates the function F (M-file F.m) with the specified arguments** *arg1 arg2,..., argn*

For example, we can evaluate previously defined functions using the command *feval*:

`>> [r1,r2]=feval('equation2',1,-6,2)`

r1 =

   5.6458

R2 =

   0.3542

`>> feval('fun1',pi)`

ans =

   23.7231

6.3 Functions and Flow Control. Loops

The use of recursive functions, conditional operations and piecewise defined functions is very common in mathematics. The handling of loops is necessary for the definition of these types of functions. Naturally, the definition of the functions will be made via M-files or through the relationship with Maple, via the symbolic math *Toolbox*.

6.4 The FOR loop

MATLAB has its own version of the DO statement (defined in the syntax of most programming languages). This statement allows you to run a command or group of commands repeatedly. For example:

`>> for i=1:3, x(i)=0, end`

x =

   0

x =

   0   0

x =

   0 0 0

The general form of a FOR loop is as follows:

```
for variable = expression
        commands
end
```

The loop always starts with the clause *for* and ends with the clause *end*, and includes in its interior a whole set of commands that are separated by commas. If any command defines a variable, it must end with a semicolon in order to avoid repetition in the output. Typically, loops are used in the syntax of M-files. Here is an example:

```
for i=1:m,
    for j=1:n,
        A(i,j)=1/(i+j-1);
    end
end
```

In this loop (Figure 6-4) we have defined the Hilbert matrix of order (m, n). If we save the M-file (Figure 6-5) as *for1.m*, we can build any Hilbert matrix by running the M-file and specifying values for the variables m and n as shown below:

```
>> m = 3, n = 4; for1; A
```

A =

1.0000	0.5000	0.3333	0.2500
0.5000	0.3333	0.2500	0.2000
0.3333	0.2500	0.2000	0.1667

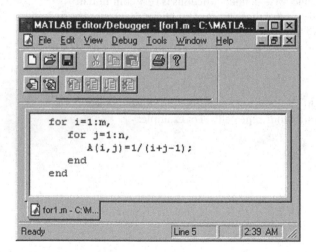

Figure 6-4.

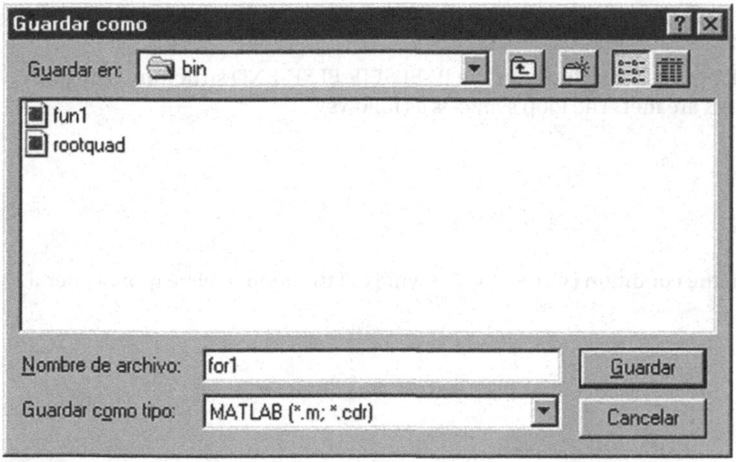

Figure 6-5.

6.5 The WHILE loop

MATLAB has its own version of the WHILE structure defined in the syntax of most programming languages.
This statement allows you to repeat a command or group of commands a number of times while a specified logical
condition is met. The general syntax of this loop is as follows:

> *While condition*
> *commands*
> *end*

The loop always starts with the clause *while*, followed by a condition, and ends with the clause *end*, and includes
in its interior a whole set of commands that are separated by commas which continually loop while the condition is
met. If any command defines a variable, it must end with a semicolon in order to avoid repetition in the output. As an
example, we write an M-file that is saved as *while1.m*, which calculates the largest number whose factorial does not
exceed 10^{100}.

```
n=1;
while prod(1:n) < 1.e100,
      n = n + 1;
end,
n
```

Now, we run the M-file:

```
>> while1

n =

   70
```

6.6 IF ELSEIF ELSE END LOOP

MATLAB, like most structured programming languages, also includes the IF-ELSEIF-ELSE-END structure. Using this structure, scripts can be run if certain conditions are met. The loop syntax is as follows:

```
If condition
    commands
end
```

In this case the commands are executed if the condition is true. But the syntax of this loop may be more general.

```
If condition
    commands1
else
    commands2
end
```

In this case, the *commands1* are executed if the condition is true, and the *commands2* are executed if the condition is false.

The IF statements, as well as FOR statements, can be nested. When multiple IF statements are nested, use the ELSEIF statement, whose general syntax is as follows:

```
if condition1
    commands1
ElseIf condition2
    commands2
ElseIf condition3
    commands3
.
.
else
end
```

In this case, the *commands1* are executed if *condition1* is true, the *commands2* are executed if *condition1* is false and *condition2* is true, the *commands3* are executed if *condition1* and *condition2* are false and *condition3* is true, and so on.

The previous nested syntax is equivalent to the following unnested syntax, but executes much faster:

```
if condition1
    commands1
else
      If condition2
          commands2
      else
            if condition3
                commands3
            else
.
.
            end
      end
end
```

Consider as an example the following M-file named *else1.m*:

```
If n < 0,
   A = 'n is negative'
elseif rem(n,2) ==0
   A = 'n is even'
else
   A = 'n is odd'
end
```

Running it, we obtain the number type (negative, odd or even) for a specified value of *n*:

```
>> n = 8; else1

A =

n is even

>> n = 7; else1

A =

n is odd

>> n =-2; else1

A =

n is negative
```

6.7 Recursive Functions

One of the applications of loops is the creation of recursive functions via M-files. For example, although the factorial function can be defined in MATLAB as $n! = prod(1:n)$, it can be also defined as a recursive function in the following way:

```
function y=factori(x)
      if x==0
       y=1;
      end
      if x==1
       y=1;
      end
      if x>1
       y=x*feval('factori',x-1);
      end
```

If we now want to calculate *40!*, we do the following:

```
>> factori(40)

ans =

  8. 1592e + 047
```

EXERCISE 6-1

The Fibonacci sequence {an} is defined by the recurrence law $a_1 = 1$, $a_2 = 1$, $a_n = a_{n-1} + a_{n-2}$. Represent this succession by a recurrent function and calculate a_2, a_5 and a_{20}.

We define the function using the M-file *fibo.m* as follows:

```
function y=fibo(x)
if x<=1
   y = 1;
else y = feval('fibo',x-1) + feval('fibo',x-2);
end
```

```
>> fibo(2)
```

ans =

    2

```
>> fibo(5)
```

ans =

    8

```
>> fibo(20)
```

ans =

    10946

EXERCISE 6-2

Newton's method for solving the equation f (x) = 0, under certain conditions on f, is via the iteration $x_{r+1} = x_r - f(x_r)/f\,'(x_r)$ for an initial value x_0 sufficiently close to a solution. Write a program that solves equations by Newton's method to a given precision and use it to calculate the root of the equation $x^3 - 10 x^2 + 29 x - 20 = 0$ close to the point x = 7 with an accuracy of 0.00005. Also search for a solution setting the precision to 0.0005.

The program code would read as follows:

```
% x is the initial value, precis is the precision required
% func is the function f and dfunc is its derivative
it=0; x0=x;
d=feval(func,x0)/feval(dfunc,x0);
while abs(d)>precis
   x1=x0-d;
   it=it+1;
   x0=x1;
   d=feval(func,x0)/feval(dfunc,x0);
end;
res = x0;
```

We save the program in the file named *fnewton.m*.

Now, we define the function f (x) = x^3 - 10 x^2 x + 29 - 20 and its derivative via the M-files named *f302.m* and *f303.m* in the following way:

```
F=x.^3-10.0*x.^2+29.0*x-20.0;
function F=f303(x);
F=3*x.^2-20*x+29;
```

To run the program that solves the given equation we type:

```
>> [x, it]=fnewton('f302','f303',7,.00005)
```

x =

    5.000

it =

    6

After 6 iterations and with an accuracy of 0.00005 we have obtained the solution x = 5. For 5 iterations and a precision of 0.0005 we get x = 5.0002 via:

```
>> [x, it] = fnewton('f302','f303',7,.0005)
```

x =

    5.0002

it =

    5

EXERCISE 6-3

Schröder's method, which is similar to Newton's method for solving the equation f (x) = 0, under certain conditions required on f, uses the iteration x = x_{r+1} = x_r -m f(x_r)/f'(x_r) for a given initial value x_0 close enough to a solution, m being the order of multiplicity of the sought root. Write a program that solves equations using Schröder's method to a given precision and use it to calculate a root with multiplicity 2 of the equation $(e^{-x} -x)^2 = 0$ close to the point x =-2 to an accuracy of 0.00005.

The program code reads as follows:

```
% m is the order of the multiplicity of the root
% x is the initial value, precis is precision
it=0; x0=x;
d=feval(func,x0)/feval(dfunc,x0);
```

```
while abs(d)>precis
    x1=x0-m*d;
    it=it+1; x0=x1;
    d=feval(func,x0)/feval(dfunc,x0);
end;
res = x 0;
```

We save the program in the file named *schroder.m*.

Now, we define the function f (x) = (e $^{-x}$ -x)^2 and its derivative and save them in files named *f304.m* and *f305.m*:

```
function F=f304(x);
F=(exp(-x)-x).^2;
```

```
function F=f305(x);
F=2.0*(exp(-x)-x).*(-exp(-x)-1);
```

To run the program that solves the stated equation type:

```
>>[x,it]=schroder('f304','f305',2,-2,.00005)
```

x =

    0.5671

it =

    5

In 5 iterations we obtain the solution x = 0.56715.

6.8 Conditional Functions

Functions defined differently on different intervals of variation in the independent variable have always played an important role in mathematics. MATLAB enables you to work with these types of functions, which are usually defined using M-files, in the majority of cases relying on FOR loops, WHILE loops, IF-ELSEIF-IF-END, etc.

EXERCISE 6-4

Define the function delta (x), which has value 1 if x = 0, and 0 if x is non-zero. Also define the function delta1 (x), which has the value 0 if x = 0, 1 if x > 0, and - 1 if x < 0, and represent it graphically.

Define *delta (x)* by creating the M-file *delta.m* as follows:

```
function y = delta (x)
If x == 0
    y = 1;
else y = 0;
end
```

To define *delta1(x)* we create the M-file *delta1.m* as follows:

```
function y = delta1 (x)
If x == 0
    y = 0;
ElseIf x > 0 and = 1;
ElseIf x < 0 and =-1;
end
```

To graph a function, we use the command *fplot*, whose syntax is as follows:

```
fplot [xmin xmax ymin ymax] ('function')
```

This represents the function in the given ranges of x and y.

Now, we represent the function *delta1 (x)*. See Figure 6-6:

```
>> fplot ('delta1(x)', [-10 10 -2 2])
```

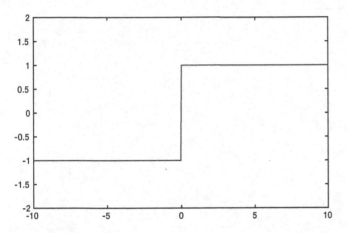

Figure 6-6.

EXERCISE 6-5

Define a function stat (v) which returns the mean and standard deviation of the elements of a given vector v. As an application, find the mean and standard deviation of the numbers 1, 5, 6, 7 and 9.

To define *stat (v)*, we create the M-file *stat.m* as follows:

```
function [media, destip] = stat(v)
[m,n]=size(v);
if m==1
    m=n;
end
media=sum(v)/m;
destip=sqrt(sum(v.^2)/m-media.^2);
```

Now we calculate the mean and standard deviation of the numbers 1, 5, 6, 7 and 9:

>> [a,s]=stat([1 5 6 7 9])

a =

   5.6000

s =

   2.6533

EXERCISE 6-6

Define and graph the piecewise function that has the value 0 if $x \le -3$, x^3 if $-3 < x < -2$, x^2 if $-2 \le x \le 2$, x if $2 < x < 3$ and 0 if $3 \le x$.

We create the function using an M-file named *piece1.m*:

```
function y=piece1(x)
if x<=-3
    y = 0;
ElseIf - 3 < x & x < - 2
      y = x ^ 3;
ElseIf - 2 < = x & x < = 2
      y = x ^ 2;
elseif 2<x & x<3
      y=x
elseif x>=3
      y = 0;
end
```

Now, we graph the function (see Figure 6-7):

>> fplot('piece1', [-5 5])

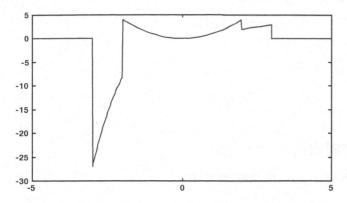

Figure 6-7.

6.9 Defining Functions Directly. Evaluating Functions

We already know that we can define and evaluate functions by making use of the relation between MATLAB and Maple, provided the symbolic mathematics *Toolbox* is available. Using this tool, you can define functions of one or severable variables using the command *maple*.

The advantage of defining functions in this way is that it is not necessary to write files to disk.

6.10 Functions of One Variable

Functions of one variable are defined in the form $f =$ *'function'* (or $f = function$ whenever its variables have previously been defined as symbolic with **syms**).

To find the value of the function f at a point, you use the command **subs**, whose syntax is as follows:

```
subs(f,a) applies the function f at the point a
```

```
subs(f,a,b) substitutes in f the value b by the value a
```

Let's see how to define the function $f(x) = x \wedge 2$:

```
>> f='x^2'   (or: syms x, f = x ^ 2)
```

$f =$

$x \wedge 2$

Now we calculate the values $f(4)$, $f(a+1)$ and $f(3x+x^2)$:

```
>> A=subs(f,4),B=subs(f,'a+1'),C=subs(f,'(3*x+x^2)')
```

$A =$

16

$B =$

$(a+1) \wedge 2$

$C =$

$(3 * x + x \wedge 2) \wedge 2$

6.11 Functions of Several Variables

Functions of one or several variables are defined using the *maple* command as follows:

```
maple('f: = x - > f (x)') defines the function f(x)
```

```
maple('f:=(x,y,z,...)- > f(x,y,z,...)') defines the function f(x,y,z,...)
```

```
maple('f:=(x,y,z,...)- > (f1(x,y,...), f2(x,y,...),...)') defines the vector function (f1(x,y,...),
f2(x,y,...),...)
```

To find the value of the function (x, y, z) -> $f(x,y,z...)$ at the point $(a, b, c,...)$ the expression ***maple ('f(a,b,c,...)')***
is used.

The value of the vector function $f:=(x,y,...)$-> $(f1(x,y,...), f2(x,y,...),...)$ at the point $(a, b,...)$ is found using the
expression ***maple ('f(a,b,...)')***.

The function $f(x,y) = 2x + y$ is defined in the following way:

```
>> maple('f:=(x,y) - > 2 * x + y');
```

$f(2,3)$ and $f(a,b)$ are calculated as follows:

```
>> maple('f(2,3)')
```

ans =

7

```
>> maple('f(a,b)')
```

ans =

$2 * a + b$

EXERCISE 6-7

Define the functions f (x) = x², g (x) = x^(1/2) and h (x) = x + sin (x). Calculate f (2), g(4) and h(a-b²).

```
>> f ='x ^ 2', g = 'x ^(1/2)', h = 'x+sin(x)'

f =

x ^ 2

g =

x ^(1/2)

h =

x+sin (x)

>> a=subs(f,2),b=subs(g,4),c=subs(h,'a-b^2')

a =

4

b =

4 ^(1/2)

c =

a-b ^ 2 + sin(a-b^2)
```

EXERCISE 6-8

Given the function h defined by h(x,y) = (cos(x²-y²), sin(x²-y²)), calculate h (1,2), h(-pi,pi) and h(cos (a²), cos (1 -a²)). As it is a vector function of two variables, we use the command *maple*:

```
>> maple('h:=(x,y) - > (cos(x^2-y^2), sin(x^2-y^2))');

>> maple('A = h (1, 2), B = h(-pi,pi), C = h(cos(a^2), cos(1-a^2))')

ans =

A = (cos (3),-sin (3)), B = (1, 0),
C = (cos (cos(a^2) ^ 2-cos(-1+a^2) ^ 2), sin(cos(a^2) ^ 2-cos(-1+a^2) ^ 2))
```

We could also define this vector function of two variables using the M-file named *vector1.m* below:

```
function [z,t] = vector1(x,y)
z = cos(x^2-y^2);
t = sin(x^2-y^2);
```

You can also build the function with the following syntax:

```
function h = vector1(x,y)
z = cos(x^2-y^2);
t = sin(x^2-y^2);
h = [z,t];
```

We calculate the values of the function at *(1,2)* and *(-pi, pi)* as follows:

```
>> A = vector1(1,2), B = vector1(-pi,pi)
```

A =

   -0.9900 - 0.1411

B =

    1 0

EXERCISE 6-9

Given the function f defined by:

$f(x,y)= 3(1-x)^2 e^{-(y+1)^2-x^2} -10(x/5-x^3-y/5)e^{-x^2-y^2}-1/3e^{-(x+1)^2-y^2}$

find f (0,0) and represent it graphically.

First, we can define it via the *maple* command:

```
>> maple ('f:=(x,y) - > 3 *(1-x) ^ 2 * exp (-(y + 1) ^ 2-x ^ 2)-
10*(x/5-x^3-y^5)*exp(-x^2-y^2)-1/3*exp(-(x+1)^2-y^2)');
```

Now, we calculate the value of *f* at *(0,0)*:

```
>> maple('f(0,0)')
```

ans =

*8/3*exp(-1)*

We can also create the M-file named *func2.m* as follows:

```
function h = func2(x,y)
h=3*(1-x)^2*exp(-(y+1)^2-x^2)-10*(x/5-x^3-y^5)*exp(-x^2-y^2)-
    1/3 * exp (-(x + 1) ^ 2 - y ^ 2);
```

Now, we calculate the value of *h* at *(0,0)*:

```
>> func2(0,0)
```

ans =

     0.9810

To graph the function, we use the command ***meshgrid*** to define the x and y ranges for the domain of the function (a neighborhood of the origin) and the command ***surfing*** to graph the surface:

```
>> [x,y] = meshgrid(-0.1:.005:0.1,-0.1:.005:0.1);
>> z = func2(x,y);
>> surf(x,y,z)
```

This yields the graph shown in Figure 6-8:

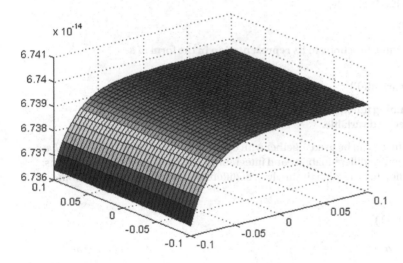

Figure 6-8.

6.12 Piecewise Functions

MATLAB provides a direct command that enables you to define conditional functions that take different values depending on different intervals of definition of the variables (*piecewise functions*). The command in question is *piecewise*, and its syntax is presented below:

maple ('piecewise(expr1, value1, expr2, value2,..., exprn, valuen)')

> Defines the piecewise function that takes *value1* if the variable satisfies *expr1*, takes *value2* if the variable satisfies *expr2*, and so on. For all values of the function not covered by the expressions the function takes the value zero.

maple ('piecewise(expr1, value1, expr2, value2,..., exprn, valuen, valuem)')

> Defines the piecewise function that takes *value1* if the variable satisfies *expr1*, takes *value2* if the variable satisfies *expr2*, and so on. For all values of the function not covered by the expressions the function takes the value *valuem*.

maple ('convert (expression,piecewise)')

> Converts the expression containing *Heaviside, abs, signum*, etc. functions to a piecewise function. The command can be applied to a list or set of expressions which is converted to a list or set.

maple ('convert (expression, piecewise variable)')

> Converts the expression containing *Heaviside, abs, signum*, etc. functions to a piecewise function according to the specified variable.

maple ('convert (expression,pwlist)')

> Converts the expression containing functions to its representation in the form of a piecewise list.

maple ('convert (expression, pwlist,variable)')

> Converts the expression containing functions to its representation in the form of a piecewise list based on the specified variable.

A great advantage of this command is that it can be used together with commands like *discont, diff, int, dsolve*. This allows you to directly analyze the continuity, differentiability and integrability of piecewise-defined functions. At the same time, it allows this type of function to be used in the analysis of differential equations. Here are some examples:

```
>> pretty(sym(maple('piecewise(x>0,x)')))
```

$$
\begin{cases} x & 0 < x \\ 0 & \text{otherwise} \end{cases}
$$

```
>> pretty(sym(maple('piecewise(x*x>4 and x<8,f(x))')))
```

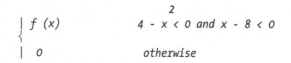

$$
\begin{cases} f(x) & 4 - x^2 < 0 \text{ and } x - 8 < 0 \\ 0 & \text{otherwise} \end{cases}
$$

```
>> pretty(sym(maple('simplify(piecewise(x*x>4 and x<8,f(x)))')))
```

$$
\begin{cases}
f\ (x) & x < - 2 \\
0 & x < = 2 \\
f(x) & x < 8 \\
0 & 8 <= x
\end{cases}
$$

```
>> pretty(sym(maple('piecewise(x<0,-1,x<1,0,1)')))
```

$$
\begin{cases}
-1 & x < 0 \\
0 & x < 1 \\
1 & otherwise
\end{cases}
$$

It is possible to define piecewise functions using the arrow operator, and to evaluate previously defined functions at different points.

```
>> pretty(sym(maple('f:=x->piecewise(x<0,-1,x<1,0,1) : f(1/2)')))
```

$$0$$

```
>> pretty(sym(maple('f(5),f(-5),f(-infinity),f(infinity)')))
```

$$1, - 1, - 1, 1$$

You can also directly simplify functions defined in terms of predefined piecewise functions

```
>> pretty(sym(maple('p:= piecewise(x<0,-x,x>0,x):p')))
```

$$
p := \begin{cases}
-x & x < 0 \\
x & 0 < x
\end{cases}
$$

```
>> pretty(sym(maple('p:= piecewise(x<0,-x,x>0,x):simplify(p^2 + 5)')))
```

$$x^2 + 5$$

However, you cannot directly simplify functions defined in terms of predefined piecewise functions that include parameters.

```
>> pretty(sym(maple('p:= piecewise(x<a,x,x>b,x*x):p')))
```

$$
p := \begin{cases}
x & x < a \\
x^2 & b < x
\end{cases}
$$

```
>> pretty(sym(maple('p:= piecewise(x<a,x,x>b,x*x):simplify(p^2)')))
```

$$
\begin{cases}
x & x < a^{\wedge} \ 2 \\
\\
x^2 & b < x
\end{cases}
$$

To simplify the above expression, we need to convert it into a piecewise function in terms of the main variable *x*.

```
>> pretty(sym(maple('convert(p,piecewise,x)')))
```

$$
\begin{cases}
x^2 & x < a \\
0 & x = a \\
x^4 & a < x
\end{cases}
$$

A piecewise function can also be expressed as a list.

```
>> pretty(sym(maple('f:=piecewise(x<0,-1,x<1,0,1):')));
>> pretty(sym(maple('convert(f,pwlist)')))
```

$$[- \ 1, \ 0, \ 0, \ 1, \ 1]$$

EXERCISE 6-10

Given the function f of a real variable defined by:

f(x)= |(1-|x|) |

express it as a piecewise-defined function and represent it graphically.

```
>> pretty(sym(maple('convert(abs(1-abs(x)),piecewise)')))
```

$$
\begin{cases}
-1 - x & x <= -1 \\
x + 1 & x <= 0 \\
1 - x & x < 1 \\
x - 1 & 1 <= x
\end{cases}
$$

Below, we represent the piecewise function using the ***ezplot*** command (see Figure 6-9) which can be used for general representations of functions of one variable.

```
>> ezplot('abs(1-abs(x))',[-2,2])
```

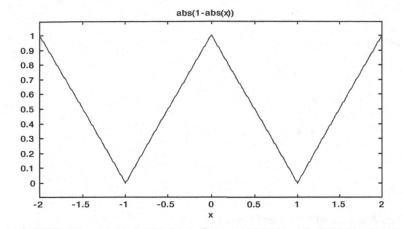

Figure 6-9.

EXERCISE 6-11

Given the function p of a real variable defined by:

p (x) =-1 if x < 0, p (x) = 2 x if x > 1 and p (x) = x² otherwise

express it as a piecewise-defined function. Find its indefinite integral and its derivative.

```
>> pretty(sym(maple('p:=piecewise(x<0, -1, x>1, 2*x, x^2):p')))
```

$$
p:= \begin{cases} -1 & x < 0 \\ 2\ x & 1 < x \\ x^2 & otherwise \end{cases}
$$

Now, let's calculate the indefinite integral of the function *p (x)*.

```
>> pretty(sym(maple('h:=int(p,x):h')))
```

$$
h:= \begin{cases} -x & x <\ = 0 \\ 1/3\ x^3 & x <= 1 \\ x^2 - 2/3 & 1 < x \end{cases}
$$

Next, we find the first derivative of p (x):

```
>> pretty(sym(maple('d:=diff(p,x):d')))
```

$$
d := \begin{cases}
0 & x <= 0 \\
2\,x & x <= 1 \\
2 & 1 < x \\
undefined & x = 1 \\
undefined & x = 0
\end{cases}
$$

Note that the function p (x) is not differentiable at the points $x = 1$ and $x = 0$.

EXERCISE 6-12

Given the function of a real variable p defined in the previous exercise, solve the following differential equation:

$$
\frac{\partial y(x)}{\partial(x)} + p y(x) = 0
$$

```
>> maple('dsolve(diff(y(x), x) + p * y(x) = 0, y(x))');
>> pretty(sym(maple('dsolve(diff(y(x), x) + p * y(x) = 0, y(x))')))
```

$$
y(x) = \begin{cases}
\_C1\ exp\ (x) & x < = 0 \\
\_C1\ exp(-1/3\ x)^{3} & x < = 1 \\
\_C1\ exp(-x + 2/3)^{2} & 1 < x
\end{cases}
$$

EXERCISE 6-13

Solve the following differential equation:

$$\frac{\partial y(x)}{\partial(x)} - |(1-|x|)| y^2(x) = 0$$

```
>> pretty(sym(maple('convert(abs(1-abs(x)),piecewise)')))
```

```
        | -1 - x        x <= -1
        |
        | 1 + x         x <= 0
       {
        | 1 - x         x <= 1
        |
        | x - 1          1 < x
```

```
>> pretty(sym(maple('dsolve(diff(y(x),x)=convert(abs(1-abs(x)),piecewise)*
y(x)^2,y(x))')))
```

```
           |              2
           | - ------------------ /         x <= -1
           |              2
           |     -2 x - x  + 2 _C1
           |
           |              2
           | - --------------------         x <= 0
           |              2
           |     2 x + 2 + x  + 2 _C1
  y(x) =  {
           |              2
           | - --------------------         x <= 1
           |              2
           |     2 x + 2 - x  + 2 _C1
           |
           |              2
           | - --------------------         1 < x
           |              2
           |     -2 x + 4 + x  + 2 _C1
```

6.13 Functional Operations

Normally, functions defined in MATLAB operate on their arguments. However, there are also functional operators that operate on other functions (i.e. functional operators have functions as arguments), for example, the inverse function operator. MATLAB also allows the classical operations between functions (sum, product, etc.).

Among the functional operators and classical operations between functions offered by MATLAB, we highlight the following:

```
syms x y z...
```

```
f = f(x,y,z,...), g = g(x,y,z,...), h = h(x,y,z,...)...
```

`symadd(f,g)` adds the functions *f* and *g* (i.e. *f* + *g*)

`symop(f,'+',g,'+',h,'+',...)` performs the sum *f+g+h+...*

`maple('f+g+h+...')` performs the sum *f+g+h +...*

`symsub(f,g)` subtracts g from *f* (i.e. *f-g*)

`symop(f,'-',g,'-',h,'-',...)` forms the successive difference *f-g-h-...*

`maple('f-g-h-...)')` forms the successive difference *f-g-h-...*

`symmul(f, g)` finds the product of *f* and *g* (i.e. *f * g*)

`symop(f,' * ',g,' * ',h,' * ',...)` forms the product *f*g*h*...*

`maple('f*g*h*,...) ')` forms the product *f * g * h *...*

`symdiv(f,g)` finds the quotient *f / g*

`symop(f,'/',g,'/ ',h,'/ ',...)` forms the successive quotient *f/(g/(h/...*

`maple('f/g/h/...) ')` forms the successive quotient *f/(g/(h/...*

`sympow(f,k)` raises f to the power k (*k* is a scalar)

`symop(f,'^',g)` raises a function f to the power of another function g

`maple('f^g')` raises a function f to the power of another function g

`compose(f,g)` composes two functions *f* and *g* (i.e. *f(g(x))*)

`compose(f,g,u)` composes the functions *f* and *g*, taking the expression *u* as the domain of *f* and *g*

`maple('f @g @h @...')` composes the functions *f, g, h...*

`maple('f(g(h(...)')))` composes the functions *f, g, h...*

`g = finverse(f)` gives the inverse of the function *f*

g = finverse(f,v) gives the inverse of the function *f* using the symbolic variable *v* as an independent variable

maple('invfunc[f(x)]') gives the inverse of the function f(x)

maple('f(x)@@(-1)') gives the inverse of the function f(x)

maple('map(function,exp)') applies the given function to each operand or element of the expression (according to the first level of operations), where *exp* is a list or set

maple('map2(f,exp,list)') applies the function *f* to the elements of the list, in such a way that the function has as its first argument the constant expression *expr*, and as the second argument, each item in the specified list

maple('unapply(expr,x1,x2,...,xn)') returns an operator from the expression *expr* in the variables *x1, x2,..., xn*

maple('applyop(f,n,expr)') applies the function to the nth operand of the expression

maple('applyop(function,{n1, n2,..., nk},expr)') applies the function to the n1, n2,..., nk-th operands of the expression

maple('applyop(function,n,expr,arg2,..., argn)') replaces the nth operand of the expression *expr* by the result of applying the given function to it, passing *arg2,..., argn* as additional arguments

Here are some examples:

```
>> maple('p: = x ^ 2 + sin (x) + 1')
```

ans =

p := x^2+sin(x)+1

```
>>  pretty(sym(maple('f:= unapply(p,x):f')))
```

$$x \rightarrow x^2 + sin(x) + 1$$

```
>> pretty(sym(maple('f(Pi/6)')))
```

$$1/36\ pi^2 + 3/2$$

```
>> maple('q:= x^2 + y^3 + 1'):
>> pretty(sym(maple('f:= unapply(q,x) :f')))
```

$$x \rightarrow x^2 + y^3 + 1$$

```
>> pretty(sym(maple('f(2)')))
```

$$5 + y^3$$

```
>> pretty(sym(maple('g:= unapply(q,x,y) :g')))
```

$$(x, y) \to x^2 + y^3 + 1$$

```
>> pretty(sym(maple('g(2,3)')))
```

$$32$$

```
>> clear all
>> maple('p:= y^2-2*y-3');
>> pretty(sym(maple('applyop(f,2,p)')))
```

$$y^2 + f(-2\ y) - 3$$

```
>> pretty(sym(maple('applyop(f,2,p,x1,x2)')))
```

$$y^2 + f(-2\ y,\ x1,\ x2) - 3$$

```
>> pretty(sym(maple('applyop(f,{2,3},p)')))
```

$$y^2 + f(-2\ y) + f\ (-\ 3)$$

```
>> pretty(sym(maple('map(f,x + y*z)')))
```

$$f\ (x) + f(y\ z)$$

```
>> pretty(sym(maple('map(f,{a,b,c})')))
```

$$\{f(a),\ f(b),\ f(c)\}$$

```
>> pretty(sym(maple('map(x -> x^2, x + y)')))
```

$$x^2 + y^2$$

```
>> pretty(sym(maple('map2(f,g,{a,b,c})')))
```

$$\{f(g,\ a),\ f(g,\ b),\ f(g,\ c)\}$$

```
>> pretty(sym(maple('map(diff,[(x+1)*(x+2),x*(x+2)],x)')))
```

$$[2\ x\ +\ 3,\ 2\ x\ +\ 2]$$

```
>> pretty(sym(maple('map2(diff,x^y/z,[x,y,z])')))
```

$$[\frac{x^y\ y}{x\ z},\ \frac{x^y\ \ln(x)}{z},\ -\frac{x^y}{z^2}]$$

EXERCISE 6-14

Let f(x) = x²+ x, g(x) = x³+ 1 and h(x) = sin (x) + cos (x). Calculate:

f (g(x)), g(f(x-1)), f(h(Pi/3)) and *f(g(h(sinx)))*.

Graph *f(g(x))* on the interval *[- 1,1]*.

```
>> syms x
>> f = x ^ 2; g = x ^ 3 + 1; h = sin (x) + cos (x); u = compose(f, g)
```

u =

(x ^ 3 + 1) ^ 2

```
>> v = subs(compose(g,f),x-1)
```

v =

(x-1)^6+1

```
>> w=subs(compose(f,h),'pi/3')
```

w =

(sin(1/3*pi) + cos(1/3*pi)) ^ 2

```
>> r = subs(compose(f,compose(g, h)), sin (x))
```

r =

((sin (sin (x)) + cos (sin (x))) ^ 3 + 1) ^ 2

This can also be solved in the following way:

```
>> maple('f: = x - > x ^ 2; g: = x - > x ^ 3 + 1, h: = x - > sin(x) + cos(x)');
>> maple('(f(g(h(sin(x)))'))))
```

ans =

((sin(sin (x)) + cos (sin (x))) ^ 3 + 1) ^ 2

To graph the function f (g (x)) we use the command ***ezplot***, which, like ***fplot***, graphs functions of a single variable as follows (see Figure 6-10):

```
>> ezplot(subs(compose(f,g),x),[-1,1])
```

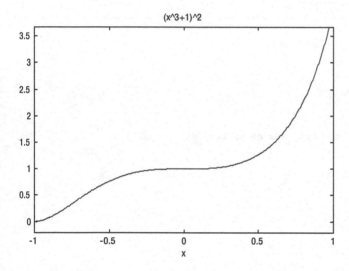

Figure 6-10.

EXERCISE 6-15

Define the functions f and g by $f(x,y) = (x^2, y^2)$ and $g(x,y) = (\sin(x), \sin(y))$. Calculate f (f (f(x,y))) and $g(f(\pi,\pi))$.

```
>> maple('f:=(x,y) - >(x^2,y^2); g:=(x,y) - > (sin(x), cos(y))');
>> a = maple('(f(f(f(x,y)))'))
```

a =

x ^ 8, y ^ 8

```
>> maple('(g(f(pi,pi)))')
```

ans =

sin(pi^2), cos(pi^2)

EXERCISE 6-16

Calculate the inverse of each of the functions f (x) = sin (cos ($x^{1/2}$) and g (x) = sqrt (tan (x^2)).

```
>> syms x, f = (cos(x ^(1/2)));
```

```
>> finverse(f)
```

ans =

arccos(arcsin(x))^2

```
>> g=sqrt(tan(x^2));
```

```
>> finverse(g)
```

Warning: finverse(sqrt(tan(x^2))) is not unique

ans =

arctan(x^2) ^(1/2)

In the latter case the program warns us of the non-uniqueness of the inverse function.

CHAPTER 7

■ ■ ■

Programming and Numerical Analysis

7.1 MATLAB and Programming

MATLAB can be used as a high-level programming language including data structures, functions, instructions for flow control, management of inputs/outputs and even object-oriented programming. MATLAB programs are usually written into files called M-files. An M-file is nothing more than a MATLAB code (*script*) that executes a series of commands or functions that accept arguments and produces an output. The M-files are created using the text editor.

7.2 The Text Editor

The *Editor/Debugger* is activated by clicking on the *create a new M-file* button ▢ in the MATLAB desktop or by selecting *File* ➤ *New* ➤ *M-file* in the MATLAB desktop (Figure 7-1) or Command Window (Figure 7-2). The *Editor/Debugger* opens a file in which we create the M-file, i.e. a blank file into which we will write MATLAB programming code (Figure 7-3). You can open an existing M-file using *File* ➤ *Open* on the MATLAB desktop (Figure 7-1) or, alternatively, you can use the command *Open* in the Command Window (Figure 7-2). You can also open the *Editor/Debugger* by right-clicking on the *Current Directory* window and choosing *New* ➤ *M-file* from the resulting pop-up menu (Figure 7-4). Using the menu option *Open*, you can open an existing M-file. You can open several M-files simultaneously, each of which will appear in a different window.

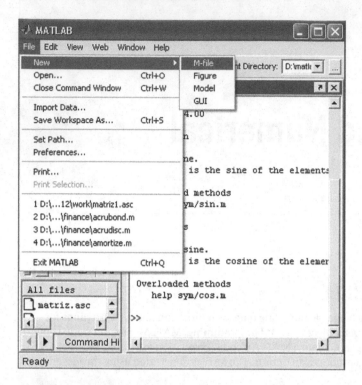

Figure 7-1.

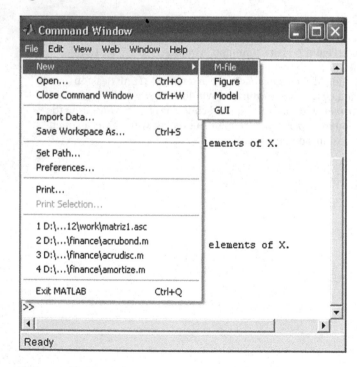

Figure 7-2.

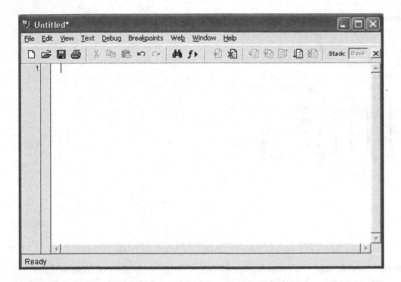

Figure 7-3.

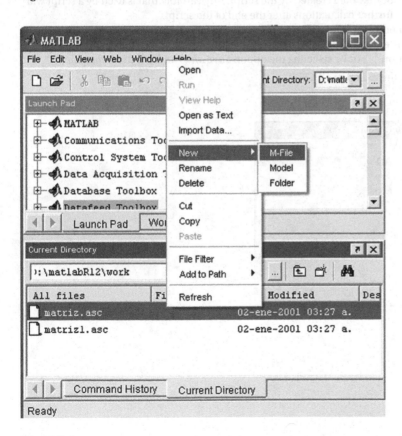

Figure 7-4.

Figure 7-5 shows the functions of the icons in the *Editor/Debugger*.

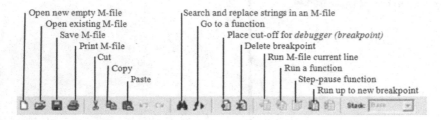

Figure 7-5.

7.3 Scripts

Scripts are the simplest possible M-files. A script has no input or output arguments. It simply consists of instructions that MATLAB executes sequentially and that could also be submitted in a sequence in the Command Window. Scripts operate with existing data on the workspace or new data created by the script. Any variable that is used by a script will remain in the workspace and can be used in further calculations after the end of the script.

Below is an example of a script that generates several curves in polar form, representing flower petals. Once the syntax of the script has been entered into the editor (Figure 7-6), it is stored in the work library (*work*) and simultaneously executes by clicking the button 🗋 or by selecting the option *Save and run* from the *Debug* menu (or pressing F5). To move from one chart to the next press ENTER.

```
%M-file script producing graphics of petals
theta = -pi:0.01:pi;
rho(1,:) = 2*sin(5*theta).^2;
rho(2,:) = cos(10*theta).^3;
rho(3,:) = sin(theta).^2;
rho(4,:) = 5*cos(3.5*theta).^3;
for i = 1:4
    polar(theta,rho(i,:))
    pause
end
```

Figure 7-6.

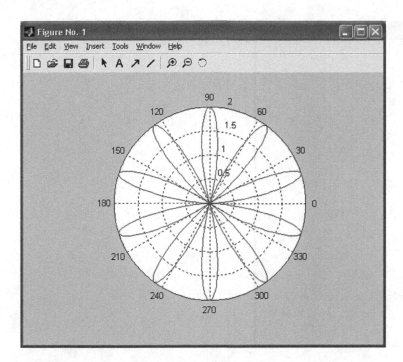

Figure 7-7.

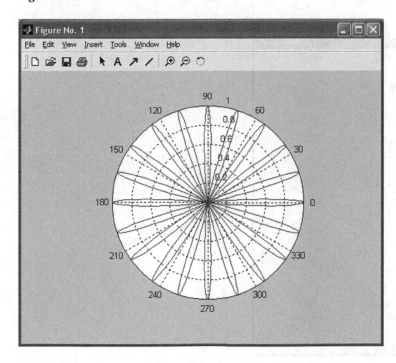

Figure 7-8.

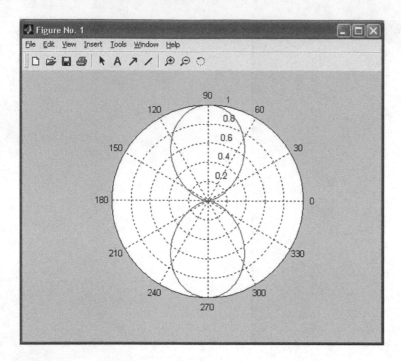

Figure 7-9.

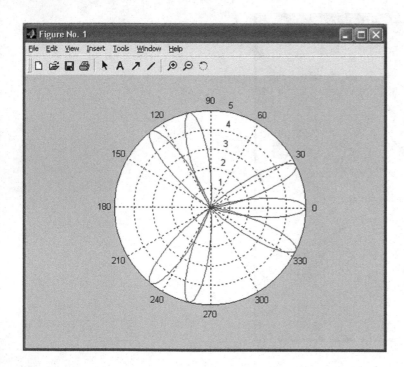

Figure 7-10.

7.4 Functions and M-files. Eval and feval

We already know that MATLAB has a wide variety of functions that can be used in everyday work with the program. But, in addition, the program also offers the possibility of custom defined functions. The most common way to define a function is to write its definition to a text file, called an M-file, which will be permanent and will therefore enable the function to be used whenever required.

MATLAB is usually used in *command mode* (or *interactive mode*), in which case a command is written in a single line in the Command Window and is immediately processed. But MATLAB also allows the implementation of sets of commands in *batch* mode, in which case a sequence of commands can be submitted which were previously written in a file. This file (M-file) must be stored on disk with the extension ".*m*" in the MATLAB subdirectory, using any ASCII editor or by selecting *M-file New* from the *File* menu in the top menu bar, which opens a text editor that will allow you to write command lines and save the file with a given name. Selecting *M-File Open* from the *File* menu in the top menu bar allows you to edit any pre-existing M-file.

To run an M-file simply type its name (without extension) in interactive mode into the Command Window and press *Enter*. MATLAB sequentially interprets all commands and statements of the M-file line by line and executes them. Normally the literal commands that MATLAB is performing do not appear on screen, except when the command *echo on* is active and only the results of successive executions of the interpreted commands are displayed. Normally, work in batch mode is useful when automating large scale tedious processes which, if done manually, would be prone to mistakes. You can enter explanatory text and comments into M-files by starting each line of the comment with the symbol %. The *help* command can be used to display comments made in a particular M-file.

The command *function* allows the definition of functions in MATLAB, making it one of the most useful applications of M-files. The syntax of this command is as follows:

    function output_parameters = function_name (input_parameters)
    the function body

Once the function has been defined, it is stored in an M-file for later use. It is also useful to enter some explanatory text in the syntax of the function (using %), which can be accessed later by using the *help* command.

When there is more than one output parameter, they are placed between square brackets and separated by commas. If there is more than one input parameter, they are separated by commas. The body of the function is the syntax that defines it, and should include commands or instructions that assign values to output parameters. Each command or instruction of the body often appears in a line that ends either with a comma or, when variables are being defined, by a semicolon (in order to avoid duplication of outputs when executing the function). The function is stored in the M-file named *function_name.m*.

Let us define the function $fun1(x) = x \wedge 3 - 2x + \cos(x)$, creating the corresponding M-file *fun1.m*. To define this function in MATLAB select *M-file New* from the *File* menu in the top menu bar (or click the button ⬜ in the MATLAB tool bar). This opens the *MATLAB Editor/Debugger* text editor that will allow us to insert command lines defining the function, as shown in Figure 7-11.

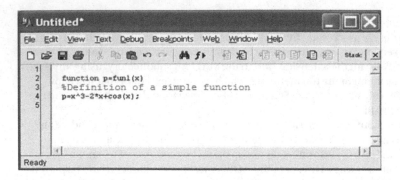

Figure 7-11.

To permanently save this code in MATLAB select the *Save* option from the *File* menu at the top of the *MATLAB Editor/Debugger*. This opens the *Save* dialog of Figure 7-12, which we use to save our function with the desired name and in the subdirectory indicated as a path in the *file name* field. Alternatively you can click on the button ⬜ or select *Save and run* from the *Debug* menu. Functions should be saved using a file name equal to the name of the function and in MATLAB's default work subdirectory *C: \MATLAB6p1\work*.

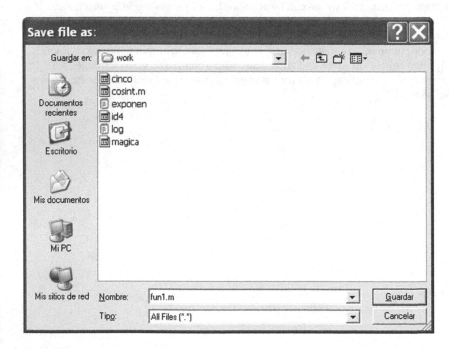

Figure 7-12.

Once a function has been defined and saved in an M-file, it can be used from the Command Window. For example, to find the value of the function at 3π-2 we write in the Command Window:

```
>> fun1(3*pi/2)

ans =

95.2214
```

For help on the previous function (assuming that comments were added to the M-file that defines it) you use the command *help*, as follows:

```
>> help fun1(x)
```

7.4.1 A Simple Function Definition

A function can also be evaluated at some given arguments (input parameters) via the *feval* command, the syntax of which is as follows:

feval ('F', arg1, arg1,..., argn)
This evaluates the function F (the M-file F.m) at the specified arguments arg1, arg2,..., argn.

As an example we build an M-file named *equation2.m* which contains the function equation2, whose arguments are the three coefficients of the quadratic equation $ax^2+bx+c = 0$ and whose outputs are the two solutions (Figure 7-13).

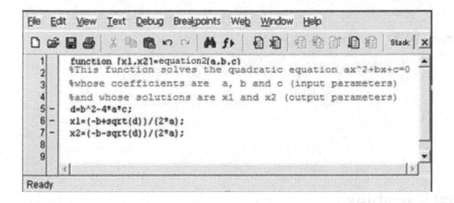

Figure 7-13.

Now if we want to solve the equation $x^2 + 2x + 3 = 0$ using *feval*, we write the following in the Command Window:

```
>> [x1, x2] = feval('equation2',1,2,3)

x1 =

-1.0000 + 1. 4142i

x2 =

-1.0000 - 1. 4142i
```

The quadratic equation can also be solved as follows:

```
>> [x1, x2] = equation2 (1,2,3)

x1 =

  -1.0000 + 1. 4142i

x2 =

-1.0000 - 1. 4142i
```

If we want to ask for help about the function equation2 we do the following:

```
>> help equation2
```

This function solves the quadratic equation $ax^2 + bx + c = 0$ whose coefficients are a, b and c (input parameters) and whose solutions are x 1 and x 2 (output parameters)

Evaluating a function when its arguments (input parameters) are strings is performed via the command *eval,* whose syntax is as follows:

```
eval (expression)
```

This executes the expression when it is a string.

As an example, we evaluate a string that defines a magic square of order 4.

```
>> n=4;
>> eval(['M' num2str(n) ' = magic(n)'])

M4 =

16 2 3 13
5 11 10 8
9 7  6 12
4 14 15 1
```

7.5 Local and Global Variables

Typically, each function defined as an M-file contains local variables, i.e., variables that have effect only within the M-file, separate from other M-files and the base workspace. However, it is possible to define variables inside M-files which can take effect simultaneously in other M-files and in the base workspace. For this purpose, it is necessary to define global variables with the GLOBAL command whose syntax is as follows:

> GLOBAL x y z...
> This defines the variables x, y and z as global.

Any variables defined as global inside a function are available separately for the rest of the functions and in the base workspace command line. If a global variable does not exist, the first time it is used, it will be initialized as an empty array. If there is already a variable with the same name as a global variable being defined, MATLAB will send a warning message and change the value of that variable to match the global variable. It is convenient to declare a variable as global in every function that will need access to it, and also in the command line, in order to access it from the base workspace. The GLOBAL command is located at the beginning of a function (before any occurrence of the variable).

As an example, suppose that we want to study the effect of the interaction coefficients α and β in the Lotka–Volterra predator-prey model:

$$y_1 = y_1 - \alpha y_1 y_2$$

$$y_2 = -y_2 - \beta y_1 y_2$$

To do this, we create the function *lotka* in the M-file *lotka.m* as depicted in Figure 7-14.

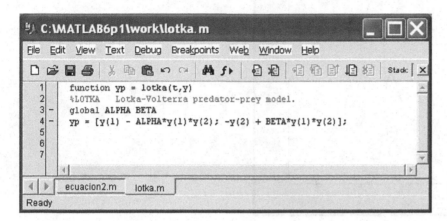

Figure 7-14.

Later, we might type the following in the command line:

```
>> global ALPHA BETA
ALPHA = 0.01
BETA = 0.02
```

These global values may then be used for α and β in the M-file *lotka.m* (without having to specify them). For example, we can generate the graph (Figure 7-15) with the following syntax:

```
>> [t, y] = ode23 ('lotka', 0.10, [1; 1]); plot(t,y)
```

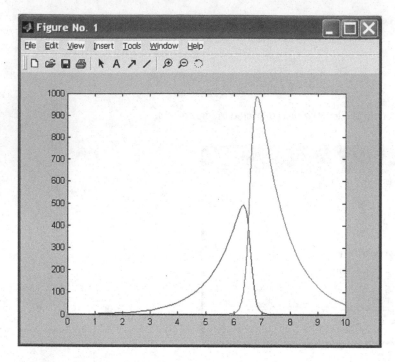

Figure 7-15.

7.6 Data Types

MATLAB has 14 different data types, summarized in Figure 7-16 below.

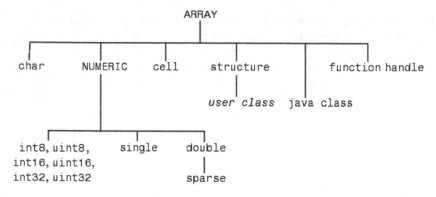

Figure 7-16.

Below are the different types of data:

Data type	Example	Description
single	3* 10 ^ 38	*Simple numerical precision. This requires less storage than double precision, but it is less precise. This type of data should not be used in mathematical operations.*
Double	3*10^300 5+6i	*Double numerical precision. This is the most commonly used data type in MATLAB.*
sparse	speye(5)	*Sparse matrix with double precision.*
int8, uint8, int16, uint16, int32, uint32	UInt8(magic (3))	*Integers and unsigned integers with 8, 16, and 32 bits. These make it possible to use entire amounts with efficient memory management. This type of data should not be used in mathematical operations.*
char	'Hello'	*Characters (each character has a length of 16 bits).*
cell	{17 'hello' eye (2)}	*Cell (contains data of similar size)*
structure	a.day = 12; a.color = 'Red'; a.mat = magic(3);	*Structure (contains cells of similar size)*
user class	inline('sin (x)')	*MATLAB class (built with functions)*
java class	Java. awt.Frame	*Java class (defined in API or own) with Java*
function handle	@humps	*Manages functions in MATLAB. It can be last in a list of arguments and evaluated with feval.*

7.7 Flow Control: FOR, WHILE and IF ELSEIF Loops

The use of recursive functions, conditional operations and piecewise defined functions is very common in mathematics. The handling of loops is necessary for the definition of these types of functions. Naturally, the definition of the functions will be made via *M-files*.

7.8 FOR Loops

MATLAB has its own version of the DO statement (defined in the syntax of most programming languages). This statement allows you to run a command or group of commands repeatedly. For example:

```
>> for i=1:3, x(i)=0, end

x =

    0

x =

    0    0

x =

    0  0  0
```

The general form of a FOR loop is as follows:

for variable = expression
commands
end

The loop always starts with the clause *for* and ends with the clause *end*, and includes in its interior a whole set of commands that are separated by commas. If any command defines a variable, it must end with a semicolon in order to avoid repetition in the output. Typically, loops are used in the syntax of M-files. Here is an example (Figure 7-17):

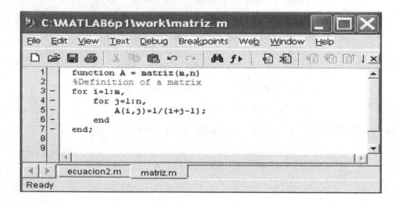

Figure 7-17.

In this loop we have defined a Hilbert matrix of order *(m, n)*. If we save it as an M-file *matriz.m*, we can build any Hilbert matrix later by running the M-file and specifying values for the variables *m* and *n* (the matrix dimensions) as shown below:

```
>> M = matriz (4,5)

M =

1.0000 0.5000 0.3333 0.2500 0.2000
0.5000 0.3333 0.2500 0.2000 0.1667
0.3333 0.2500 0.2000 0.1667 0.1429
0.2500 0.2000 0.1667 0.1429 0.1250
```

7.9 WHILE Loops

MATLAB has its own version of the WHILE structure defined in the syntax of most programming languages. This statement allows you to repeat a command or group of commands a number of times while a specified logical condition is met. The general syntax of this loop is as follows:

While condition
commands
end

The loop always starts with the clause *while*, followed by a condition, and ends with the clause *end*, and includes in its interior a whole set of commands that are separated by commas which continually loop while the condition is met. If any command defines a variable, it must end with a semicolon in order to avoid repetition in the output. As an example, we write an M-file (Figure 7-18) that is saved as *while1.m*, which calculates the largest number whose factorial does not exceed 10^{100}.

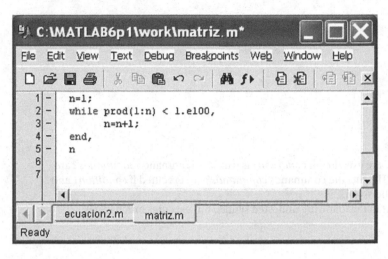

Figure 7-18.

Now now run the M-file.

```
>> while1

n =

    70
```

7.10 IF ELSEIF ELSE END Loops

MATLAB, like most structured programming languages, also includes the IF-ELSEIF-ELSE-END structure. Using this structure, scripts can be run if certain conditions are met. The loop syntax is as follows:

```
if condition
commands
end
```

In this case the commands are executed if the condition is true. But the syntax of this loop may be more general.

```
if condition
    commands1
else
    commands2
end
```

In this case, the commands *commands1* are executed if the condition is true, and the commands *commands2* are executed if the condition is false.

IF statements and FOR statements can be nested. When multiple IF statements are nested using the ELSEIF statement, the general syntax is as follows:

```
if condition1
    commands1
elseif condition2
    commands2
elseif condition3
    commands3
.
.
else
end
```

In this case, the commands *commands1* are executed if c*ondition1* is true, the commands *commands2* are executed if *condition1* is false and *condition2* is true, the commands *commands3* are executed if *condition1* and *condition2* are false and *condition3* is true, and so on.

The previous nested syntax is equivalent to the following unnested syntax, but executes much faster:

```
if condition1
    commands1
else
        if condition2
            commands2
        else
                if condition3
                    commands3
                else
                .
                .
                .
                end
        end
end
```

Consider, for example, the M-file *else1.m* (see Figure 7-19).

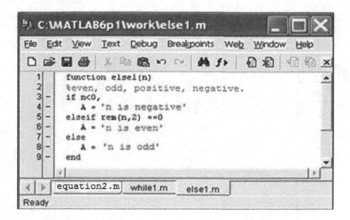

```
function else1(n)
%even, odd, positive, negative.
if n<0,
    A = 'n is negative'
elseif rem(n,2) ==0
    A = 'n is even'
else
    A = 'n is odd'
end
```

Figure 7-19.

When you run the file it returns negative, odd or even according to whether the argument *n* is negative, non-negative and odd, or non-negative and even, respectively:

>> else1 (8), else1 (5), else1 (-10)

A =

n is even

A =

n is odd

A =

n is negative

7.11 SWITCH and CASE

The *switch* statement executes certain statements based on the value of a variable or expression. Its basic syntax is as follows:

```
switch expression (scalar or string)
case value1
statements % runs if expression is value1
case value2
statements % runs if expression is value2
.
.
.
otherwise
statements % runs if neither case is satisfied

end
```

Below is an example of a function that returns 'minus one', 'zero', 'one', or 'another value' according to whether the input is equal to -1,0,1 or something else, respectively (Figure 7-20).

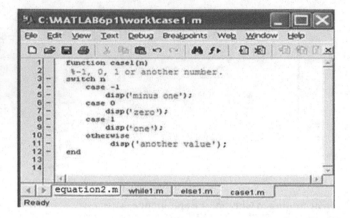

Figure 7-20.

Running the above example we get:

>> case1 (25)
another value

>> case1 (- 1)
minus one

7.12 CONTINUE

The *continue* statement passes control to the next iteration in a *for* loop or *while* loop in which it appears, ignoring the remaining instructions in the body of the loop. Below is an M-file *continue.m* (Figure 7-21) that counts the lines of code in the file *magic.m*, ignoring the white lines and comments.

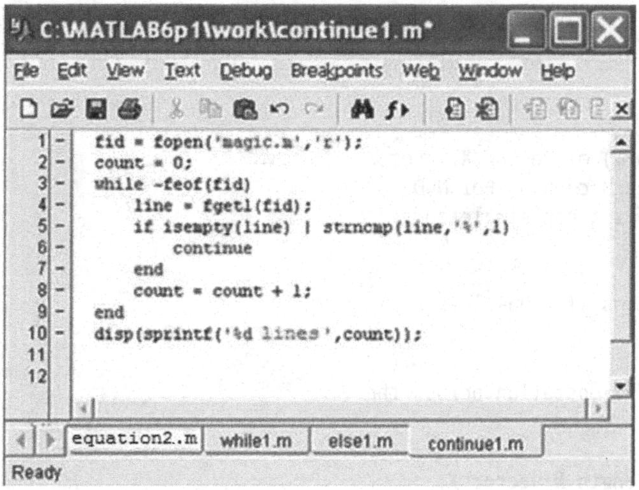

Figure 7-21.

Running the M-file, we get:

```
>> continue1
25 lines
```

7.13 BREAK

The *break* statement terminates the execution of a *for* loop or *while* loop, skipping to the first instruction which appears outside of the loop. Below is an M-file *break1.m* (Figure 7-22) which reads the lines of code in the file *fft.m*, exiting the loop as soon as it encounters the first empty line.

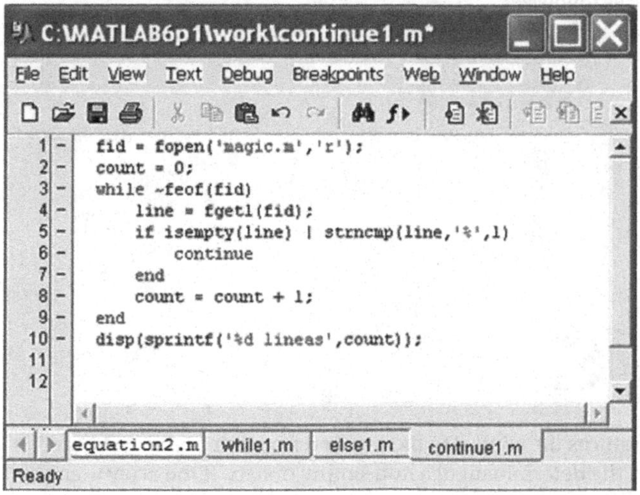

Figure 7-22.

Running the M-file we get:

```
>> break1
```

```
%FFT Discrete Fourier transform.
%    FFT(X) is the discrete Fourier transform (DFT) of vector X.  For
%    matrices, the FFT operation is applied to each column. For N-D
%    arrays, the FFT operation operates on the first non-singleton
%    dimension.
%
%    FFT(X,N) is the N-point FFT, padded with zeros if X has less
%    than N points and truncated if it has more.
%
%    FFT(X,[],DIM) or FFT(X,N,DIM) applies the FFT operation across the
%    dimension DIM.
%
%    For length N input vector x, the DFT is a length N vector X,
%    with elements
%                     N
%       X(k) =       sum  x(n)*exp(-j*2*pi*(k-1)*(n-1)/N), 1 <= k <= N.
%                    n=1
%    The inverse DFT (computed by IFFT) is given by
%                     N
%       x(n) = (1/N) sum  X(k)*exp( j*2*pi*(k-1)*(n-1)/N), 1 <= n <= N.
%                    k=1
%
%    See also IFFT, FFT2, IFFT2, FFTSHIFT.
```

7.14 TRY ... CATCH

The instructions between *try* and *catch* are executed until an error occurs. The instruction *lasterr* is used to show the cause of the error. The general syntax of the command is as follows:

```
try,
instruction
...,
instruction
catch,
instruction
...,
instruction
end
```

7.15 RETURN

The *return* statement terminates the current script and returns the control to the invoked function or the keyboard. The following is an example (Figure 7-23) that computes the determinant of a non-empty matrix. If the array is empty it returns the value 1.

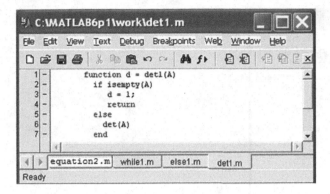

Figure 7-23.

Running the function for a non-empty array we get:

```
>> A = [- 1, - 1, 1; 1,0,1; 1,1,1]

A =

-1 -1 -1
 1  0  1
 1 -1 -1

>> det1 (A)

ans =

2
```

Now we apply the function to an empty array:

```
>> B =[]

B =

   []

>> det1 (B)

ans =

   1
```

7.16 Subfunctions

M-file-defined functions can contain code for more than one function. The main function in an M-file is called a *primary function*, which is precisely the function which invokes the M-file, but subfunctions hanging from the primary function may be added which are only visible for the primary function or another subfunction within the same M-file. Each subfunction begins with its own function definition. An example is shown in Figure 7-24.

Figure 7-24.

The subfunctions *mean* and *median* calculate the arithmetic mean and the median of the input list. The primary function *newstats* determines the length *n* of the list and calls the subfunctions with the list as the first argument and *n* as the second argument. When executing the main function, it is enough to provide as input a list of values for which the arithmetic mean and median will be calculated. The subfunctions are executed automatically, as shown below.

```
>> [mean, median] = newstats ([10,20,3,4,5,6])

mean =

    8

median =

    5.5000
```

7.17 Commands in M-files

MATLAB provides certain procedural commands which are often used in M-file scripts. Among them are the following:

echo on	*View on-screen commands of an M-file script while it is running.*
echo off	*Hides on-screen commands of an M-file script (this is the default setting).*
pause	*Interrupts the execution of an M-file until the user presses a key to continue.*
pause(n)	*Interrupts the execution of an M-file for n seconds.*

(continued)

pause off	*Disables pause and pause (n).*
pause on	*Enables pause and pause (n).*
keyboard	*Interrupts the execution of an M-file and passes the control to the keyboard so that the user can perform other tasks. The execution of the M-file can be resumed by typing the* return *command into the Command Window and pressing Enter.*
return	*Resumes execution of an M-file after an outage.*
break	*Prematurely exits a loop.*
CLC	*Clears the Command Window.*
Home	*Hides the cursor.*
more on	*Enables paging of the MATLAB Command Window output.*
more off	*Disables paging of the MATLAB Command Window output.*
more(N)	*Sets page size to N lines.*
menu	*Offers a choice between various types of menu for user input.*

7.18 Functions relating to Arrays of Cells

An array is a well-ordered collection of individual items. It is simply a list of elements, each of which is associated with a positive integer called its index, which represents the position of that element in the list. It is essential that each element is associated with a unique index, which can be zero or negative, which identifies it fully, so that to make changes to any elements of the array it suffices to refer to their indices. Arrays can be of one or more dimensions, and correspondingly they have one or more sets of indices that identify their elements. The most important commands and functions that enable MATLAB to work with arrays of cells are the following:

c = cell(n)	*Creates an n×n array whose cells are empty arrays.*
c = cell(m,n)	*Creates an m×n array whose cells are empty arrays.*
c = cell([m n])	*Creates an m×n array whose cells are empty arrays.*
c = cell(m,n,p,...)	*Creates an m×n×p×... array of empty arrays.*
c = cell([m n p ...])	*Creates an m×n×p×... array of empty arrays.*
c = cell(size(A))	*Creates an array of empty arrays of the same size as A.*
D = cellfun('f',C)	*Applies the function f (isempty, islogical, isreal, length, ndims, or prodofsize) to each element of the array C.*
D = cellfun('size',C,k)	*Returns the size of each element of dimension k in C.*
D = cellfun('isclass',C,class)	*Returns true for each element of C corresponding to class.*
C=cellstr(S)	*Places each row of the character array S into separate cells of C.*
S = cell2struct(C,fields,dim)	*Converts the array C to a structure array S incorporating field names 'fields' and the dimension 'dim' of C.*
celldisp (C)	*Displays the contents of the array C.*
celldisp(C, name)	*Assigns the contents of the array C to the variable name.*

(continued)

cellplot(C)	*Shows a graphical representation of the array C.*
cellplot(C,'legend')	*Shows a graphical representation of the array C and incorporates a legend.*
C = num2cell(A)	*Converts a numeric array A to the cell array C*
C = num2cell(A,dims)	*Converts a numeric array A to a cell array C placing the given dimensions in separate cells.*

As a first example, we create an array of cells of the same size as the unit square matrix of order two.

```
>> A = ones(2,2)

A =

1    1
1    1

>> c = cell(size(A))

c =

[]    []
[]    []
```

We then define and present a 2 × 3 array of cells element by element, and apply various functions to the cells.

```
>> C{1.1} = [1 2; 4 5];
C{1,2} = 'Name';
C{1,3} = pi;
C{2,1} = 2 + 4i;
C{2,2} = 7;
C{2,3} = magic(3);

>> C

C =

[2x2 double]    'Name'    [    3.1416]
[2.0000+ 4.0000i]    [    7]    [3x3 double]

>> D = cellfun('isreal',C)

D =

1    1    1
0    1    1
```

```
>> len = cellfun('length',C)

len =

2   4   1
1   1   3

>> isdbl = cellfun('isclass',C,'double')

isdbl =

1 0 1
1 1 1
```

The contents of the cells in the array C defined above are revealed using the command *celldisp*.

```
>> celldisp(C)

C{1,1} =

1   2
4   5

C{2,1} =

2.0000 + 4.0000i

C{1,2} =

Name

C {2,2} =

7

C {1,3} =

3.1416

C {2,3} =

8 1 6
3 5 7
4 9 2
```

The following displays a graphical representation of the array C (Figure 7-25).

```
>> cellplot(C)
```

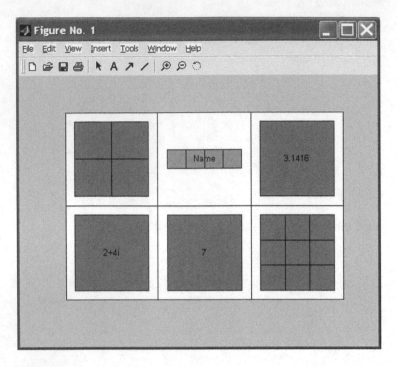

Figure 7-25.

7.19 Functions of Multidimensional Arrays

The following group of functions is used by MATLAB to work with multidimensional arrays:

C = cat(dim,A,B)	*Concatenates arrays A and B according to the dimension dim.*
C = cat(dim,A1,A2,A3,A4...)	*Concatenates arrays A1, A2,... according to the dimension dim.*
B = flipdim (A, dim)	*Flips the array A along the specified dimension dim.*
[I,J] = ind2sub(*siz*,IND)	*Returns the matrices I and J containing the equivalent row and column subscripts corresponding to each index in the matrix IND for a matrix of size siz.*
[I1,I2,I3,...,In] = ind2sub(*siz*,IND)	*Returns matrices I1, I2,...,In containing the equivalent row and column subscripts corresponding to each index in the matrix IND for a matrix of size siz.*
A = ipermute(B,*order*)	*Inverts the dimensions of the multidimensional array D according to the values of the vector order.*
[X1, X2, X3,...] = ndgrid(x1,x2,x3,...)	*Transforms the domain specified by vectors x1, x2,... into the arrays X1, X2,... which can be used for evaluation of functions of several variables and interpolation.*
[X 1, X 2,...] = ndgrid (x)	*Equivalent to ndgrid(x,x,x,...).*

(continued)

n = ndims(A)	*Returns the number of dimensions in the array A.*
B = permute(A,order)	*Swaps the dimensions of the array A specified by the vector order.*
B = reshape(A,m,n)	*Defines an m×n matrix B whose elements are the columns of a.*
B = reshape(A,m,n,p,...)	*Defines an array B whose elements are those of the array A restructured according to the dimensions m×n×p×...*
B = reshape(A,[m n p...])	*Equivalent to B = reshape(A,m,n,p,...)*
B = reshape(A,siz)	*Defines an array B whose elements are those of the array A restructured according to the dimensions of the vector siz.*
B = shiftdim(X,n)	*Shifts the dimensions of the array X by n, creating a new array B.*
[B,nshifts] = shiftdim(X)	*Defines an array B with the same number of elements as X but with leading singleton dimensions removed.*
B=squeeze(A)	*Creates an array B with the same number of elements as A but with all singleton dimensions removed.*
IND = sub2ind(siz,I,J)	*Gives the linear index equivalent to the row and column indices I and J for a matrix of size siz.*
IND = sub2ind(siz,I1,I2,...,In)	*Gives the linear index equivalent to the n indices I1, I2,..., in a matrix of size siz.*

As a first example we concatenate a magic square and Pascal matrix of order 3.

```
>> A = magic (3); B = pascal (3);
>> C = cat (4, A, B)

C(:,:,1,1) =

8 1 6
3 5 7
4 9 2

C(:,:,1,2) =

1 1 1
1 2 3
1 3 6
```

The following example flips the Rosser matrix.

```
>> R=rosser
```

```
R =

    611    196   -192    407     -8    -52    -49     29
    196    899    113   -192    -71    -43     -8    -44
   -192    113    899    196     61     49      8     52
    407   -192    196    611      8     44     59    -23
     -8    -71     61      8    411   -599    208    208
    -52    -43     49     44   -599    411    208    208
    -49     -8      8     59    208    208     99   -911
     29    -44     52    -23    208    208   -911     99
```

```
>> flipdim(R,1)
```

```
ans =

ans =

     29    -44     52    -23    208    208   -911     99
    -49     -8      8     59    208    208     99   -911
    -52    -43     49     44   -599    411    208    208
     -8    -71     61      8    411   -599    208    208
    407   -192    196    611      8     44     59    -23
   -192    113    899    196     61     49      8     52
    196    899    113   -192    -71    -43     -8    -44
    611    196   -192    407     -8    -52    -49     29
```

Now we define an array by concatenation and permute and inverse permute its elements.

```
>> a = cat(3,eye(2),2*eye(2),3*eye(2))
```

```
a(:,:,1) =

1 0
0 1
```

```
a(:,:,2) =

2 0
0 2
```

```
a(:,:,3) =

3 0
0 3
```

```
>> B = permute(a,[3 2 1])
```

```
B(:,:,1) =

1 0
2 0
3 0
```

```
B(:,:,2) =

0 1
0 2
0 3
```

```
>> C = ipermute(B,[3 2 1])
```

```
C(:,:,1) =

1 0
0 1
```

```
C(:,:,2) =

2 0
0 2
```

```
C(:,:,3) =

3 0
0 3
```

The following example evaluates the function $f(x_1, x_2) = x_1 e^{-x^2_1 - x^2_2}$ in the square $[-2, 2] \times [-2, 2]$ and displays it graphically (Figure 7-26).

```
>> [X 1, X 2] = ndgrid(-2:.2:2,-2:.2:2);
Z = X 1. * exp(-X1.^2-X2.^2);
mesh (Z)
```

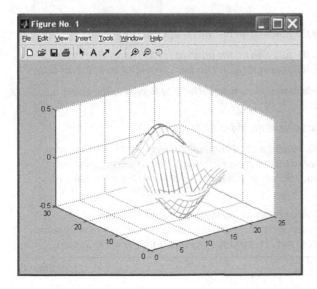

Figure 7-26.

In the following example we resize a 3 × 4 random matrix to a 2 × 6 matrix.

```
>> A = rand(3,4)

A =

0.9501    0.4860    0.4565    0.4447
0.2311    0.8913    0.0185    0.6154
0.6068    0.7621    0.8214    0.7919

>> B = reshape(A,2,6)

B =

  0.9501 0.6068 0.8913 0.4565 0.8214 0.6154
  0.2311 0.4860 0.7621 0.0185 0.4447 0.7919
```

7.20 Numerical Analysis Methods in MATLAB

MATLAB programming techniques allow you to implement a wide range of numerical algorithms. It is possible to design programs which perform numerical integration and differentiation, solve differential equations, optimize non-linear functions, etc. However, MATLAB's Basic module already has a number of tailor-made functions which implement some of these algorithms. These functions are set out in the following subsections. In the next chapter we will give some examples showing how these functions can be used in practice.

7.21 Zeros of Functions and Optimization

The commands (functions) that enables MATLAB's Basic module to optimize functions and find the zeros of functions are as follows:

x = **fminbnd(fun,x1,x2)**	*Minimizes the function on the interval (x1 x2).*
x = **fminbnd(fun,x1,x2,options)**	*Minimizes the function on the interval (x1 x2) according to the option given by optimset (...). This last command is explained later.*
x = **fminbnd(fun,x1,x2,options,P1,P2,...)**	*Specifies additional parameters P1, P2,... to pass to the target function fun(x,P1,P2,...).*
[x, fval] = **fminbnd (...)**	*Returns the value of the objective function at x.*
[x, fval, f] = **fminbnd (...)**	*In addition, returns an indicator of convergence f (f > 0 indicates convergence to the solution, f < 0 indicates no convergence and f = 0 indicates the algorithm exceeded the maximum number of iterations).*
[x,fval,f,output] = **fminbnd(...)**	*Provides further information (output.algorithm gives the algorithm used, output.funcCount gives the number of evaluations of fun and output.iterations gives the number of iterations).*

(*continued*)

x = fminsearch(fun,x0) x = fminsearch(fun,x0,options) x = fminsearch(fun,x0,options,P1,P2,...) [x,fval] = fminsearch(...) [x,fval,f] = fminsearch(...) [x,fval,f,output] = fminsearch(...)	*Returns the minimum of a scalar function of several variables, starting at an initial estimate x0. The argument x0 can be an interval [a, b]. To find the minimum of fun in [a, b], x = fminsearch (fun, [a, b]) is used.*
x = fzero(fun,x0) x = fzero(fun,x0,options) x = fzero(fun,x0,options,P1,P2,...) [x, fval] = fzero (...) [x, fval, exitflag] = fzero (...) [x,fval,exitflag,output] = fzero(...)	*Finds zeros of the function fun, with initial estimate x0, by finding a point where fun changes sign. The argument x0 can be an interval [a, b]. Then, to find a zero of fun in [a, b], we use x = fzero (fun, [a, b]), where fun has opposite signs at a and b.*
options = optimset('p1',v1,'p2',v2,...)	*Creates optimization parameters p1, p2,... with values v1, v2... The possible parameters are Display (with possible values 'off', 'iter','final','notify') to respectively not display the output, display the output of each iteration, display only the final output, and display a message if there is no convergence); MaxFunEvals, whose value is an integer indicating the maximum number of evaluations; MaxIter whose value is an integer indicating the maximum number of iterations; TolFun, whose value is an integer indicating the tolerance in the value of the function, and TolX, whose value is an integer indicating the tolerance in the value of x.*
val = optimget (options, 'param')	*Returns the value of the parameter specified in the optimization options structure.*
g = inline (*expr*)	*Transforms the string expr into a function.*
g = inline(*expr,arg1,arg2, ...*)	*Transforms the string expr into a function with given input arguments.*
g = inline (*expr, n*)	*Transforms the string expr into a function with n input arguments.*
f = @function	*Enables the function to be evaluated.*

As a first example we find the value of x that minimizes the function $\cos(x)$ in the interval (3,4).

```
>> x = fminbnd(@cos,3,4)

x =

3.1416
```

We could also have used the following syntax:

```
>> x = fminbnd(inline('cos(x)'),3,4)

x =
3.1416
```

In the following example we find the above minimum to 8 decimal places and find the value of x that minimizes the cosine in the given interval, presenting information relating to all iterations of the process.

```
>> [x,fval,f] = fminbnd(@cos,3,4,optimset('TolX',1e-8,...          'Display','iter'));
```

```
Func-count      x          f(x)        Procedure
1          3.38197     -0.971249    initial
2          3.61803     -0.888633    golden
3          3.23607     -0.995541    golden
4          3.13571     -0.999983    parabolic
5           3.1413          -1      parabolic
6          3.14159          -1      parabolic
7          3.14159          -1      parabolic
8          3.14159          -1      parabolic
9          3.14159          -1      parabolic
```

```
Optimization terminated successfully:
the current x satisfies the termination criteria using OPTIONS.TolX of 1.000000e-008
```

In the following example, taking (- 1, 2; 1) as initial values, we find the minimum and target value of the following function of two variables:

$$f(x) = 100\left(x_2 - x^2_1\right)^2 + \left(1 - x_1\right)^2$$

```
>> [x,fval] = fminsearch(inline('100*(x(2)-x(1)^2)^2+...
(((1-x (1)) ^ 2'), [- 1.2, 1])
```

```
x =
```

```
1.0000 1.0000
```

```
fval =
```

```
8. 1777e-010
```

The following example computes a zero of the sine function with an initial estimate of 3, and a zero of the cosine function between 1 and 2.

```
>> x = fzero(@sin,3)
```

```
x =
```

```
3.1416
```

```
>> x = fzero(@cos,[1 2])
```

```
x =
```

```
    1.5708
```

7.22 Numerical Integration

MATLAB contains functions that allow you to perform numerical integration using Simpson's method and Lobatto's method. The syntax of these functions is as follows:

q = quad(f,a,b)	*Finds the integral of f between a and b by Simpson's method with an error of 10⁻⁶.*
q = quad(f,a,b,tol)	*Find the integral of f between a and b by Simpson's method with the tolerance tol instead of 10⁻⁶.*
q = quad(f,a,b,tol,trace)	*Find the integral of f between a and b by Simpson's method with the tolerance tol and presents the trace of iterations.*
q = quad(f,a,b,tol,trace,p1,p2,...)	*Passes additional arguments p1, p2,... to the function f, f(x,p1,p2,...).*
[q, fcnt] = quadl(f,a,b,...)	*Additionally returns the number of evaluations of f.*
q = quadl(f,a,b)	*Finds the integral of f between a and b by Lobatto's quadrature method with a 10⁻⁶ error.*
q = quadl(f,a,b,tol)	*Finds the integral of f between a and b by Lobatto's quadrature method with the tolerance tol instead of 10⁻⁶.*
q = quadl(f,a,b,tol,trace)	*Finds the integral of f between a and b by Lobatto's quadrature method with the tolerance tol and presents the trace of iterations.*
q = quad(f,a,b,tol,trace,p1,p2,...)	*Passes additional arguments p1, p2,... to the function f, f(x,p1,p2,...).*
[q, fcnt] = quadl(f,a,b,...)	*Additionally returns the number of evaluations of f.*
q = dblquad (f, xmin, xmax, ymin, ymax)	*Evaluates the double integral f(x,y) in the rectangle specified by the given parameters, with an error of 10⁻⁶. dblquad will be removed in future releases and replaced by integral2.*
q = dblquad (f, xmin, xmax, ymin,ymax,tol)	*Evaluates the double integral f(x,y) in the rectangle specified by the given parameters, with tolerance tol.*
q = dblquad (f, xmin, xmax, ymin,ymax,tol,@quadl)	*Evaluates the double integral f(x,y) in the rectangle specified by the given parameters, with tolerance tol and using the quadl method.*
q = dblquad (f, xmin, xmax, ymin,ymax,tol,method,p1,p2,...)	*Passes additional arguments p1, p2,... to the function f.*

As a first example, we calculate $\int_0^2 \frac{1}{x^3-2x-5}\,dx$ using Simpson's method.

```
>> F = inline('1./(x.^3-2*x-5)');
>> Q = quad(F,0,2)

Q =

-0.4605
```

Then we observe that the integral remains unchanged even if we increase the tolerance to 10^{-18}.

```
>> Q = quad(F,0,2,1.0e-18)
```

Q =

-0.4605

In the following example we evaluate the same integral using Lobatto's method.

```
>> Q = quadl(F,0,2)
```

Q =

-0.4605

We evaluate the double integral $\int\limits_{\pi}^{2\pi}\int\limits_{0}^{\pi}(y\sin(x)+x\cos(y))dydx$.

```
>> Q = dblquad (inline (' y * sin (x) + x * cos (y)'), pi, 2 * pi, 0, pi)
```

Q =

   -9.8696

7.23 Numerical Differentiation

The derivative $f'(x)$ of a function $f(x)$ can simply be defined as the rate of change of $f(x)$ with respect to x. The derivative can be expressed as a ratio between the change in $f(x)$, denoted by $df(x)$, and the change in x, denoted by dx. The derivative of a function f at the point x_k can be estimated by using the expression:

$$f'(x_k)=\frac{f(x_k)-f(x_{k-1})}{x_k-x_{k-1}}$$

provided the values x_k, x_{k-1} are close to each other. Similarly the second derivative $f''(x)$ of the function $f(x)$ can be estimated as the first derivative of $f'(x)$, i.e.:

$$f''(x_k)=\frac{f'(x_k)-f'(x_{k-1})}{x_k-x_{k-1}}$$

MATLAB includes in its Basic module the function $diff$, which allows you to approximate derivatives. The syntax is as follows:

Y = diff(X)	*Calculates the differences between adjacent elements in the vector X:[X(2) - X(1), X(3) - X (2),..., X(n) - X(n-1)]. If X is an m×n matrix, diff (X) returns the array of differences by rows: [X(2:m,:)-X(1:m-1,:)]*
Y = diff(X,n)	*Finds differences of order n, for example: diff(X,2) = diff (diff (X)).*

As an example we consider the function $f(x) = x^5-3x^4-11x^3+27x^2+10x-24$, find the difference vector of [-4,-3.9,-3.8, ...,4.8,4.9,5] the difference vector of [$f(-4),f(-3.9),f(-3.8),...,f(4.8),f(4.9),f(5)$] and the elementwise quotient of the latter by the former, and graph the function in the interval [-4,5]. See Figure 7-27.

```
>> x =-4:0.1: 5;
>> f = x.^5-3*x.^4-11*x.^3 + 27*x.^2 + 10*x-24;
>> df=diff(f)./diff(x)
```

df =

  1.0e+003 *

Columns 1 through 7

    1.2390   1.0967   0.9655   0.8446   0.7338   0.6324   0.5400

Columns 8 through 14

    0.4560   0.3801   0.3118   0.2505   0.1960   0.1477   0.1053

Columns 15 through 21

    0.0683   0.0364   0.0093   -0.0136   -0.0324   -0.0476   -0.0594

Columns 22 through 28

   -0.0682   -0.0743   -0.0779   -0.0794   -0.0789   -0.0769   -0.0734

Columns 29 through 35

   -0.0687   -0.0631   -0.0567   -0.0497   -0.0424   -0.0349   -0.0272

Columns 36 through 42

   -0.0197   -0.0124   -0.0054   0.0012   0.0072   0.0126   0.0173

Columns 43 through 49

    0.0212   0.0244   0.0267   0.0281   0.0287   0.0284   0.0273

Columns 50 through 56

    0.0253   0.0225   0.0189   0.0147   0.0098   0.0044   -0.0014

Columns 57 through 63

   -0.0076   -0.0140   -0.0205   -0.0269   -0.0330   -0.0388   -0.0441

Columns 64 through 70

   -0.0485   -0.0521   -0.0544   -0.0553   -0.0546   -0.0520   -0.0472
```
```

```
Columns 71 through 77
```

```
-0.0400   -0.0300   -0.0170   -0.0007   0.0193   0.0432   0.0716
```

```
Columns 78 through 84
```

```
  0.1046   0.1427   0.1863   0.2357   0.2914   0.3538   0.4233
```

```
Columns 85 through 90
```

```
  0.5004   0.5855   0.67910.7816   0.8936   1.0156
```

```
>> plot (x, f)
```

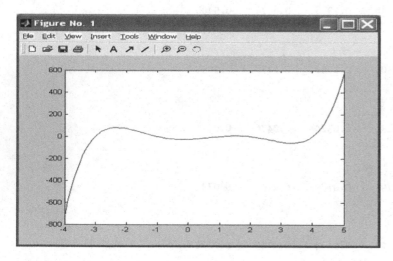

Figure 7-27.

7.24 Approximate Solutions of Differential Equations

MATLAB provides commands in its Basic module allowing for the numerical solution of ordinary differential equations (ODEs), differential algebraic equations (DAEs) and boundary value problems. It is also possible to solve systems of differential equations with boundary values and parabolic and elliptic partial differential equations.

7.25 Ordinary Differential Equations with Initial Values

An ordinary differential equation contains one or more derivatives of the dependent variable y with respect to the independent variable t. A first order ordinary differential equation with an initial value for the independent variable can be represented as:

$$y' = f(t, y)$$
$$y(t_0) = y_0$$

The previous problem can be generalized to the case where y is a vector, $y = (y_1, y_2, ..., y_n)$.

MATLAB's Basic module commands relating to ordinary differential equations and differential algebraic equations with initial values are presented in the following table:

Command	Class of problem solving, numerical method and syntax
ode45	*Ordinary differential equations by the Runge–Kutta method*
ode23	*Ordinary differential equations by the Runge–Kutta method*
ode113	*Ordinary differential equations by Adams' method*
ode15s	*Differential algebraic equations and ordinary differential equations using NDFs (BDFs)*
ode23s	*Ordinary differential equations by the Rosenbrock method*
ode23t	*Ordinary differential and differential algebraic equations by the trapezoidal rule*
ode23tb	*Ordinary differential equations using TR-BDF2*

The common syntax for the previous seven commands is the following:

```
[T, y] = solver(odefun,tspan,y0)
[T, y] = solver(odefun,tspan,y0,options)
[T, y] = solver(odefun,tspan,y0,options,p1,p2...)
[T, y, TE, YE, IE] = solver(odefun,tspan,y0,options)
```

In the above, solver can be any of the commands ode45, ode23, ode113, ode15s, ode23s, ode23t, or ode23tb.

The argument *odefun* evaluates the right-hand side of the differential equation or system written in the form $y' = f(t, y)$ or $M(t, y)y' = f(t, y)$, where $M(t, y)$ is called a mass matrix. The command *ode23s* can only solve equations with constant mass matrix. The commands *ode15s* and *ode23t* can solve algebraic differential equations and systems of ordinary differential equations with a singular mass matrix. The argument *tspan* is a vector that specifies the range of integration $[t_0, t_f]$ (*tspan*= $[t_0, t_1,...,t_f]$, which must be either an increasing or decreasing list, is used to obtain solutions for specific values of t). The argument y_0 specifies a vector of initial conditions. The arguments $p1$, $p2$,... are optional parameters that are passed to *odefun*. The argument *options* specifies additional integration options using the command options *odeset* which can be found in the program manual. The vectors T and Y present the numerical values of the independent and dependent variables for the solutions found.

As a first example we find solutions in the interval $[0,12]$ of the following system of ordinary differential equations:

$$y'_1 = y_2 y_3 \qquad y_1(0) = 0$$
$$y'_2 = -y_1 y_3 \qquad y_2(0) = 1$$
$$y'_3 = -0.51 y_1 y_2 \qquad y_3(0) = 1$$

For this, we define a function named *system1* in an M-file, which will store the equations of the system. The function begins by defining a column vector with three rows which are subsequently assigned components that make up the syntax of the three equations (Figure 7-28).

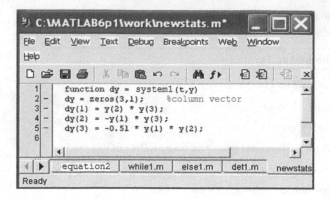

```
function dy = system1(t,y)
dy = zeros(3,1);        %column vector
dy(1) = y(2) * y(3);
dy(2) = -y(1) * y(3);
dy(3) = -0.51 * y(1) * y(2);
```

Figure 7-28.

We then solve the system by typing the following in the Command Window:

```
>> [T, Y] = ode45(@system1,[0 12],[0 1 1])

T =

0
0.0001
0.0001
0.0002
0.0002
0.0005
.
.
.
11.6136
11.7424
11.8712
12.0000

Y =
0 1.0000 1.0000
0.0001 1.0000 1.0000
0.0001 1.0000 1.0000
0.0002 1.0000 1.0000
0.0002 1.0000 1.0000
0.0005 1.0000 1.0000
0.0007 1.0000 1.0000
0.0010 1.0000 1.0000
0.0012 1.0000 1.0000
0.0025 1.0000 1.0000
0.0037 1.0000 1.0000
0.0050 1.0000 1.0000
0.0062 1.0000 1.0000
0.0125 0.9999 1.0000
0.0188 0.9998 0.9999
```

```
0.0251 0.9997 0.9998
0.0313 0.9995 0.9997
0.0627 0.9980 0.9990
.

.
0.8594  -0.5105 0.7894
0.7257  -0.6876 0.8552
0.5228  -0.8524 0.9281
0.2695  -0.9631 0.9815
-0.0118 -0.9990 0.9992
-0.2936 -0.9540 0.9763
-0.4098 -0.9102 0.9548
-0.5169 -0.8539 0.9279
-0.6135 -0.7874 0.8974
-0.6987 -0.7128 0.8650
```

To better interpret the results, the above numerical solution can be graphed (Figure 7-29) by using the following command:

```
>> plot (T, Y(:,1), '-', T, Y(:,2),'-', T, Y(:,3),'. ')
```

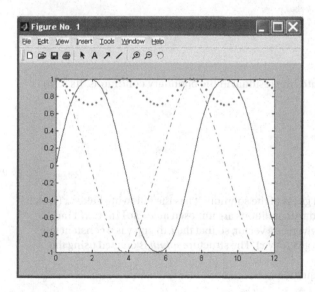

Figure 7-29.

7.26 Ordinary Differential Equations with Boundary Conditions

MATLAB also allows you to solve ordinary differential equations with boundary conditions. The boundary conditions specify a relationship that must hold between the values of the solution function at the end points of the interval on which it is defined. The simplest problem of this type is the system of equations

$$y' = f(x,y)$$

where x is the independent variable, y is the dependent variable and y' is the derivative *with respect to* x (i.e., $y' = dy/dx$). In addition, the solution on the interval $[a, b]$ has to meet the following boundary condition:

$$g\big(y(a), y(b)\big) = 0$$

More generally this type of differential equation can be expressed as follows:

$$y' = f(x, y, P)$$
$$g\big(y(a), y(b), P\big) = 0$$

where the vector p consists of parameters which have to be determined simultaneously with the solution via the boundary conditions.

The command that solves these problems is *bvp4c*, whose syntax is as follows:

```
Sol = bvp4c (odefun, bcfun, solinit)
Sol = bvp4c (odefun, bcfun, solinit, options)
Sol = bvp4c(odefun,bcfun,solinit,options,p1,p2...)
```

In the syntax above *odefun* is a function that evaluates $f(x, y)$. It may take one of the following forms:

```
dydx = odefun(x,y)
dydx = odefun(x,y,p1,p2,...)
dydx = odefun (x, y, parameters)
dydx = odefun(x,y,parameters,p1,p2,...)
```

The argument *bcfun* in *Bvp4c* is a function that computes the residual in the boundary conditions. Its form is as follows:

```
Res = bcfun (ya, yb)
Res = bcfun(ya,yb,p1,p2,...)
Res = bcfun (ya, yb, parameters)
Res = bcfun(ya,yb,parameters,p1,p2,...)
```

The argument *solinit* is a structure containing an initial guess of the solution. It has the following fields: x (which gives the ordered nodes of the initial mesh so that the boundary conditions are imposed at $a = $ solinit.x(1) and b = solinit.x(end)) and y (the initial guess for the solution, given as a vector, so that the i-th entry is a constant guess for the i-th component of the solution at all the mesh points given by x). The structure *solinit* is created using the command *bvpinit*. The syntax is solinit = bvpinit(x,y).

As an example we solve the second order differential equation:

$$y'' + |y| = 0$$

whose solutions must satisfy the boundary conditions:

$$y(0) = 0$$
$$y(4) = -2$$

This is equivalent to the following problem (where $y_1 = y$ and $y_2 = y'$):

$$y_1' = y_2$$
$$y_2' = -|y_1|$$

We consider a mesh of five equally spaced points in the interval [0,4] and our initial guess for the solution is $y_1 = 1$ and $y_2 = 0$. These assumptions are included in the following syntax:

```
>> solinit = bvpinit (linspace (0,4,5), [1 0]);
```

The M-files depicted in Figures 7-30 and 7-31 show how to enter the equation and its boundary conditions.

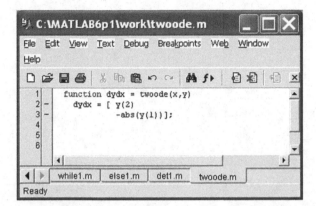

Figure 7-30.

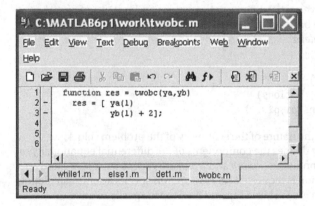

Figure 7-31.

The following syntax is used to find the solution of the equation:

```
>> Sun = bvp4c (@twoode, @twobc, solinit);
```

The solution can be graphed (Figure 7-32) using the command *bvpval* as follows:

```
>> y = bvpval (Sun, linspace (0,4));
>> plot (x, y(1,:));
```

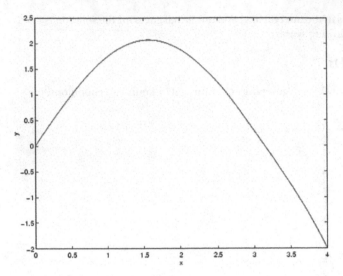

Figure 7-32.

7.27 Partial Differential Equations

MATLAB's Basic module has features that enable you to solve partial differential equations and systems of partial differential equations with initial boundary conditions. The basic function used to calculate the solutions is *pedepe*, and the basic function used to evaluate these solutions is *pdeval*.

The syntax of the function *pedepe* is as follows:

```
Sol = pdepe (m, pdefun, icfun, bcfun, xmesh, tspan)
Sol = pdepe (m, pdefun, icfun, bcfun, xmesh, tspan, options)
Sun = pdepe(m,pdefun,icfun,bcfun,xmesh,tspan,options,p1,p2...)
```

The parameter m takes the value 0, 1 or 2 according to the nature of the symmetry of the problem (block, cylindrical or spherical, respectively). The argument *pdefun* defines the components of the differential equation, *icfun* defines the initial conditions, *bcfun* defines the boundary conditions, *xmesh* and *tspan* are vectors $[x_0, x_1,...,x_n]$ and $[t_0, t_1,...,t_f]$ that specify the points at which a numerical solution is requested (n, $f{\geq}3$), *options* specifies some calculation options of the underlying solver (RelTol, AbsTol, NormControl, InitialStep and MaxStep to specify relative tolerance, absolute tolerance, norm tolerance, initial step and max step, respectively) and $p1$, $p2$,... are parameters to pass to the functions *pdefun, icfun* and *bcfun.*

pdepe solves partial differential equations of the form:

$$c\left(x,t,u,\frac{\partial u}{\partial x}\right)\frac{\partial u}{\partial t} = x^{-m}\frac{\partial}{\partial x}\left(x^m f\left(x,t,u,\frac{\partial u}{\partial x}\right)\right) + s\left(x,t,u,\frac{\partial u}{\partial x}\right)$$

where $a{\leq}x{\leq}b$ and $t_0{\leq}t{\leq}t_f$. Moreover, for $t = t_0$ and for all x the solution components meet the initial conditions:

$$u(x,t_0) = u_0(x)$$

and for all t and each $x = a$ or $x = b$, the solution components satisfy the boundary conditions of the form:

$$p(x,t,u) + q(x,t)f\left(x,t,u,\frac{\partial u}{\partial x}\right) = 0$$

In addition, we have that $a =$ xmesh (1), $b =$ xmesh (end), tspan (1) $= t_0$ and tspan (end) $= t_f$. Moreover *pdefun* finds the terms c, f and s of the partial differential equation, so that:

```
[c, f, s] = pdefun (x, t, u, dudx)
```

Similiarly *icfun* evaluates the initial conditions

```
u = icfun (x)
```

Finally, *bcfun* evaluates the terms p and q of the boundary conditions:

```
[pl, ql, pr, qr] = bcfun (xl, ul, xr, ur, t)
```

As a first example we solve the following partial differential equation ($x \in [0,1]$ and $t \geq 0$):

$$\pi^2 \frac{\partial u}{\partial t} = \frac{\partial}{\partial x}\left(\frac{\partial u}{\partial x}\right)$$

satisfying the initial condition:

$$u(x,0) = \sin \pi x$$

and the boundary conditions:

$$u(0,t) \equiv 0$$

$$\pi e^{-t} + \frac{\partial u}{\partial x}(1,t) = 0$$

We begin by defining functions in M-files as shown in Figures 7-33 to 7-35.

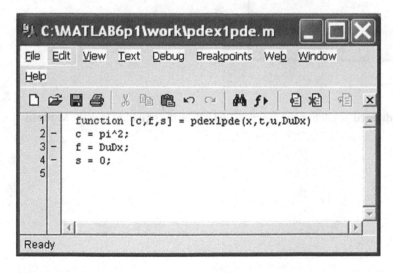

Figure 7-33.

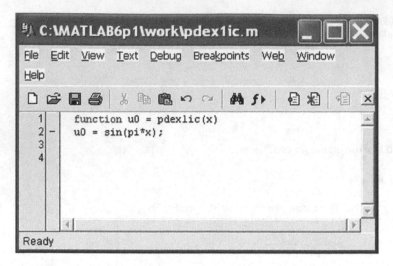

Figure 7-34.

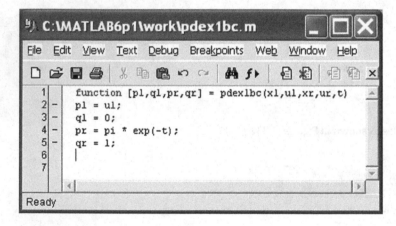

Figure 7-35.

Once the support functions have been defined, we define the function that solves the equation (see the M-file in Figure 7-36).

```
C:\MATLAB6p1\work\pdex1.m

File  Edit  View  Text  Debug  Breakpoints  Web  Window  Help

 1    function pdex1
 2
 3 -  m = 0;
 4 -  x = linspace(0,1,20);
 5 -  t = linspace(0,2,5);
 6
 7 -  sol = pdepe(m,@pdex1pde,@pdex1ic,@pdex1bc,x,t);
 8    %Extracts the first component of the solution as u
 9 -  u = sol(:,:,1);
10
11    %The solution is represented graphically as a surface
12 -  figure(1)
13 -  surf(x,t,u)
14 -  title('Numerical solution with 20 grid points.')
15 -  xlabel('Distance x')
16 -  ylabel('Time t')
17
18    %Profile of the solution
19 -  figure(2)
20 -  plot(x,u(end,:))
21 -  title('Solution in t=2')
22 -  xlabel('Distance x')
23 -  ylabel('u(x,2)')
24

Ready
```

Figure 7-36.

To view the solution (Figures 7-37 and 7-38), we enter the following into the MATLAB Command Window:

>> pdex1

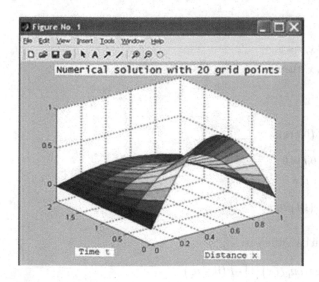

Figure 7-37.

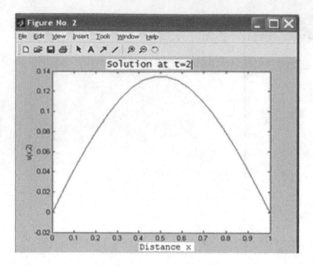

Figure 7-38.

As a second example we solve the following system of partial differential equations ($x \in [0,1]$ and $t \geq 0$):

$$\frac{\partial u_1}{\partial t} = 0.024 \frac{\partial^2 u_1}{\partial x^2} - F(u_1 - u_2)$$

$$\frac{\partial u_2}{\partial t} = 0.170 \frac{\partial^2 u_2}{\partial x^2} - F(u_1 - u_2)$$

$$F(y) = \exp(5.73y) - \exp(-11.46y)$$

satisfying the initial conditions:

$$u_1(x,0) \equiv 1$$
$$u_2(x,0) \equiv 0$$

and the boundary conditions:

$$\frac{\partial u_1}{\partial x}(0,t) \equiv 0$$
$$u_2(0,t) \equiv 0$$
$$u_1(1,t) \equiv 1$$
$$\frac{\partial u_2}{\partial x}(1,t) \equiv 0$$

To conveniently use the function *pdepe*, the system can be written as:

$$\begin{bmatrix} 1 \\ 1 \end{bmatrix} \cdot * \frac{\partial}{\partial t} \begin{bmatrix} u_1 \\ u_2 \end{bmatrix} = \frac{\partial}{\partial x} \begin{bmatrix} 0.024(\partial u_1 / \partial x) \\ 0.170(\partial u_2 / \partial x) \end{bmatrix} + \begin{bmatrix} -F(u_1 - u_2) \\ F(u_1 - u_2) \end{bmatrix}$$

The left boundary condition can be written as:

$$\begin{bmatrix} 0 \\ u_2 \end{bmatrix} + \begin{bmatrix} 1 \\ 0 \end{bmatrix} .* \begin{bmatrix} 0.024(\partial u_1 / \partial x) \\ 0.170(\partial u_2 / \partial x) \end{bmatrix} = \begin{bmatrix} 0 \\ 0 \end{bmatrix}$$

and the right boundary condition can be written as:

$$\begin{bmatrix} u_1 - 1 \\ 0 \end{bmatrix} + \begin{bmatrix} 1 \\ 0 \end{bmatrix} .* \begin{bmatrix} 0.024(\partial u_1 / \partial x) \\ 0.170(\partial u_2 / \partial x) \end{bmatrix} = \begin{bmatrix} 0 \\ 0 \end{bmatrix}$$

We start by defining the functions in M-files as shown in Figures 7-39 to 7-41.

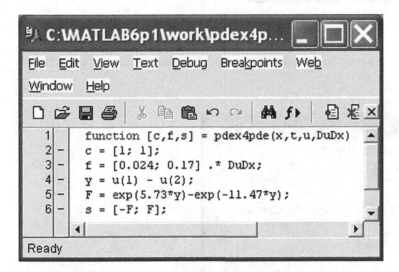

```
function [c,f,s] = pdex4pde(x,t,u,DuDx)
c = [1; 1];
f = [0.024; 0.17] .* DuDx;
y = u(1) - u(2);
F = exp(5.73*y)-exp(-11.47*y);
s = [-F; F];
```

Figure 7-39.

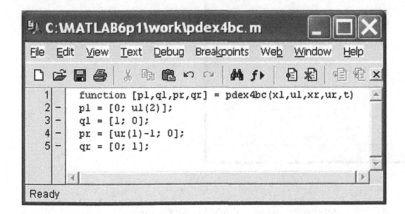

```
function [pl,ql,pr,qr] = pdex4bc(xl,ul,xr,ur,t)
pl = [0; ul(2)];
ql = [1; 0];
pr = [ur(1)-1; 0];
qr = [0; 1];
```

Figure 7-40.

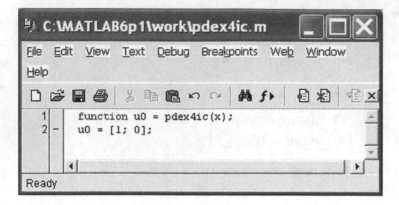

Figure 7-41.

Once the support functions are defined, the function that solves the system of equations is given by the M-file shown in Figure 7-42.

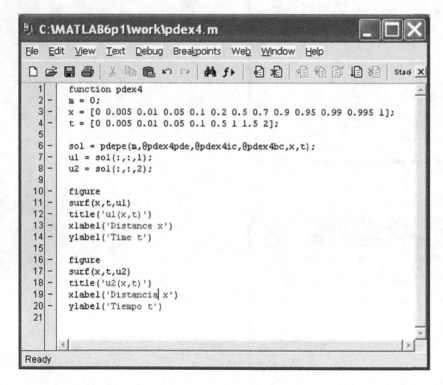

Figure 7-42.

To view the solution (Figures 7-43 and 7-44), we enter the following in the MATLAB Command Window:

```
>> pdex4
```

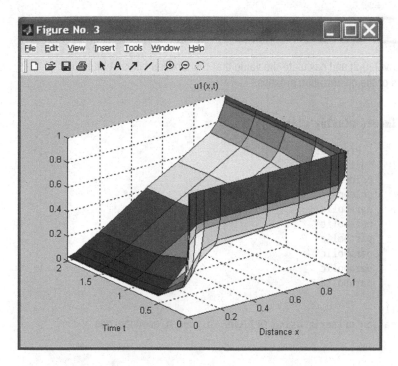

Figure 7-43.

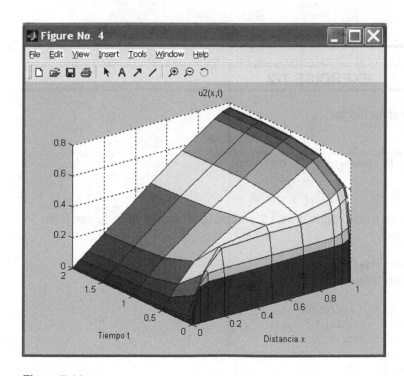

Figure 7-44.

EXERCISE 7-1

Minimize the function x^3-2x-5 in the interval (0,2) and calculate the value that the function takes at that point, displaying information about all iterations of the optimization process.

```
>> f = inline('x.^3-2*x-5');
>> [x,fval] = fminbnd(f, 0, 2,optimset('Display','iter'))
```

Func-count	x	f(x)	Procedure
1	0.763932	-6.08204	initial
2	1.23607	-5.58359	golden
3	0.472136	-5.83903	golden
4	0.786475	-6.08648	parabolic
5	0.823917	-6.08853	parabolic
6	0.8167	-6.08866	parabolic
7	0.81645	-6.08866	parabolic
8	0.816497	-6.08866	parabolic
9	0.81653	-6.08866	parabolic

```
Optimization terminated successfully:
the current x satisfies the termination criteria using OPTIONS.TolX of 1.000000e-004

x =

0.8165

fval =

-6.0887
```

EXERCISE 7-2

Find in a neighborhood of $x = 1.3$ a zero of the function:

$$f(x)=\frac{1}{(x-0.3)^2+0.01}+\frac{1}{(x-0.9)^2+0.04}-6.$$

Minimize this function on the interval (0,2).

First we find a zero of the function using the initial estimate of $x=1.3$, presenting information about the iterations and checking that the result is indeed a zero.

```
>> [x,feval]=fzero(inline('1/((x-0.3)^2+0.01)+...
1/((x-0.9)^2+0.04)-6'),1.3,optimset('Display','iter'))
```

Func-count	x	f(x)	Procedure
1	1.3	-0.00990099	initial
2	1.26323	0.882416	search

```
Looking for a zero in the interval [1.2632, 1.3]
```

```
3        1.29959   -0.00093168      interpolation
4        1.29955   1.23235e-007     interpolation
5        1.29955   -1.37597e-011    interpolation
6        1.29955          0         interpolation
Zero found in the interval: [1.2632, 1.3].

x =

1.2995

feval =

0
```

Secondly, we minimize the function specified in the interval [0,2] and also present information about the iterative process, terminating the process when the value of *x* which minimizes the function is found. In addition, the value of the function at this point is calculated.

```
>> [x,feval]=fminbnd(inline('1/((x-0.3)^2+0.01)+...
1/((x-0.9)^2+0.04)-6'),0,2,optimset('Display','iter'))
```

```
Func-count    x          f(x)       Procedure
    1      0.763932    15.5296      initial
    2      1.23607     1.66682      golden
    3      1.52786     -3.03807     golden
    4      1.8472      -4.51698     parabolic
    5      1.81067     -4.41339     parabolic
    6      1.90557     -4.66225     golden
    7      1.94164     -4.74143     golden
    8      1.96393     -4.78683     golden
    9      1.97771     -4.81365     golden
   10      1.98622     -4.82978     golden
   11      1.99148     -4.83958     golden
   12      1.99474     -4.84557     golden
   13      1.99675     -4.84925     golden
   14      1.99799     -4.85152     golden
   15      1.99876     -4.85292     golden
   16      1.99923     -4.85378     golden
   17      1.99953     -4.85431     golden
   18      1.99971     -4.85464     golden
   19      1.99982     -4.85484     golden
   20      1.99989     -4.85497     golden
   21      1.99993     -4.85505     golden
   22      1.99996     -4.85511     golden
```

```
Optimization terminated successfully:
the current x satisfies the termination criteria using OPTIONS.TolX of 1.000000e-004
```

x =

2.0000

feval =

-4.8551

EXERCISE 7-3

The intermediate value theorem says that if f is a continuous function on the interval [a, b] and L is a number between f(a) and f(b), then there is a c (a < c < b) such that f(c) = L. For the function f(x) = cos(x-1), find the value c in the interval [1, 2.5] such that f(c)= 0.8.

The question asks us to solve the equation cos(x - 1) - 0.8 = 0 in the interval [1, 2.5].

```
>> c = fzero (inline ('cos (x-1) - 0.8'), [1 2.5])
```

c =

1.6435

EXERCISE 7-4

Calculate the following integral using both Simpson's and Lobatto's methods:

$$\int_1^6 \left(2+\sin\left(2\sqrt{x}\right)dx\cdot\right)$$

For the solution using Simpson's method we have:

```
>> quad(inline('2+sin(2*sqrt(x))'),1,6)
```

ans =

8.1835

For the solution using Lobatto's method we have:

```
>> quadl(inline('2+sin(2*sqrt(x))'),1,6)
```

ans =

8.1835

EXERCISE 7-5

Calculate the area under the normal curve (0,1) between the limits - 1.96 and 1.96.

The integral we need to calculate is

$$\int_{-196}^{196} \frac{e^{\frac{-x^2}{2}}}{\sqrt{2\pi}} dx$$

The calculation is done in MATLAB using Lobatto's method as follows:

```
>> quadl(inline('exp(-x.^2/2)/sqrt(2*pi)', - 1.96,1.96)
```

ans =

0.9500

EXERCISE 7-6

Calculate the volume of the hemisphere-function defined in [-1,1]×[-1,1] by

$$f(x,y) = \sqrt{1 - \left(x^2 + y^2\right)}.$$

```
>> dblquad(inline('sqrt(max(1-(x.^2+y.^2),0))'),-1,1,-1,1)
```

ans =

2.0944

The calculation could also have been done in the following way:

```
>> dblquad(inline('sqrt(1-(x.^2+y.^2)).*(x.^2+y.^2<=1)'),-1,1,-1,1)
```

ans =

2.0944

EXERCISE 7-7

Evaluate the following double integral:

$$\int_3^4 \int_1^2 \frac{1}{(x+y)^2} \, dx \, dy$$

```
>> dblquad(inline('1./(x+y).^2'),3,4,1,2)
```

ans =

    0.0408

EXERCISE 7-8

Solve the following Van der Pol system of equations:

$$y'_1 = y_2 \qquad\qquad y_1(0) = 0$$
$$y'_2 = 1000\left(1 - y^2_1\right)y_2 - y_1 \quad y_2(0) = 1$$

We begin by defining a function named *vdp100* in an M-file, where we will store the equations of the system. This function begins by defining a vector column with two empty rows which are subsequently assigned the components which make up the equation (Figure 7-45).

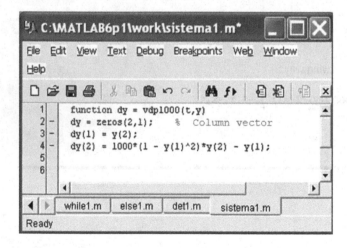

Figure 7-45.

We then solve the system and plot the solution $y_1 = y_1(t)$ given by the first column (Figure 7-46) by typing the following into the Command Window:

```
>> [T, Y] = ode15s(@vdp1000,[0 3000],[2 0]);
>> plot (T, Y(:,1),'-')
```

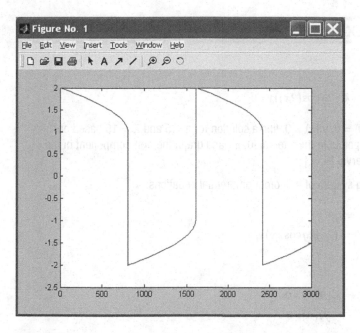

Figure 7-46.

Similarly we plot the solution $y_2 = y_2(t)$ (Figure 7-47) by using the syntax:

```
>> plot (T, Y(:,2),'-')
```

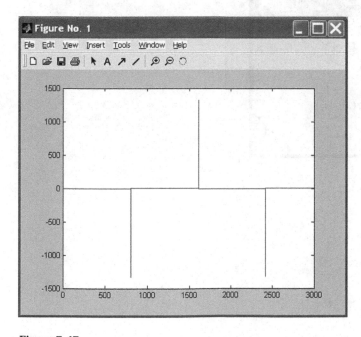

Figure 7-47.

EXERCISE 7-9

Given the following differential equation

$$y'' + \left(\lambda - 2q\cos(2x)\right)y = 0$$

subject to the boundary conditions y(0) = 1, y'(0) = 0, y'(π) = 0, find a solution for q = 5 and λ = 15 based on an initial solution defined on 10 equally spaced points in the interval [0, π] and graph the first component of the solution on 100 equally spaced points in the interval [0, π].

The given equation is equivalent to the following system of first order differential equations:

$$y'_1 = y_2$$
$$y_2' = -\left(\lambda - 2q\cos 2x\right)y_1$$

with the following boundary conditions:

$$y_1(0) - 1 = 0$$
$$y_2(0) = 0$$
$$y_2(\pi) = 0$$

The system of equations is introduced in the M-file shown in Figure 7-48, the boundary conditions are given in the M-file shown in Figure 7-49, and the M-file in Figure 7-50 sets up the initial solution.

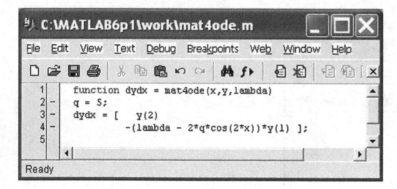

```
function dydx = mat4ode(x,y,lambda)
q = 5;
dydx = [    y(2)
           -(lambda - 2*q*cos(2*x))*y(1) ];
```

Figure 7-48.

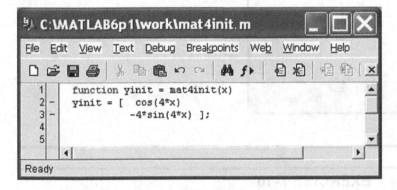

Figure 7-49.

```
function res = mat4bc(ya,yb,lambda)
res = [  ya(2)
         yb(2)
         ya(1)-1 ];
```

Figure 7-50.

```
function yinit = mat4init(x)
yinit = [  cos(4*x)
          -4*sin(4*x) ];
```

The initial solution for $\lambda = 15$ and 10 equally spaced points in $[0, \pi]$ is calculated using the following MATLAB syntax:

```
>> lambda = 15;
solinit = bvpinit (linspace(0,pi,10), @mat4init, lambda);
```

The numerical solution of the system is calculated using the following syntax:

```
>> sol = bvp4c(@mat4ode,@mat4bc,solinit);
```

To graph the first component on 100 equally spaced points in the interval $[0, \pi]$ we use the following syntax:

```
>> xint = linspace(0,pi);
Sxint = bvpval (ground, xint);
plot (xint, Sxint(1,:)))
axis([0 pi-1 1.1])
xlabel ('x')
ylabel('solution y')
```

The result is shown in Figure 7-51.

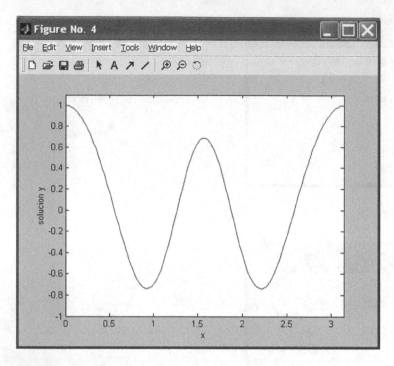

Figure 7-51.

EXERCISE 7-10

Solve the following differential equation

$$y'' + \left(1 - y^2\right)y' + y = 0$$

in the interval [0,20], taking as initial solution y = 2, y' = 0. Solve the more general equation

$$y'' + \mu\left(1 - y^2\right)y' + y = 0 \quad \mu > 0.$$

The general equation above is equivalent to the following system of first-order linear equations:

$$y'_1 = y_2$$
$$y'_2 = \mu\left(1 - y_1^2\right)y_2 - y_1$$

which is defined for $m = 1$ in the M-file shown in Figure 7-52.

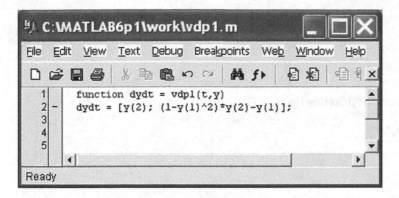

```
function dydt = vdpl(t,y)
dydt = [y(2); (1-y(1)^2)*y(2)-y(1)];
```

Figure 7-52.

Taking the initial solution $y_1 = 2$ and $y_2 = 0$ in the interval [0,20], we can solve the system using the following MATLAB syntax:

```
>> [t, y] = ode45(@vdp1,[0 20],[2; 0])
```

```
t =

0
0.0000
0.0001
0.0001
0.0001
0.0002
0.0004
0.0005
0.0006
0.0012
.
.
19.9559
19.9780
20.0000


y =

2.0000   0
2.0000 - 0.0001
2.0000 - 0.0001
2.0000 - 0.0002
2.0000 - 0.0002
2.0000 - 0.0005
.
.
1.8729 1.0366
1.9358 0.7357
1.9787 0.4746
```

```
2.0046 0.2562
2.0096 0.1969
2.0133 0.1413
2.0158 0.0892
2.0172 0.0404
```

We can graph the solutions using the following syntax (see Figure 7-53):

```
>> plot (t, y(:,1),'-', t, y(:,2),'-')
>> xlabel ('time t')
>> ylabel('solution y')
>> legend ('y_1', 'y_2')
```

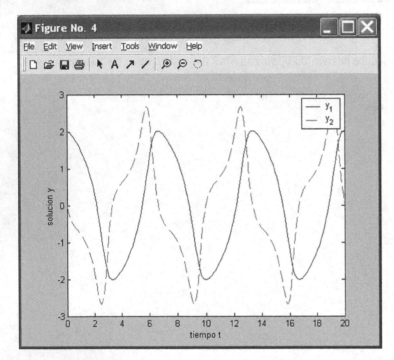

Figure 7-53.

To solve the general system with the parameter *m*, we define the system in the M-file shown in Figure 7-54.

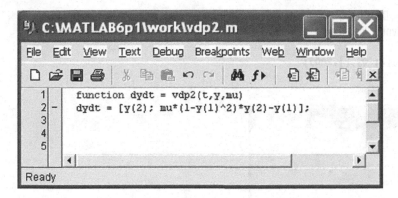

Figure 7-54.

Now we can graph the first solution $y_1 = 2$ and $y_2 = 0$ corresponding to m = 1000 in the interval [0,1500] using the following syntax (see Figure 7-55):

```
>> [t, y] = ode15s(@vdp2,[0 1500],[2; 0],[],1000);
>> xlabel ('time t')
>> ylabel ('solution y_1')
```

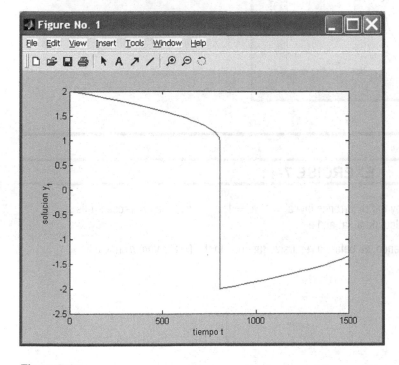

Figure 7-55.

To graph the first solution $y_1 = 2$ and $y_2 = 0$ for another value of the parameter, for example $m = 100$, in the interval [0,1500], we use the following syntax (see Figure 7-56):

```
>> [t, y] = ode15s(@vdp2,[0 1500],[2; 0],[],100);
>> plot (t, y(:,1),'-');
```

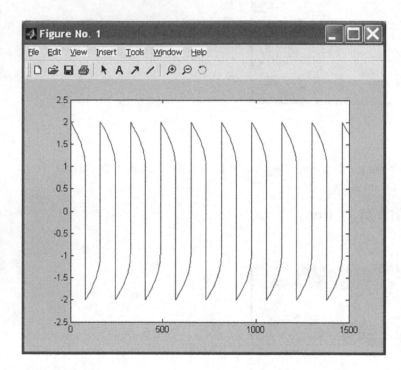

Figure 7-56.

EXERCISE 7-11

The Fibonacci sequence {an} is defined by the recurrence law $a_1 = 1$, $a_2 = 1$, $a_{n+1} = a_{n-1} + a_n$. Represent this sequence by a recursive function and calculate a_2, a_5 and a_{20}.

To generate terms of the Fibonacci sequence we define a recursive function in the M-file *fibo.m* shown in Figure 7-57.

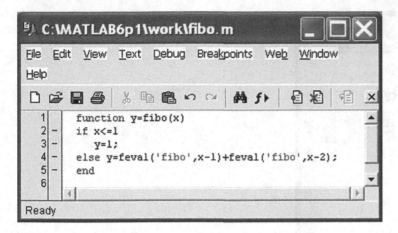

Figure 7-57.

Terms 2, 5 and 20 of the sequence are now calculated using the syntax:

➤ [fibo(2), fibo(5), fibo(20)]

ans =

2 8 10946

EXERCISE 7-12

Define the Kronecker delta, which equals 1 if x = 0 and 0 otherwise. Define the modified Kronecker delta function, which is 0 if x = 0, 1 if x> 0 and -1 if x <0 and graph it. Lastly, define the piecewise function that is equal to 0 if x ≤ -3, x^3 if -3 <x <-2, x^2 if -2≤x≤2, x if 2<x<3 and 0 if 3≤x, and graph it.

The Kronecker delta *delta(x)* is defined in the M-file *delta.m* shown in Figure 7-58. The modified Kronecker delta *delta1(x)* is defined in the M-file *delta1.m* shown in Figure 7-59. To define the third function *piece1(x)* of the exercise, we create the M-file *piece1.m* shown in Figure 7-60.

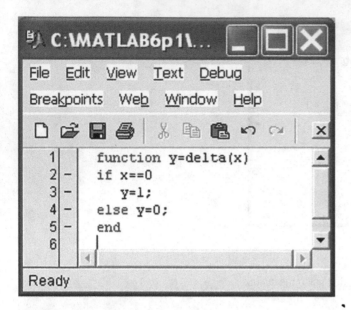

Figure 7-58.

Figure 7-59.

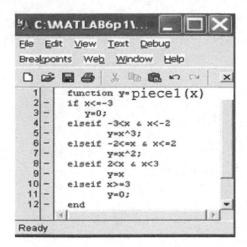

Figure 7-60.

To graphically represent the modified Kronecker delta on the domain [-10, 10] (and with codomain [-2, 2]) we use the following syntax (see Figure 7-61):

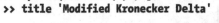

```
>> fplot ('delta1 (x)', [- 10 10 - 2-2])
>> title 'Modified Kronecker Delta'
```

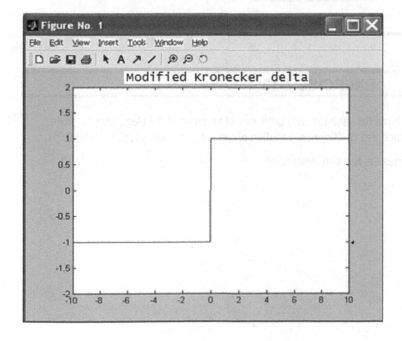

Figure 7-61.

To graphically represent the piecewise function on the interval [- 5,5] we use the following syntax (see Figure 7-62):

```
>> fplot ('piece1 (x)', [- 5 5]);
>> title 'Piecewise function'
```

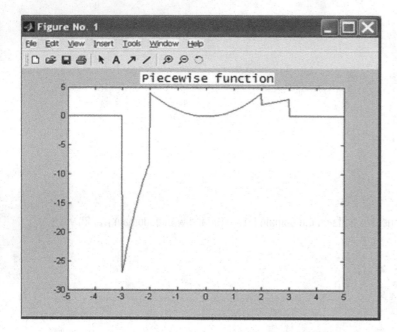

Figure 7-62.

EXERCISE 7-13

Define a function descriptive(v) which returns the variance and coefficient of variation of the elements of a given vector v. As an application, find the variance and coefficient of variation of the set of numbers 1, 5, 6, 7 and 9.

Figure 7-63 shows the M-file which defines the function *descriptive*.

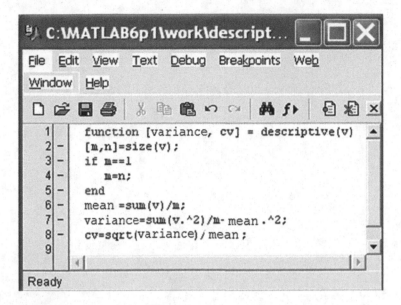

```
function [variance, cv] = descriptive(v)
[m,n]=size(v);
if m==1
    m=n;
end
mean =sum(v)/m;
variance=sum(v.^2)/m- mean .^2;
cv=sqrt(variance)/ mean ;
```

Figure 7-63.

To find the variance and coefficient of variation of the given set of numbers, we use the following syntax:

>> [variance, cv] = descriptive([1 5 6 7 9])

variance =

    7.0400

cv =

    0.4738

■ ■ ■

Numerical Algorithms: Equations, Derivatives, Integrals and Differential Equations

8.1 Solving Non-Linear Equations

MATLAB is able to implement a number of algorithms which provide numerical solutions to certain problems which play a central role in the solution of non-linear equations. Such algorithms are easy to construct in MATLAB and are stored as M-files. From previous chapters we know that an M-file is simply a sequence of MATLAB commands or functions that accept arguments and produces output. The M-files are created using the text editor.

8.1.1 The Fixed Point Method for Solving x = g(x)

The fixed point method solves the equation $x = g(x)$, under certain conditions on the function g, using an iterative method that begins with an initial value p_0 (a first approximation to the solution) and defines $p_{k+1} = g(p_k)$. The fixed point theorem ensures that, in certain circumstances, this sequence will converges to a solution of the equation $x = g(x)$. In practice the iterative process will stop when the absolute or relative error corresponding to two consecutive iterations is less than a preset value (*tolerance*). The smaller this value, the better the approximation to the solution of the equation.

This simple iterative method can be implemented using the M-file shown in Figure 8-1.

As an example we solve the following non-linear equation:

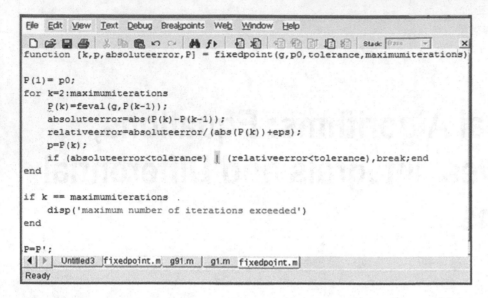

```
File  Edit  View  Text  Debug  Breakpoints  Web  Window  Help

function [k,p,absoluteerror,P] = fixedpoint(g,p0,tolerance,maximumiterations)

P(1)= p0;
for k=2:maximumiterations
    P(k)=feval(g,P(k-1));
    absoluteerror=abs(P(k)-P(k-1));
    relativeerror=absoluteerror/(abs(P(k))+eps);
    p=P(k);
    if (absoluteerror<tolerance) | (relativeerror<tolerance),break;end
end

if k == maximumiterations .
    disp('maximum number of iterations exceeded')
end

P=P';
```
Untitled3 fixedpoint.m g91.m g1.m fixedpoint.m
Ready

Figure 8-1.

$$x - 2^{-x} = 0.$$

In order to apply the fixed point algorithm we write the equation in the form $x = g(x)$ as follows:

$$x - 2^{-x} = g(x).$$

We will start by finding an approximate solution which will be the first term p_0. To plot the x axis and the curve defined by the given equation on the same graph we use the following syntax (see Figure 8-2):

```
>> fplot ('[x-2^(-x), 0]',[0, 1])
```

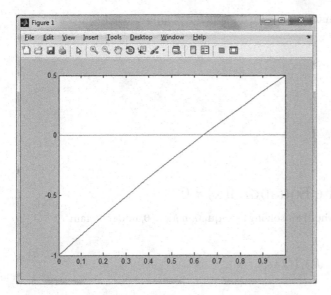

Figure 8-2.

The graph shows that one solution is close to $x = 0.6$. We can take this value as the initial value. We choose $p_0 = 0.6$. If we consider a tolerance of 0.0001 for a maximum of 1000 iterations, we can solve the problem once we have defined the function $g(x)$ in the M-file *g1.m* (see Figure 8-3).

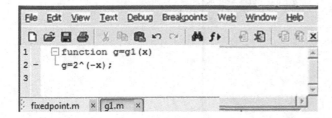

Figure 8-3.

We can now solve the equation using the MATLAB syntax:

```
>> [k, p] = fixedpoint('g1',0.6,0.0001,1000)

k =

    10

p =

    0.6412
```

We obtain the solution $x = 0.6412$ at the 1000th iteration. To check if the solution is approximately correct, we must verify that g1(0.6412) is close to 0.6412.

```
>> g1 (0.6412)

ans =

    0.6412
```

Thus we observe that the solution is acceptable.

8.1.2 Newton's Method for Solving the Equation f(x) = 0

Newton's method (also called the Newton–Raphson method) for solving the equation $f(x) = 0$, under certain conditions on f, uses the iteration

$$x_{r+1} = x_r - f(x_r)/f'(x_r)$$

for an initial value x_0 close to a solution.

The M-file in Figure 8-4 shows a program which solves equations by Newton's method to a given precision.

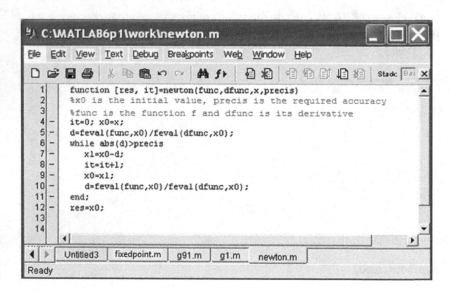

```
function [res, it]=newton(func,dfunc,x,precis)
%x0 is the initial value, precis is the required accuracy
%func is the function f and dfunc is its derivative
it=0; x0=x;
d=feval(func,x0)/feval(dfunc,x0);
while abs(d)>precis
    x1=x0-d;
    it=it+1;
    x0=x1;
    d=feval(func,x0)/feval(dfunc,x0);
end;
res=x0;
```

Figure 8-4.

As an example we solve the following equation by Newton's method:

$$x^2 - x - \sin(x + 0.15) = 0.$$

The function $f(x)$ is defined in the M-file *f1.m* (see Figure 8-5), and its derivative $f'(x)$ is given in the M-file *derf1.m* (see Figure 8-6).

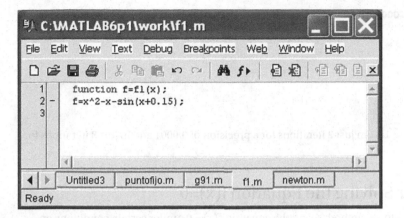

Figure 8-5.

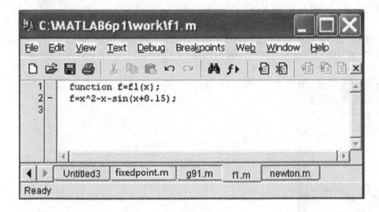

Figure 8-6.

We can now solve the equation up to an accuracy of 0.0001 and 0.000001 using the following MATLAB syntax, starting with an initial estimate of 1.5:

```
>> [x,it]=newton('f1','derf1',1.5,0.0001)

x =

1.6101

it =

2
```

```
>> [x,it]=newton('f1','derf1',1.5,0.000001)
x =

1.6100

it =

3
```

Thus we have obtained the solution $x = 1.61$ in just 2 iterations for a precision of 0.0001 and in just 3 iterations for a precision of 0.000001.

8.1.3 Schröder's Method for Solving the Equation f(x)=0

Schröder's method, which is similar to Newton's method, solves the equation $f(x) = 0$, under certain conditions on f, via the iteration

$$X_{r+1} = X_r - mf(X_r) / f'(X_r)$$

for an initial value x_0 close to a solution, and where m is the order of multiplicity of the solution being sought.

The M-file shown in Figure 8-7 gives the function that solves equations by Schröder's method to a given precision.

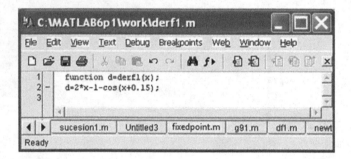

Figure 8-7.

8.2 Systems of Non-Linear Equations

As for differential equations, it is possible to implement algorithms with MATLAB that solve systems of non-linear equations using classical iterative numerical methods.

Among a diverse collection of existing methods we will consider the Seidel and Newton–Raphson methods.

8.2.1 The Seidel Method

The Seidel method for solving systems of equations is a generalization of the fixed point iterative method for single equations.

In the case of a system of two equations $x = g_1(x,y)$ and $y = g_2(x,y)$ the terms of the iteration are defined as:

$$P_{k+1} = g_1(p_k, q_k) \text{ and } q_{k+1} = g_2(p_k, q_k).$$

Similarly, in the case of a system of three equations $x=g_1(x,y,z)$,

$y = g_2(x,y,z)$ and $z = g_3(x,y,z)$ the terms of the iteration are defined as:

$p_k+_1= g_1(p_k,q_k,r_k)$, $q_k+_1= g_2(p_k,q_k,r_4)$ and $r_k+_1= g_3(p_k,q_k,r_4)$.

The M-file shown in Figure 8-8 gives a function which solves systems of equations using Seidel's method up to a specified accuracy.

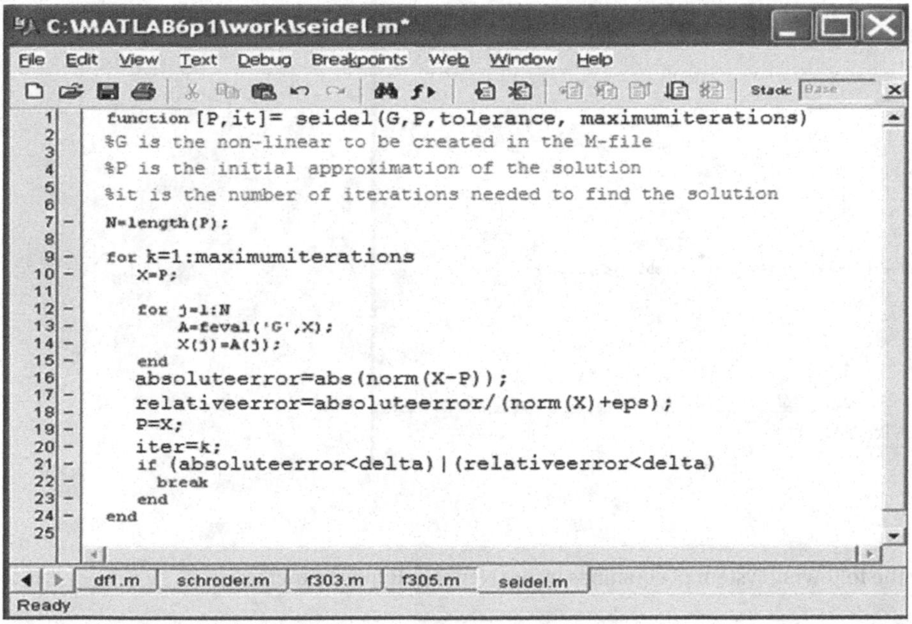
C:\MATLAB6p1\work\seidel.m*
File Edit View Text Debug Breakpoints Web Window Help
Stack Base
function [P,it]= seidel(G,P,tolerance, maximumiterations)
%G is the non-linear to be created in the M-file
%P is the initial approximation of the solution
%it is the number of iterations needed to find the solution
N=length(P);
for k=1:maximumiterations
X=P;
for j=1:N
A=feval('G',X);
X(j)=A(j);
end
absoluteerror=abs(norm(X-P));
relativeerror=absoluteerror/(norm(X)+eps);
P=X;
iter=k;
if (absoluteerror<delta)|(relativeerror<delta)
break
end
end
df1.m
schroder.m
f303.m
f305.m
seidel.m
Ready

Figure 8-8.

8.2.2 The Newton-Raphson Method

The Newton-Raphson method for solving systems of equations is a generalization of Newton's method for single equations.

The idea behind the algorithm is familiar. The solution of the system of non-linear equations $F(X) = 0$ is obtained by generating from an initial approximation P_0 a sequence of approximations P_k which converges to the solution. Figure 8-9 shows the M-file containing the function which solves systems of equations using the Newton-Raphson method up to a specified degree of accuracy.

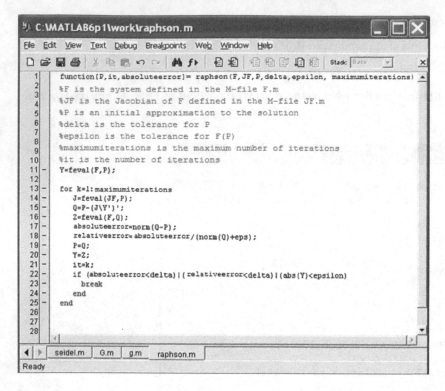

```
C:\MATLAB6p1\work\raphson.m

File  Edit  View  Text  Debug  Breakpoints  Web  Window  Help

1    function[P,it,absoluteerror]= raphson(F,JF,P,delta,epsilon, maximumiterations)
2    %F is the system defined in the M-file F.m
3    %JF is the Jacobian of F defined in the M-file JF.m
4    %P is an initial approximation to the solution
5    %delta is the tolerance for P
6    %epsilon is the tolerance for F(P)
7    %maximumiterations is the maximum number of iterations
8
9    %it is the number of iterations
10   Y=feval(F,P);
11
12
13   for k=1:maximumiterations
14       J=feval(JF,P);
15       Q=P-(J\Y')';
16       Z=feval(F,Q);
17       absoluteerror=norm(Q-P);
18       relativeerror= absoluteerror/(norm(Q)+eps);
19       P=Q;
20       Y=Z;
21       it=k;
22       if (absoluteerror<delta)|(relativeerror<delta)|(abs(Y)<epsilon)
23          break
24       end
25   end
26
27
28

seidel.m   G.m   g.m   raphson.m
Ready
```

Figure 8-9.

As an example we solve the following system of equations by the Newton–Raphson method:

$$x^2 - 2x - y = -0.5$$
$$x^2 + 4y^2 - 4 = 0$$

taking as an initial approximation to the solution $P = [2\ 3]$.

We start by defining the system $F(X) = 0$ and its Jacobian matrix JF according to the M-files $F.m$ and $JF.m$ shown in Figures 8-10 and 8-11.

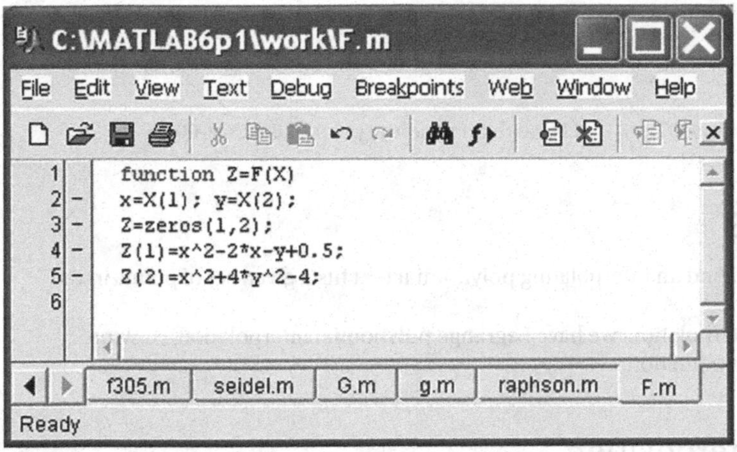

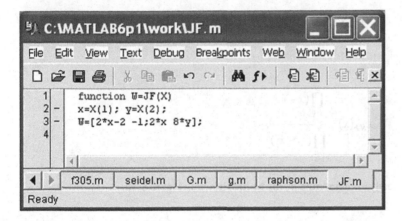

Figure 8-10.

Figure 8-11.

Then the system is solved with a tolerance of 0.00001 and with a maximum of 100 iterations using the following MATLAB syntax:

```
>> [P,it,absoluteerror]=raphson('F','JF',[2 3],0.00001,0.00001,100)
```

P =

1.9007 0.3112

it =

6

absoluteerror =

8. 8751e-006

The solution obtained in 6 iterations is $x = 1.9007$, $y = 0.3112$, with an absolute error of 8.8751e-006.

8.3 Interpolation Methods

There are many different methods available to find an interpolating polynomial that fits a given set of points in the best possible way.

Among the most common methods of interpolation, we have Lagrange polynomial interpolation, Newton polynomial interpolation and Chebyshev approximation.

8.3.1 Lagrange Polynomial Interpolation

The Lagrange interpolating polynomial which passes through the $N+1$ points (x_k, y_k), $k = 0, 1, ..., N$, is defined as follows:

$$P(x) = \sum_{k=0}^{N} y_k L_{N,k}(x)$$

where:

$$L_{N,k}(x) = \frac{\displaystyle\prod_{\substack{j=0 \\ j \neq k}}^{N} (x - x_j)}{\displaystyle\prod_{\substack{j=0 \\ j \neq k}}^{N} (x_k - x_j)}.$$

The algorithm for obtaining P and L is easily implemented by the M-file shown in Figure 8-12.

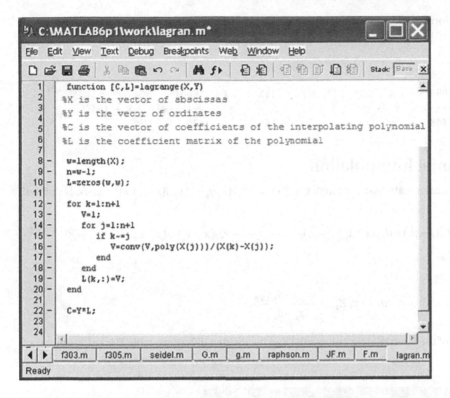

Figure 8-12.

As an example we find the Lagrange interpolating polynomial that passes through the points (2,3), (4,5), (6,5), (7,6), (8,8), (9,7).

We will simply use the following MATLAB syntax:

>> [F, L] = lagrange([2 4 6 7 8 9],[3 5 5 6 8 7])

C =

-0.0185 0.4857 -4.8125 22.2143 -46.6690 38.8000

L =

-0.0006 0.0202 -0.2708 1.7798 -5.7286 7.2000
0.0042 -0.1333 1.6458 -9.6667 26.3500 -25.2000
-0.0208 0.6250 -7.1458 38.3750 -94.8333 84.0000
0.0333 -0.9667 10.6667 -55.3333 132.8000 -115.2000
-0.0208 0.5833 -6.2292 31.4167 -73.7500 63.0000
0.0048 -0.1286 1.3333 -6.5714 15.1619 -12.8000

We can obtain the symbolic form of the polynomial whose coefficients are given by the vector *C* by using the following MATLAB command:

```
>> pretty(poly2sym(C))
```

$$\frac{31}{1680} x^5 + \frac{1093731338075689}{2251799813685248} x^4 - \frac{77}{16} x^3 + \frac{311}{14} x^2 - \frac{19601}{420} x + 194/5$$

8.3.2 Newton Polynomial Interpolation

The Newton interpolating polynomial that passes through the *N*+1 points $(x_k, y_k) = (x_k, f(x_k))$, *k*= 0,1,..., *N*, is defined as follows:

$$P(x) = d_{0,0} + d_{1,1}(x - x_0) + d_{2,2}(x - x_0)(x - x_1) + \cdots + d_{N,N}(x - x_0)(x - x_1)\cdots(x - x_{N-1})$$

where:

$$d_{k,j} = y_k \quad d_{k,j} = \frac{d_{k,j-1} - d_{k-1,j-1}}{x_k - d_{k-1}}.$$

Obtaining the coefficients *C* of the interpolating polynomial and the divided difference table *D* is easily done via the M-file shown in Figure 8-13.

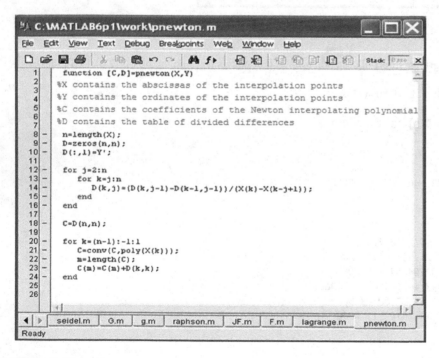

Figure 8-13.

As an example we apply Newton's method to the same interpolation problem solved by the Lagrange method in the previous section. We will use the following MATLAB syntax:

```
>> [C, D] = pnewton([2 4 6 7 8 9],[3 5 5 6 8 7])

C =

-0.0185 0.4857 - 4.8125 22.2143 - 46.6690 38.8000

D =

3.0000        0          0          0        0        0
5.0000     1.0000        0          0        0        0
5.0000        0       - 0.2500      0        0        0
6.0000     1.0000      0.3333     0.1167     0        0
8.0000     2.0000      0.5000     0.0417  - 0.0125    0
7.0000   - 1.0000    - 1.5000   - 0.6667  - 0.1417  - 0.0185
```

The interpolating polynomial in symbolic form is calculated as follows:

```
>> pretty(poly2sym(C))

   31        5  17    4  77    3  311   2   19601
- ----  x  + --  x  - --  x  + ---  x  - -----  x + 194/5
  1680       35       16       14        420
```

Observe that the results obtained by both interpolation methods are similar.

8.4 Numerical Derivation Methods

There are various different techniques available for numerical derivation. These are of great importance when developing algorithms to solve problems involving ordinary or partial differential equations.

Among the most common methods for numerical derivation are derivation using limits, derivation using extrapolation and derivation using interpolation on N-1 nodes.

8.4.1 Numerical Derivation via Limits

This method consists in building a sequence of numerical approximations to $f'(x)$ via the generated sequence:

$$f'(x) \approx D_k = \frac{f(x+10^{-k}h) - f(x-10^{-k}h)}{2(10^{-k}h)}.$$

The iterations continue until $|D_{n+1}-D_n| \geq |D_n-D_{n-1}|$ or $|D_n-D_{n-1}| <$ tolerance. This approach approximates $f'(x)$ by D_n. The algorithm to obtain the derivative D is easily implemented by the M-file shown in Figure 8-14.

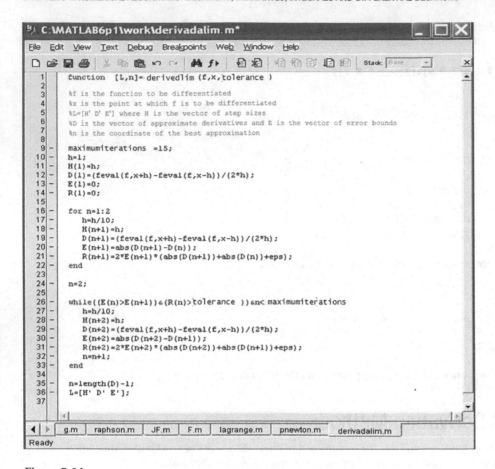

Figure 8-14.

As an example, we approximate the derivative of the function:

$$f(x) = \sin\left(\cos\left(\frac{1}{x}\right)\right)$$

at the point $\dfrac{1-\sqrt{5}}{2}$.

To begin we define the function *f* in an M-file named funcion (see Figure 8-15). (Note: we use *funcion* rather than *function* here since the latter is a protected term in MATLAB.)

Figure 8-15.

The derivative is then given by the following MATLAB command:

```
>> [L, n] = derivedlim ('funcion', (1-sqrt (5)) / 2,0.01)

L =

1.0000 - 0.7448 0
0.1000 - 2.6045 1.8598
0.0100 - 2.6122 0.0077
0.0010 - 2.6122 0.0000
0.0001 - 2.6122 0.0000

n =

4
```

Thus we see that the approximate derivative is – 2.6122, which can be checked as follows:

```
>> f = diff ('sin (cos (x))')

f =

cos (cos (x)) * sin (x) / x ^ 2

>> subs (f, (1-sqrt (5)) / 2).

ans =

  -2.6122
```

8.4.2 Richardson's Extrapolation Method

This method involves building numerical approximations to $f'(x)$ via the construction of a table of values $D(j, k)$ with $k £ j$ that yield a final solution to the derivative $f'(x) = D(n, n)$. The values $D(j, k)$ form a lower triangular matrix, the first column of which is defined as:

$$D(j,1) = \frac{f(x+2^{-j}h) - f(x-2^{-j}h)}{2^{-j+1}h}$$

and the remaining elements are defined by:

$$D(j,k) = D(j,k-1) + \frac{D(j,k-1) - D(j-1,k-1)}{4^k - 1} \quad (2 \leq k \leq j)$$

The corresponding algorithm for D is implemented by the M-file shown in Figure 8-16.

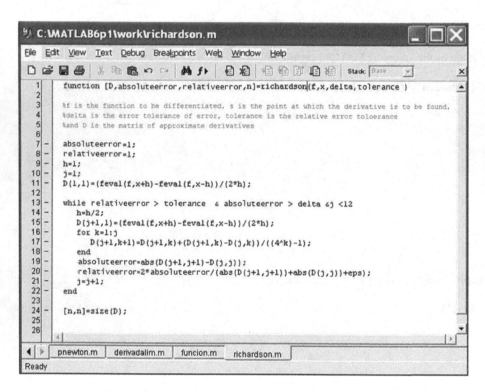

Figure 8-16.

As an example, we approximate the derivative of the function:

$$f(x) = \sin\left(\cos\left(\frac{1}{x}\right)\right)$$

at the point $\dfrac{1-\sqrt{5}}{2}$.

As the M-file that defines the function *f* has already been defined in the previous section, we can find the approximate derivative using the MATLAB syntax:

```
>> [D, relativeerror, absoluteerror, n] = richardson ('funcion', (1-sqrt(5))/2,0.001,0.001)
```

D =

-0.7448	0	0	0	0	0
-1.1335	- 1.2631	0	0	0	0
-2.3716	- 2.7843	- 2.8857	0	0	0
-2.5947	- 2.6691	- 2.6614	- 2.6578	0	0
-2.6107	- 2.6160	- 2.6125	- 2.6117	- 2.6115	0
-2.6120	- 2.6124	- 2.6122	- 2.6122	- 2.6122	- 2.6122

relativeerror =

6. 9003e-004

absoluteerror =

2. 6419e-004

n =

6

Thus we get the same result as before when we used the limit method.

8.4.3 Derivation Using Interpolation (n + 1 Nodes)

This method consists in building the Newton interpolating polynomial of degree *N*:

$$P(x) = a_0 + a_1(x - x_0) + a_2(x - x_0)(x - x_1) + \cdots + a_N(x - x_0)(x - x_1) \cdots (x - x_{N-1})$$

and numerically approximating $f'(x_0)$ by $P'(x_0)$.

The algorithm for the derivative *D* is easily implemented by the M-file shown in Figure 8-17.

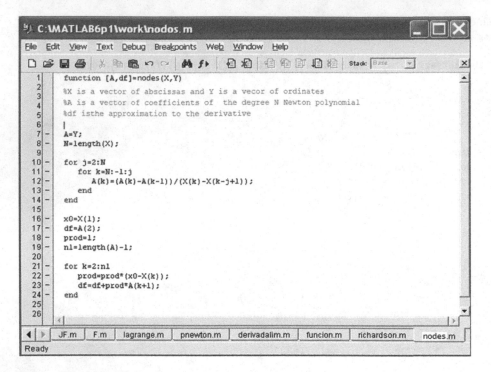

Figure 8-17.

As an example, we approximate the derivative of the function:

$$f(x) = \sin\left(\cos\left(\frac{1}{x}\right)\right)$$

at the point $\dfrac{1-\sqrt{5}}{2}$.

As the M-file that defines the function *f* has already been constructed in the previous section, we can calculate the approximate derivative using the MATLAB command:

>> [A, df] = nodes([2 4 6 7 8 9],[3 5 5 6 8 7])

A =

3.0000   1.0000   - 0.2500   0.1167   - 0.0125   - 0.0185

df =

-1.4952

8.5 Numerical Integration Methods

Given the difficulty of obtaining an exact primitive for most functions, numerical integration methods are especially important. There are many different ways to numerically approximate definite integrals, among them the trapezium method, Simpson's method and Romberg's method (all implemented in MATLAB's Basic module).

8.5.1 The Trapezium Method

The trapezium method for numerical integration has two variants: the trapezoidal rule and the recursive trapezoidal rule.

The trapezoidal rule approximates the definite integral of the function $f(x)$ between a and b as follows:

$$\int_a^b f(x)dx \approx \frac{h}{2}(f(a)+f(b))+h\sum_{k=1}^{M-1} f(x_k)$$

calculating $f(x)$ at equidistant points $x_k = a+kh$, $k = 0,1,...,M$ where $x_0 = a$ and $x_M = b$.

The trapezoidal rule is implemented by the M-file shown in Figure 8-18.

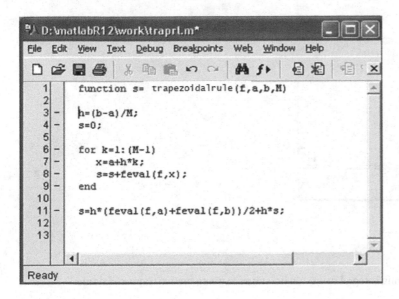

```
function s= trapezoidalrule(f,a,b,M)

h=(b-a)/M;
s=0;

for k=1:(M-1)
    x=a+h*k;
    s=s+feval(f,x);
end

s=h*(feval(f,a)+feval(f,b))/2+h*s;
```

Figure 8-18.

The *recursive trapezoidal rule* considers the points $x_k = a+kh$, $k = 0,1,...,M$, where $x_0 = a$ and $x_M = b$, dividing the interval $[a, b]$ into $2J = M$ subintervals of the same size $h = (b-a)/2J$. We then consider the following recursive formula:

$$T(0) = \frac{h}{2}(f(a)+f(b))$$

$$T(J) = \frac{T(J-1)}{2} + h\sum_{k=1}^{M} f(x_{2k-1})$$

and the integral of the function $f(x)$ between a and b can be calculated as:

$$\int_a^b f(x)dx \approx \frac{h}{2}\sum_{k=1}^{2^J}(f(x_k)+f(x_{k-1}))$$

using the trapezoidal rule as the number of sub-intervals $[a, b]$ increases, taking at the J-th iteration a set of $2J+1$ equally spaced points.

The recursive trapezoidal rule is implemented via the M-file shown in Figure 8-19.

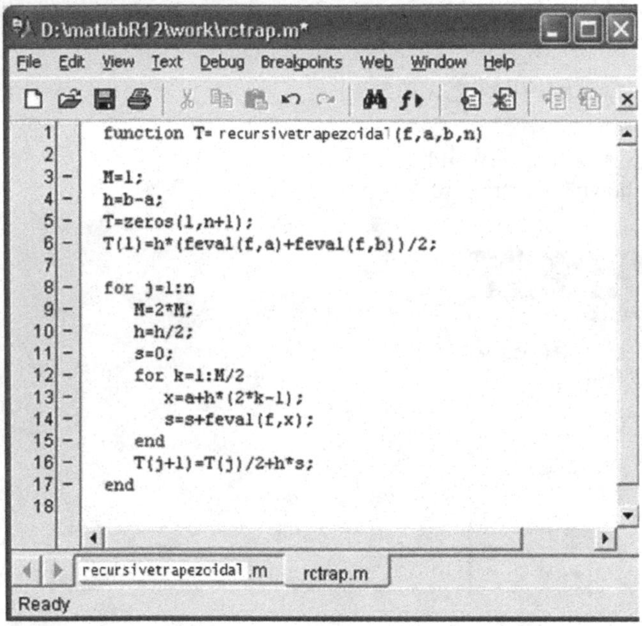
D:\matlabR12\work\rctrap.m*
File Edit View Text Debug Breakpoints Web Window Help
function T= recursivetrapezoidal(f,a,b,n)
M=1;
h=b-a;
T=zeros(1,n+1);
T(1)=h*(feval(f,a)+feval(f,b))/2;
for j=1:n
M=2*M;
h=h/2;
s=0;
for k=1:M/2
x=a+h*(2*k-1);
s=s+feval(f,x);
end
T(j+1)=T(j)/2+h*s;
end
recursivetrapezoidal.m
rctrap.m
Ready

Figure 8-19.

As an example, we calculate the following integral using 100 iterations of the recursive trapezoidal rule:

$$\int_0^2 \frac{1}{x^2+\frac{1}{10}}dx.$$

We start by defining the integrand by means of the M-file *integrand1.m* shown in Figure 8-20.

Figure 8-20.

We then calculate the requested integral as follows:

>> *recursivetrapezoidal('integrand1',0,2,14)*

ans =

Columns 1 through 4

10.24390243902439   6.03104212860310   4.65685845031979   4.47367657743630

Columns 5 through 8

4.47109102437123 4.47132194954670 4.47138003053334 4.47139455324593

Columns 9 through 12

4.47139818407829 4.47139909179602 4.47139931872606 4.47139937545860

Columns 13 through 15

4.47139938964175 4.47139939318754 4.47139939407398

This shows that after 14 iterations an accurate value for the integral is 4.47139939407398.
We calculate the same integral using the trapezoidal rule, using M = 14, using the following MATLAB command:

>> **trapezoidalrule('integrand1',0,2,14)**

ans =

4.47100414648074

The result is now the less accurate 4.47100414648074.

8.5.2 Simpson's Method

Simpson's method for numerical integration is generally considered in two variants: the simple Simpson's rule and the composite Simpson's rule.

Simpson's simple approximation of the definite integral of the function $f(x)$ between the points a and b is the following:

$$\int_a^b f(x)dx \approx \frac{h}{3}(f(a)+f(b)+4f(c))\, c = \frac{a+b}{2}$$

This can be implemented using the M-file shown in Figure 8-21.

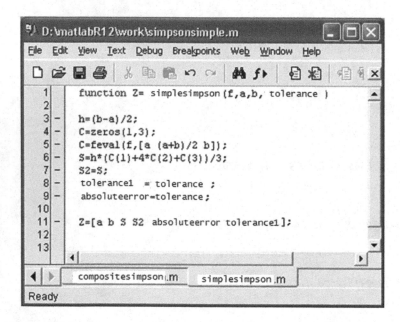

Figure 8-21.

The *composite Simpson's rule* approximates the definite integral of the function $f(x)$ between points a and b as follows:

$$\int_a^b f(x)dx \approx \frac{h}{3}(f(a)+f(b))+\frac{2h}{3}\sum_{k=1}^{M-1} f(x_{2k})+\frac{4h}{3}\sum_{k=1}^{M} f(x_{2k-1})$$

calculating $f(x)$ at equidistant points $x_k = a+kh$, k = 0, 1,..., 2_M, where $x_0 = a$ and $x_{2M} = b$.

The composite Simpson's rule is implemented using the M-file shown in Figure 8-22.

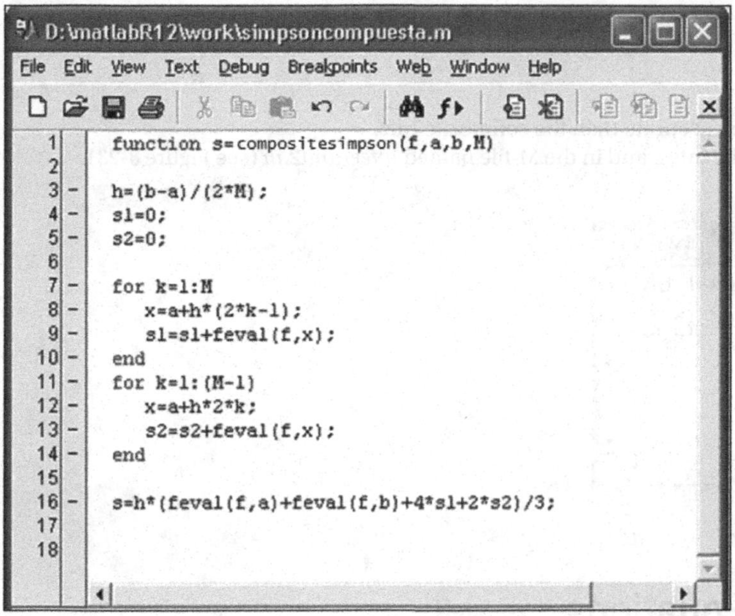

```
     D:\matlabR12\work\simpsoncompuesta.m                    _ □ X
 File  Edit  View  Text  Debug  Breakpoints  Web  Window  Help

  D  ☞ 🖫 🖨  | X 🖻 🛍 ⌐ ⌐ | 🏦 ƒ▸ | 🖹 🗐 | 🗐 🗐 📄 X
  1       function s=compositesimpson(f,a,b,M)
  2
  3 -     h=(b-a)/(2*M);
  4 -     s1=0;
  5 -     s2=0;
  6
  7 -     for k=1:M
  8 -         x=a+h*(2*k-1);
  9 -         s1=s1+feval(f,x);
 10 -     end
 11 -     for k=1:(M-1)
 12 -         x=a+h*2*k;
 13 -         s2=s2+feval(f,x);
 14 -     end
 15
 16 -     s=h*(feval(f,a)+feval(f,b)+4*s1+2*s2)/3;
 17
 18
```

Figure 8-22.

As an example, we calculate the following integral by the composite Simpson's rule taking M = 14:

$$\int_0^2 \frac{1}{x^2+\frac{1}{10}}dx.$$

We use the following syntax:

>> compositesimpson('integrand1',0,2,14)

ans =

   4.47139628125498

Next we calculate the same integral using the simple Simpson's rule:

>> Z=simplesimpson('integrand2',0,2,0.0001)

Z =

Columns 1 through 4

0 2.00000000000000 4.62675535846268 4.62675535846268

Columns 5 through 6

0.00010000000000 0.00010000000000

As we see, the simple Simpson's rule is less accurate than the composite rule.

In this case, we have previously defined the integrand in the M-file named *integrand2.m* (see Figure 8-23).

Figure 8-23.

8.6 Ordinary Differential Equations

Obtaining exact solutions of ordinary differential equations is not a simple task. There are a number of different methods for obtaining approximate solutions of ordinary differential equations. These numerical methods include, among others, Euler's method, Heun's method, the Taylor series method, the Runge–Kutta method (implemented in MATLAB's Basic module), the Adams–Bashforth–Moulton method, Milne's method and Hamming's method.

8.6.1 Euler's Method

Suppose we want to solve the differential equation $y' = f(t, y)$, $y(a)=y_0$, on the interval $[a, b]$. We divide the interval $[a, b]$ into M subintervals of the same size using the partition given by the points $t_k = a+kh$, k = 0,1,..., M, $h = (b-a)/M$. Euler's method then finds the solution of the differential equation iteratively by calculating $y_{k+1} = y_k+hf(t_k, y_k)$, $k = 0,1, ..., M-1$.

Euler's method is implemented using the M-file shown in Figure 8-24.

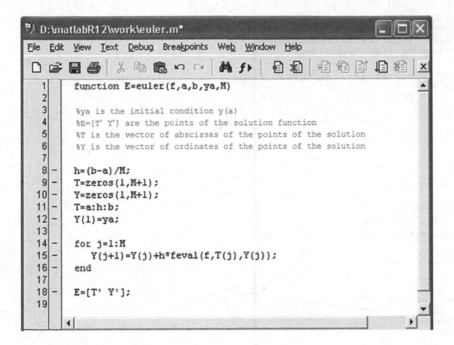

Figure 8-24.

8.6.2 Heun's Method

Suppose we want to solve the differential equation $y' = f(t, y)$, $y(a) = y_0$, on the interval $[a, b]$. We divide the interval $[a, b]$ into M subintervals of the same size using the partition given by the points $t_k = a + kh$, $k = 0,1,...,M$, $h = (b-a)/M$. Heun's method then finds the solution of the differential equation iteratively by calculating $y_{k+1} = y_k + h(f(t_k, y_k) + f(t_{k+1}, y_k + f(t_k, y_k))) / 2$, $k = 0,1,..., M-1$.

Heun's method is implemented using the M-file shown in Figure 8-25.

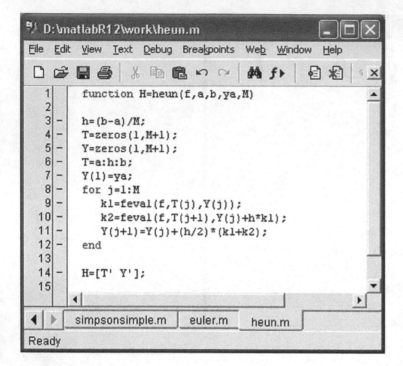

```
function H=heun(f,a,b,ya,M)

h=(b-a)/M;
T=zeros(1,M+1);
Y=zeros(1,M+1);
T=a:h:b;
Y(1)=ya;
for j=1:M
    k1=feval(f,T(j),Y(j));
    k2=feval(f,T(j+1),Y(j)+h*k1);
    Y(j+1)=Y(j)+(h/2)*(k1+k2);
end

H=[T' Y'];
```

Figure 8-25.

8.6.3 The Taylor Series Method

Suppose we want to solve the differential equation $y' = f(t, y)$, $y(a) = y_0$, on the interval $[a, b]$. We divide the interval $[a, b]$ into M subintervals of the same size using the partition given by the points $t_k = a + kh$, $k = 0,1,\ldots, M$, $h = (b-a)/M$. The Taylor series method (let us consider here the method to order 4) finds a solution to the differential equation by evaluating y', y'', y''' and y'''' to give the 4th order Taylor series for y at each partition point.

The Taylor series method is implemented using the M-file shown in Figure 8-26.

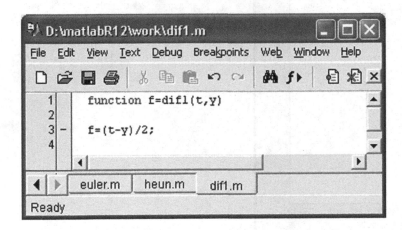

```
function T4=taylor(df,a,b,ya,M)

% df=[y' y'' y''' y''''] is the string 'df'
% T4=[T' Y']

h=(b-a)/M;
T=zeros(1,M+1);
Y=zeros(1,M+1);
T=a:h:b;
Y(1)=ya;

for j=1:M
    D=feval(df,T(j),Y(j));
    Y(j+1)=Y(j)+h*(D(1)+h*(D(2)/2+h*(D(3)/6+h*D(4)/24)));
end

T4=[T' Y'];
```

Figure 8-26.

As an example we solve the differential equation $y'(t) = (t - y) / 2$ on the interval [0,3], with $y(0) = 1$, using Euler's method, Heun's method and by the Taylor series method.

We will begin by defining the function $f(t, y)$ via the M-file shown in Figure 8-27.

```
function f=dif1(t,y)

f=(t-y)/2;
```

| euler.m | heun.m | dif1.m |

Ready

Figure 8-27.

The solution of the equation using Euler's method in 100 steps is calculated as follows:

```
>> E = euler('dif1',0,3,1,100)
```

E =

0 1.00000000000000

```
0.03000000000000  0.98500000000000
0.06000000000000  0.97067500000000
0.09000000000000  0.95701487500000
0.12000000000000  0.94400965187500
0.15000000000000  0.93164950709688
0.18000000000000  0.91992476449042
.
.
.
2.85000000000000  1.56377799005910
2.88000000000000  1.58307132020821
2.91000000000000  1.60252525040509
2.94000000000000  1.62213737164901
2.97000000000000  1.64190531107428
3.00000000000000  1.66182673140816
```

This solution can be graphed as follows (see Figure 8-28):

```
>> plot (E (:,2))
```

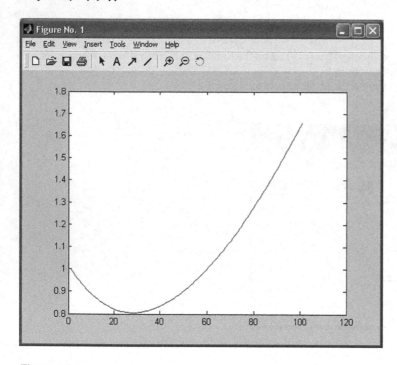

Figure 8-28.

The solution of the equation by Heun's method in 100 steps is calculated as follows:

```
>> H = heun('dif1',0,3,1,100)
```

H =

0 1.00000000000000
0.03000000000000 0.98533750000000
0.06000000000000 0.97133991296875
0.09000000000000 0.95799734001443
0.12000000000000 0.94530002961496
.
.
.
2.88000000000000 1.59082209379464
2.91000000000000 1.61023972987327
2.94000000000000 1.62981491089478
2.97000000000000 1.64954529140884
3.00000000000000 1.66942856088299

The solution using the Taylor series method requires the previously defined function $df = [y'\ y''\ y'''\ y'''']$ using the M-file shown in Figure 8-29.

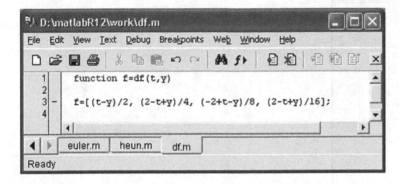

Figure 8-29.

The differential equation is solved by the Taylor series method via the command:

```
>> T = taylor('df',0,3,1,100)
```

T =

0 1.00000000000000
0.03000000000000 0.98533581882813
0.06000000000000 0.97133660068283
0.09000000000000 0.95799244555443
0.12000000000000 0.94529360082516
.
.

.
```
2.88000000000000  1.59078327648360
2.91000000000000  1.61020109213866
2.94000000000000  1.62977645599332
2.97000000000000  1.64950702246046
3.00000000000000  1.66939048087422
```

EXERCISE 8-1

Solve the following non-linear equation using the fixed point Iterative method:

$$x = \cos(\sin(x)).$$

We will start by finding an approximate solution to the equation, which we will use as the initial value p_0. To do this we show the x axis and the curve y = x-cos(sin(x)) on the same graph (Figure 8-30) by using the following command:

```
>> fplot ([x-cos (sin (x)), 0], [- 2, 2])
```

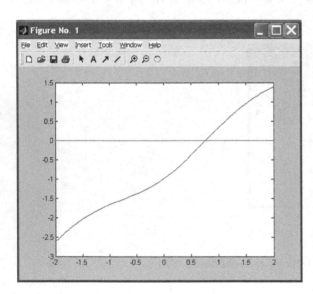

Figure 8-30.

The graph indicates that there is a solution close to $x = 1$, which is the value that we shall take as our initial approximation to the solution, i.e. $p_0 = 1$. If we consider a tolerance of 0.0001 for a maximum number of 100 iterations, we can solve the problem once we have defined the function $g(x) = \cos(\sin(x))$ via the M-file *g91.m* shown in Figure 8-31.

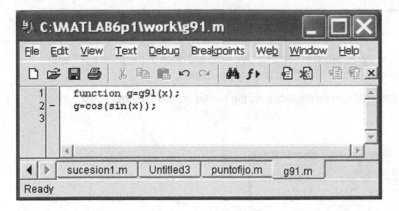

Figure 8-31.

We can now solve the equation using the MATLAB command:

```
>> [k, p, absoluteerror, P]=fixedpoint('g91',1,0.0001,1000)

k =

    13

p =

    0.7682

absoluteerror =

  6. 3361e-005

P =

1.0000
0.6664
0.8150
0.7467
0.7781
0.7636
0.7703
0.7672
0.7686
0.7680
0.7683
0.7681
0.7682
```

The solution is $x = 0.7682$, which has been found in 13 iterations with an absolute error of $6.3361e-005$. Thus, the convergence to the solution is particularly fast.

EXERCISE 8-2

Using Newton's method calculate the root of the equation $x^3 - 10x^2 + 29x - 20 = 0$ close to the point $x = 7$ with an accuracy of 0.00005. Repeat the same calculation but with an accuracy of 0.0005.

We define the function $f(x) = x^3 - 10x^2 + 29x - 20$ and its derivative via the M-files named f302.m and f303.m shown in Figures 8-32 and 8-33.

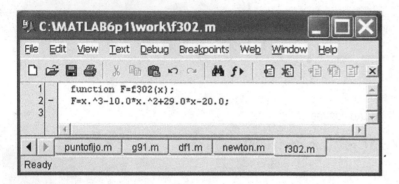

Figure 8-32.

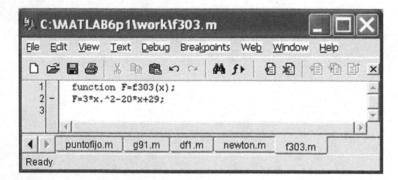

Figure 8-33.

To run the program that solves the equation, type:

```
>> [x, it]=newton('f302','f303',7,.00005)

x =

5.0000

it =

6
```

In 6 iterations and with an accuracy of 0.00005 the solution $x = 5$ has been obtained. In 5 iterations and with an accuracy of 0.0005 we get the solution $x = 5.0002$:

```
>> [x, it] = newton('f302','f303',7,.0005)
x =

5.0002

it =

5
```

EXERCISE 8-3

Write a program that calculates a root with multiplicity 2 of the equation $(e^{-x} -x)^2 = 0$ close to the point $x = -2$ to an accuracy of 0.00005.

We define the function $f(x)=(e^x - x)^2$ and its derivative via the M-files *f304.m* and *f305.m* shown in Figures 8-34 and 8-35:

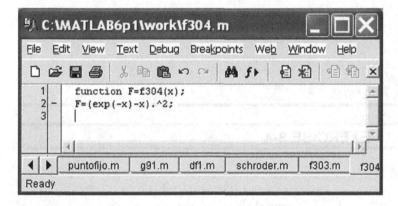

Figure 8-34.

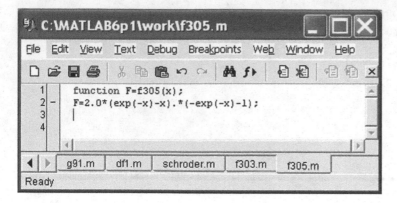

Figure 8-35.

We solve the equation using Schröder's method. To run the program we enter the command:

>> [x,it]=schroder('f304','f305',2,-2,.00005)

x =

0.5671

it =

5

In 5 iterations we have found the solution $x = 0.56715$.

EXERCISE 8-4

Approximate the derivative of the function

$$f(x) = \tan\left(\cos\left(\frac{\sqrt{5} + \sin(x)}{1 + x^2}\right)\right)$$

at the point $\dfrac{1 - \sqrt{5}}{3}$.

To begin we define the function *f* in the M-file *funcion1.m* shown in Figure 8-36.

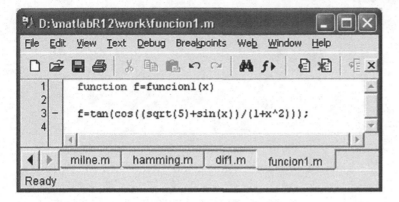

Figure 8-36.

The derivative can be found using the method of numerical derivation with an accuracy of 0.0001 via the following MATLAB command:

```
>> [L, n] = derivedlim ('funcion1', (1 + sqrt (5)) / 3,0.0001)

L =

1.00000000000000  0.94450896913313  0
0.10000000000000  1.22912035588668  0.28461138675355
0.01000000000000  1.22860294102802  0.00051741485866
0.00100000000000  1.22859747858110  0.00000546244691
0.00010000000000  1.22859742392997  0.00000005465113

n =

4
```

We see that the value of the derivative is approximated by 1.22859742392997.

Using Richardson's method, the derivative is calculated as follows:

```
>> [D, absoluteerror, relativeerror, n] = ('funcion1' richardson,(1+sqrt(5))/3,0.0001,0.0001)

D =

Columns 1 through 4

   0.94450896913313                0                                0
0
   1.22047776163545  1.31246735913623                0                            0
   1.23085024935646  1.23430774526347  1.22909710433862                0
   1.22938849854454  1.22890124827389  1.22854081514126  1.22853198515400
   1.22880865382036  1.22861537224563  1.22859631384374  1.22859719477553
```

Column 5

        0
        0
        0
        0
   1.22859745049954

absoluteerror =

6. *546534553897310e-005*

relativeerror =

   5. *328603742973844e-005*

n =
     5

EXERCISE 8-5

Approximate the following integral:

$$\int_1^{\frac{2\pi}{3}} \tan\left(\cos\left(\frac{\sqrt{5}+\sin(x)}{1+x^2}\right)\right) dx.$$

We can use the composite Simpson's rule with M=100 using the following command:

>> s = compositesimpson('function1',1,2*pi/3,100)

s =

0.68600990924332

If we use the trapezoidal rule instead, we get the following result:

>> s = trapezoidalrule('function1',1,2*pi/3,100)

s =

0.68600381840334

EXERCISE 8-6

Find an approximate solution of the following differential equation in the interval [0, 0.8]:

$$y' = t^2 + y^2 \quad y(0) = 1.$$

We start by defining the function $f(t, y)$ via the M-file in Figure 8-37.

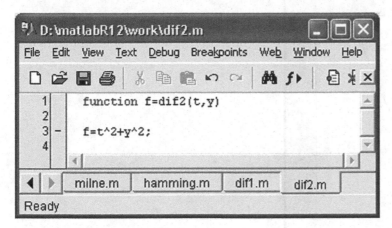

Figure 8-37.

We then solve the differential equation by Euler's method, dividing the interval into 20 subintervals using the following command:

```
>> E = euler('dif2',0,0.8,1,20)

E =
0                 1.00000000000000
0.04000000000000  1.04000000000000
0.08000000000000  1.08332800000000
0.12000000000000  1.13052798222336
0.16000000000000  1.18222772296696
0.20000000000000  1.23915821852503
0.24000000000000  1.30217874214655
0.28000000000000  1.37230952120649
0.32000000000000  1.45077485808625
0.36000000000000  1.53906076564045
0.40000000000000  1.63899308725380
0.44000000000000  1.75284502085643
0.48000000000000  1.88348764754208
0.52000000000000  2.03460467627982
0.56000000000000  2.21100532382941
0.60000000000000  2.41909110550949
0.64000000000000  2.66757117657970
0.68000000000000  2.96859261586445
0.72000000000000  3.33959030062305
0.76000000000000  3.80644083566367
0.80000000000000  4.40910450907999
```

315

The solution can be graphed as follows (see Figure 8-38):

```
>> plot (E (:,2))
```

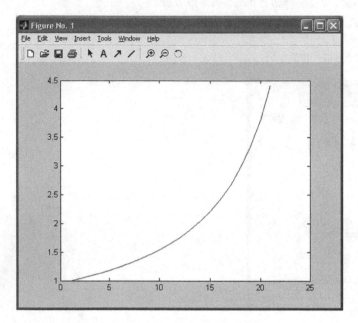

Figure 8-38.

Get the eBook for only $10!

Now you can take the weightless companion with you anywhere, anytime. Your purchase of this book entitles you to 3 electronic versions for only $10.

This Apress title will prove so indispensible that you'll want to carry it with you everywhere, which is why we are offering the eBook in 3 formats for only $10 if you have already purchased the print book.

Convenient and fully searchable, the PDF version enables you to easily find and copy code—or perform examples by quickly toggling between instructions and applications. The MOBI format is ideal for your Kindle, while the ePUB can be utilized on a variety of mobile devices.

Go to www.apress.com/promo/tendollars to purchase your companion eBook.

All Apress eBooks are subject to copyright. All rights are reserved by the Publisher, whether the whole or part of the material is concerned, specifically the rights of translation, reprinting, reuse of illustrations, recitation, broadcasting, reproduction on microfilms or in any other physical way, and transmission or information storage and retrieval, electronic adaptation, computer software, or by similar or dissimilar methodology now known or hereafter developed. Exempted from this legal reservation are brief excerpts in connection with reviews or scholarly analysis or material supplied specifically for the purpose of being entered and executed on a computer system, for exclusive use by the purchaser of the work. Duplication of this publication or parts thereof is permitted only under the provisions of the Copyright Law of the Publisher's location, in its current version, and permission for use must always be obtained from Springer. Permissions for use may be obtained through RightsLink at the Copyright Clearance Center. Violations are liable to prosecution under the respective Copyright Law.